a Year in Niagara

a Year in Niagara

THE PEOPLE AND FOOD OF WINE COUNTRY

Kathleen Sloan-McIntosh

foreword by Tony Aspler

whitecap

Edited by Elaine Jones
Proofread by Marial Shea
Cover design and art direction by Roberta Batchelor
Colour landscape photographs on cover and in interior by Steven Elphick
Colour recipe photographs on cover and in interior by Christopher Freeland
  [The Good Earth Heritage Tomatoes in a Fresh Corn Crust on p. 200 (front cover left); Panna Cotta
  with Strewn Wines Cabernet Sauvignon Raspberry Sauce on p. 302 (right); Sea Bass with Cilantro
  Cream on p. 56 (back cover, middle)]
Food styling by Rosemarie Superville
Prop styling by Marc-Philippe Gagne and Oksana Slavutych
Black and white photographs by Kathleen Sloan-McIntosh
Author photograph on back cover by Mark Shapiro
Interior design by Warren Clark
Map provided by the Wine Council of Ontario

Printed and bound in Canada

National Library of Canada Cataloguing in Publication Data

Sloan-McIntosh, Kathleen
    A year in Niagara : the people and food of wine country / Kathleen Sloan-McIntosh.

    Includes index.
    ISBN 1-55285-398-5

    1. Niagara Peninsula (Ont.)—Description and travel. 3. Cookery, Canadian—Ontario—Niagara
Peninsula. I. Title.
FC3095.N5S56 2002   917.13'38044   C2002-911064-5
F1059.N5S56 2002

The publisher acknowledges the support of the Canada Council for the Arts and the Cultural Services
Branch of the Government of British Columbia for our publishing program. We acknowledge the
financial support of the Government of Canada through the Book Publishing Industry Development
Program for our publishing activities.

Contents

Acknowledgements

A heartfelt thank you to Robert McCullough, Alison Maclean, Robin Rivers and all at Whitecap Books for providing the opportunity to recount my year in my way.

Thank you to editor Elaine Jones for her skill, care and attention to detail.

And to photographer Steven Elphick whose magnificent pictures tell the beautiful story of Niagara without words. I am grateful for the combined efforts of food photographer Christopher Freeland, food stylist Rosemarie Superville and prop stylists Marc-Philippe Gagne and Oksana Slavutych.

Thanks and appreciation to Denise Schon for her guidance, her listening ear and her friendship. And to Tony Aspler, a sincere thank you for his lovely foreword.

Love and gratitude always to my beloved Tosh for his magnanimous support, for everything he does and everything he gives, and for his deft and skillful wine and beer recommendations for each recipe in this book.

To my friend "in need," Joe Callus, who rescued me and the manuscript from techno-hell more than once.

Grateful thanks to Zenia Curzon, my good friend, for her help during the final rounds.

Appreciation, gratitude and love to my wonderfully supportive in-laws and good friends, Win & Mac McIntosh.

There are so many people in the region of Niagara to thank for their willing assistance with this book. To you all (and to any I may have missed) please know how grateful I am, for your enthusiasm for this book and for your help and generosity.

And a widespread thanks to all the unsung heroes of the wine and hospitality industries in Niagara—here's to you.

Arden Vaughn of Lake Land Game Meats

Chef Andy Dymond, the Oban Inn

Chef Anna Olson of Inn on the 20 Restaurant

Chef Catherine O'Donnell, Hillebrand Estates & Peller Estates

Chef David Berggren of Vineland Estates Winery

Chef Izabela Kalabis of Inniskillin

Chef Jan-Willem Stulp of Vineland Estates Winery

Chef Jason Rosso of Peller Estates

Chef Mark Hand of Niagara College

Chef Mark Picone of Vineland Estates Winery

Chef Michael Olson of Niagara College

Chef Neal Noble of Senses Restaurant

Chef Ray Poitras of Peninsula Ridge Winery

Chef Rob Fracchioni of Inn on the Twenty Restaurant

Chef Stephen Treadwell of Queen's Landing inn

Chef Tony de Luca of Hillebrand Estates

Chef Virginia Marr, the Pillar & Post

Daniel Lenko of Daniel Lenko Estate Winery

Helen Lenko

Debi Pratt of Inniskillin

Del Rollo of Jackson-Triggs

Johanna Burkhard of Peninsula Ridge Winery

Karl Kaiser of Inniskillin

Maria Moessner of Inniskillin

Matthew Speck, Henry of Pelham Family Estate Winery

Michelle Seaborn of Quacker Box Ducks

Niagara Brewing Company

Niagara Oyster Company

Niagara Wine Festival

Paul Speck, Henry of Pelham Family Estate Winery

Ron Giesbrecht, Henry of Pelham Family Estate Winery

Taste of Niagara

Odette Yazbeck at the Shaw Festival

Wine Council of Ontario

Dedication

To touch the cup with eager lips and taste, not drain it;
To woo and tempt and court a bliss—and not attain it;
To fondle and caress a joy, yet hold it lightly,
Lest it become necessity and cling too tightly;

To watch the sun set in the west without regretting;
To hail its advent in the east—the night forgetting;
To smother care in happiness and grief in laughter;
To hold the present close—not questioning hereafter;

To have enough to share—to know the joy of giving;
To thrill with all the sweets of life—is living.

Anon.

To our combined treasures, the "sweets" in my life—
Alysa, Jenna, Andrew, Ian, Emma and Colsen

Foreword

The Niagara escarpment, where Kathleen Sloan-McIntosh now lives overlooking Lake Ontario, is roughly on the same latitude as Bilbao, Marseilles and Siena. But geography is not the measure of a place; it's climate and soil that define our landscape and the people who sow and reap there.

In the millenium year when soul-searching was the order of the day, Kathleen and her husband Ted made the decision to escape the hurly-burly of Toronto. They bought a pre-Confederation house on land that 430 million years ago was the shoreline of the Michigan Basin.

Beyond the Falls Kathleen rediscovered a pastoral community that is Canada's Eden, a place where you can plant a walking stick and it will take root and blossom. Maybe not, but it's easier to catalogue what does not grow in this fertile crescent of land than what does. "Towards the end of the month [July]," she writes, "I toss a handful of arugula seeds in a large planter on my sunny side doorstep. It's no exaggeration to say green shoots come up within 24 hours."

Niagara, for most Canadians who love food and wine, means vineyards. Wine is the grape's quest for immortality. No other agricultural product, including grain, evokes such a passionate response and is so heavily invested in myth and merriment. It was the burgeoning of Ontario's wine industry here in the Niagara Peninsula that created a flourishing agri-tourism—the consumers' desire to visit wine country and taste the wines where they are made. The flow of tourists fuelled the need for restaurants, and with the restaurants came talented chefs, chefs who demanded only the best and freshest local products. And the region responded….

Kathleen kept a journal and documented her year in Niagara, following the rhythms of the season with a poet's sensibility. Through her eyes we tour the area, discovering the local purveyors of fine foods, bakers, brewers, makers of jams, oyster suppliers, innkeepers, winemakers and chefs, particularly the chefs who have a special place in her heart. And always we come back to her kitchen where she is constantly busy creating meals based on the seasonal ingredients she has grown herself, foraged for in the wild or purchased from local growers. She teaches us how to make a mayonnaise without it curdling, prepares for us a delicious wine punch and shares with us Helen Lenko's recipe for apple pie (a must-try at Daniel Lenko Winery). Husband

Ted, a trained sommelier, has matched her dishes, and those of Niagara's chefs, with wines from local wineries.

As a counterpoint to Kathleen's gardening instincts we learn how a commercial winery operates as Matthew Speck of Henry of Pelham gives us a monthly commentary on the workings of his family winery. But what informs this book that is part journal, part cookbook for all seasons and part guidebook is Kathleen Sloan-McIntosh's inner journey as she learns country lore with her hands in the earth. En route she unwittingly maps her own spiritual transition from city sophisticate to country gardener through contact with the land—a trowel in one hand and *The Old Farmer's Almanac* in the other. Through her limpid prose you too will experience "the magnetic pull of this comparatively little piece of Canada."

Tony Aspler

Introduction

"to drink a glass of wine in the country where the grape is grown . . ."

My ongoing love affair with the region of Ontario known as Niagara has had three distinct phases.

As a boomer kid growing up in Toronto, the name Niagara simply meant one thing. As for most everyone else on the planet, Niagara and "the Falls" were synonymous. My parents would often make late-summer forays there, showing it off to any of my Mum's visiting relatives from England. "So much nicer than the other side, we think," she would point out. Afterwards we would cross the bridge to the U.S. on foot, so that I could straddle the border, stretching my legs so as to place a foot in each country at once. Over there, Dad could sample a little fizzy canned American beer and Mum could buy clothes for the return to a new school year. Layered in new duds, I always fretted that the customs people would point out that I appeared a good deal fatter on my return to Canada. Back on our side of the border, we would spread out a blanket in stately Queen Victoria Park and enjoy our packed lunch of egg salad sandwiches, potato chips, butter tarts, lemonade and flasked tea before heading home on the Queen Elizabeth Highway. And that was it.

Years later, after living in England, I returned to discover the area around the historic town of Niagara-on-the-Lake and lived in the town itself during the late 1970s. A favoured weekend activity included "going over the river" to Niagara Falls, New York, where we would sit in funny little dark bars and order Genesee Cream Ale and containerloads of chicken wings. At that time, Niagara-on-the-Lake had the relatively stuffy-and-stately Oban Inn at one end and the relatively snooty Prince of Wales at the other. The pseudo-English Angel Inn lay betwixt the two and there was a sort of biker bar down by the river where we'd listen to CCR cover bands.

Lashings of roast beef or steak and kidney pie were to be had at he Oban, while the dining room at the newly revamped Prince featured skinny, gawky young servers culled from local farms self-consciously serving plates of veal medallions blanketed in thick cream sauces, with limp broccoli and carrots in attendance. Because summertime brought the inevitable hordes of tourists, we avoided the main drag at all costs, except to visit Greaves for their wonderful jams, jellies and chili sauce and the local bakery. My small daughters wouldn't let me pass by without stopping for a bag of their legendary warm doughnuts, split and filled with real whipped cream.

Besides those doughnuts, my girls devoured baskets of fruit: Red Haven peaches, plums, apricots, cherries and apples. The growing of fruit was what Niagara was all about then.

Niagara was pretty, mostly quiet and renowned for its lush farmland that brought forth the province's finest produce, including those cute little Concord grapes that we turned into jelly or juice. Other grapes were grown by a handful of estate wineries— Inniskillin, Château des Charmes and Hillebrand. We who lived there thought it pretty neat that wine was being made locally, and every now and then we'd actually buy a bottle on a whim—deeply purple Marechal Foch, as I remember. Smiling at each other's equally purple teeth we'd inevitably say, "Well, not bad considering it's made in Ontario."

In the summer of 2000, I returned to Niagara. I was updating research for an article I was writing for *The Globe & Mail* and a feature on the Niagara wine region for an Australian publication called the *Wine Magazine*. I also wanted to visit West Niagara, where many of the newer wineries were to be found, an area quite removed from the hustle of Niagara proper, but one, as I was to discover, with its own particular charm.

I was looking to taste wines from estate wineries that weren't even a sparkle in anyone's eye when I lived there, sleep in revamped versions of the hotels I remembered and eat, this time, on our side of the border.

After much time spent familiarizing myself with winding country roads and lanes, experiencing the visual and visceral pleasures of the region with its softly rounded hills and lush green landscapes, enjoying food at winery restaurants matched with the exemplary wines themselves, I find myself, once again, a Niagara resident. Such was the magnetic pull of this comparatively little piece of Canada that we decided to trade our home in downtown Toronto for a quiet green piece of land on the other side of Lake Ontario and live in a house whose age predates Confederation.

This land has no equal in Canada. Positioned in the northernmost segment of the Carolinian Zone, an area that extends from the coast of the American Carolinas northward, Niagara is home to more unique and rare species of plants and wildlife than any other place in Canada. It is because of this uniqueness that the United Nations dubbed it a World Biosphere Reserve back in 1990.

After our first year in this beautiful area, we can hardly imagine living anywhere else. Already we feel connected to and part of everything that goes on here. Watching the vineyard workers in fields close by our property, whether in January, July or September, pruning and tying vines, thinning flower clusters and the like, we've come to understand that the business of producing quality wine is a year-long, day-in, day-out affair demanding passion, dedication, knowledge and skill in equal measure. Similarly, the farmers who grow the area's famed peaches, plums, pears, apricots and apples are always busy, even in the depths of winter. We have visited wineries and dined in their restaurants. We have often hiked along the Bruce Trail to the restored Morningstar Mill, just a short walk from our home, to buy a little bag of their stone-ground whole wheat flour for my bread baking. We've sat at the edge of the Henry of Pelham winery vineyard to enjoy their annual Shakespeare in the Vineyard productions. At outdoor backyard summer soirées with friends we've slurped fresh oysters from Niagara Oyster Company, enjoying them with Vineland Estates wonderful sparkling Riesling. I've spent the year making everything I can using local fruits, vegetables, meat and game, eggs, cheese and wine. In the summer, two of our daughters, Jenna and Emma, picked the tiny wild cherries on the edge of our property and turned them into pies and jam. As I write this on a frigid January day, chickadees, woodpeckers and cardinals are busy at the bird feeders that my husband Ted has strung to hang beneath the grape arbour. During the summer, I used those grapes to make chutney, jam and croustades, but now the strong, sleeping, tangled vine is coated with snow and serves as a command post central for all the wild birds.

Perhaps best of all, we had the pleasure of growing many of our own foods: tomatoes, potatoes, greens and beans. If there is anything to equal the joy of unearthing the first crop of potatoes, boiling them quickly on an outdoor fire and devouring them slathered with butter, I haven't found it. Sowing seed and planting trees and bulbs in this special soil truly make this home.

Traipsing through Short Hills Provincial Park or along the Bruce Trail with our black Lab Casey and our collective of kids and grandson, we count ourselves blessed to have all this quiet beauty on our doorstep. Sitting in our gazebo after a summer dinner, perhaps with a soft rain falling, we finish our wine and gaze around us, pledging never to take any of it for granted.

All of this and much more have combined in our first year to form the inspiration for this book. In it you will find a personal collection of recipes, some of my own and many from the area's residents, workers, growers, chefs. Each one has been paired with a particular wine (or, in some cases, beer) from the Niagara region, chosen by my husband, Ted McIntosh. Though he has a sommelier background and is passionate about wine, he works for the venerable Niagara Brewing Company, the area's only microbrewery and one of the nation's oldest.

To satisfy my own curiosity, each chapter also contains capsule comments from Matthew Speck, viticulturist and vice-president of the well-respected Henry of Pelham Family Estate Winery located on the Niagara Bench. As everyone in the region knows, he is one of the three Speck brothers who own and operate the winery that produces some of the best wines in the country. Matthew, his brother Paul and winemaker Ron Giesbrecht all generously gave of their time for this book, helping me to outline in simple terms a typical year in the life of an Ontario winery, from January to December. The business of wine-making is, at the least, a year-long affair.

My hope is that this book will inspire you to look at Niagara and all it has to offer with new eyes, and to regularly visit the region throughout the year.

To appreciate the myriad products that emanate from it, travel the Niagara Wine Route that begins at Stoney Creek in the west and runs through to Niagara Falls itself; there are more than 40 wineries to visit. Stop to sample the wines, meet the talented, dedicated vintners and ask them about their wines. Buy a few bottles to take home and introduce them to your friends. Dine in a couple of the restaurants and cafés, visit the little shops and plan to stay overnight in one of the many B & Bs. In the morning, hike the trails, saunter along the small-town streets or leave the roads most travelled and pull up alongside a roadside farmer's fruit stand to load up your trunk with baskets of magnificent peaches, pears, grapes, tomatoes or peppers. Talk to the hardworking and dedicated farmers who grew them to find out what it takes to do what they do. And, above all, treasure, as we do, this blessed bit of Canada.

Kathleen Sloan-McIntosh
Niagara Peninsula, 2002

Legend

The Wineries of the Niagara Peninsula

1   Puddicombe Estate Farms and Winery
2   Kittling Ridge Estate Wines and Spirits
3   Peninsula Ridge Estates Winery
4   Angels Gate Winery
5   Thirty Bench Wines
6   EastDell Estates
7   Magnotta Beamsville
8   Crown Bench Estates
9   De Sousa Wine Cellars
10 Maple Grove Vinoteca Estate Winery
11 Lakeview Cellars Estate Winery
12 Willow Heights Estate Winery
13 Royal DeMaria Wines
14 Birchwood Estate Wines
15 Vineland Estates Winery
16 Kacaba Vineyards
17 Stoney Ridge Cellars
18 Cave Spring Cellars
19 Harbour Estates Winery
20 Creekside Estate Winery
21 Rockway Glen Golf Course & Estate Winery
22 Hernder Estate Wines
23 Henry of Pelham Family Estate Winery
24 Maleta Estate Winery
25 Château des Charmes
26 Hillebrand Estates Winery
27 Stonechurch Vineyards
28 Konzelmann Estate Winery
29 Strewn Winery
30 Pillitteri Estates Winery
31 Joseph's Estate Wines
32 Sunnybrook Farm Estate Winery
33 Jackson-Triggs Niagara Estate Winery
34 Peller Estates Winery
35 Lailey Vineyard
36 Reif Estate Winery
37 Inniskillin Wines
38 Marynissen Estates Winery
39 Riverview Cellars Winery

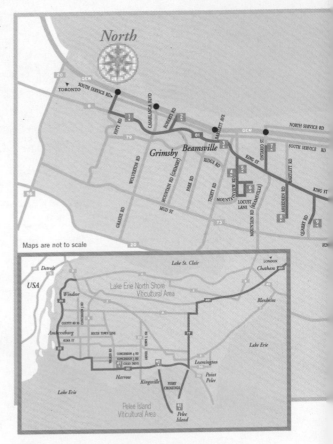

Maps are not to scale

The Wineries of Lake Erie North Shore & Pelee Island

40 Pelee Island Winery
41 Colio Estate Wines
42 Pelee Island Winery Pavilion

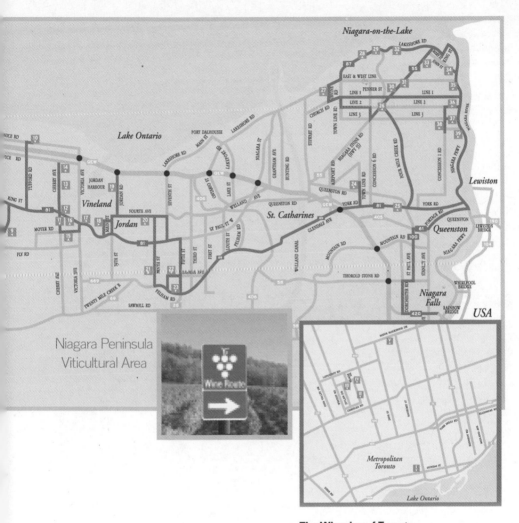

Niagara Peninsula
Viticultural Area

The Wineries of Toronto

I   De Sousa Wine Cellars
II   Magnotta Winery
III Vinoteca Inc. Premium Winery
IV Cilento Wines
V   Southbrook Farm and Winery

Think globally—
cook, eat and drink locally

White Nights & Wine Cellars

This is the start of our first year in the Niagara Peninsula. Quite removed from city life, our old house, circa 1850, is situated along a lovely, winding country road that climbs to the top of the Niagara escarpment. We live near a number of communities—Pelham, Fonthill, Thorold and the city of St. Catharines. Just west of us is Decew Falls and Morningstar Mill, a handsome old refurbished flour mill. To the east can be found the remnants of militia officer Captain John DeCou's stone house, where an inscription reads, *". . . To which came Laura Secord through the woods and swamps below the Niagara Escarpment from Queenston on June 24th, 1813, to warn of the American advance."*

The beginning of January marks one month here. And because it seems fitting, surrounded by lakes as we are, we name our house Grasmere, after my Mum's childhood home in England.

Our new home is 150 years old—older than any house in which we have lived in Canada—and the property backs onto a beautiful segment of the Bruce Trail. It winds through tall pines, wild fruit trees, rose and berry bushes, and ancient vines entangle trunks and branches. Today, every length of branch, each limb, whether sturdy or slight, is cotton-tufted with snow. My boots crunch the snow as Casey steams on ahead, snuffling at real and imagined animal scents, his sheer blackness startling against the sea of white. He is clearly in his glory. A former urban canine, now in his tenth year, he is a renewed pup in retirement. Flinging himself into the drifts, he rolls around on his back making dog angels in the powdery snow. Cartooning across the ice, legs splayed, he'll happily venture into any bit of icy water he may find, so impervious to the cold is he. I half expect him to get up on his hind legs and do a little dog cha cha cha for joy.

A slash of crimson from a fleet cardinal streaks the white. He alights on a branch, only to be frightened away by a typically obstreperous blue jay. A huge hawk effortlessly performs a sweeping arc above the lake, showing off for me. The Canada geese are an audible constant throughout the day, endlessly, noisily winging back and forth across the sky over our house between the two nearby lakes: Gibson just over the road and Lake Moodie to the rear. Their waters seem solidly frozen right now.

New Year's day is brilliant, blue sky and crystal clear air. We grab the morning to take our first hike through Short Hills Provincial Park, so near as to be almost on our doorstep. It is huge and handsome with its crisp, cross-country trails and well-marked pathways that go on forever. On the way home, looking at the frozen farmland and row upon row of dormant vine it is hard to imagine anything will ever grow again. Back home, Ted builds a fire and pours Eisbock, the robust seasonal beer from the brewery he works for, Niagara Brewing. My favourite, and quite delicious with Oka cheese and fresh walnuts. There is a sense of well-being to be felt after a bundled winter walk that I never experience during any other time of the year—of course, the Eisbock could have something to do with it.

JANUARY 8. This day finds me contemplative, sitting by the fire, thumbing through *The Old Farmer's Almanac* and reading the weather predictions for the year ahead. What an extraordinary little publication. I read with real wonder about natural remedies for what may ail plants (trap snails and slugs in shallow pans filled with beer). There's a little treatise on the visual appeal of a self-created woodpile, information about gestation and mating periods for ewes, planting and gardening by the phases of the moon and everything I've ever wanted to know about tides. Fascinating reading for a city girl.

We have been told that we will find weak-spirited winters here but you can't judge by the last few weeks: it is cold, snowy and typically Canadian. I am happy because I stubbornly hold to the old-fashioned view that that's the way winter should be in this country. It just doesn't feel right otherwise. We are surrounded by beauty, complete with that special quiet hush that only a cloak of snow provides.

Two magnificent old horse chestnut trees stand at the front of our house, long, thin, knobbly black arms coated with ice and snow. And in the rear, by the gazebo, are two stately black walnut trees with perfectly straight trunks, side by side like a couple at the altar. I learn later that their wood has always been prized by furniture makers because of that very straightness and that these days they are almost an endangered species.

The harvesting of the icewine grapes came especially early this year, not long after we moved in on December 1. Usually the picking gets underway sometime between Christmas and New Year's, making the holidays extra busy for those involved in the wine business. For wine lovers like us, it is wonderful to be so near to the land where the grape is grown. Our closest winery is Henry of Pelham Family Estate Winery, the small but distinctive premium estate winery owned and run by the Speck brothers. The last time we visited, we learned that their icewine was chosen by British Airways to be served in Business Class on their North American flights—quite the coup.

FEBRUARY 10. I received one of my favourite things today: fragrant purple hyacinths from Ted to sit in the window of the light-filled room where I work. He shows me packets of vegetable seeds: two types of tomato, Sicilian eggplant, flat-leaf parsley. I show him the list I have made after studying the Stokes seed catalogue and he says we will have to become full-time farmers to grow everything I have earmarked. I watch as he sows seeds in starter trays and soon—so soon!—tiny seedlings like pale green threads emerge, pushing up through the soil. They sit in my office window as the snow comes down heavily and the hyacinth's scent feeds my soul.

Out of the corner of my eye I think someone has tied a dozen red bows on a tree outside my window, then realize that a convention of cardinals has decided to collectively strut their stuff. So artfully arranged, I think they must know how lovely they look. Sweet little chickadees, jays, more cardinals, woodpeckers and, once in a while, a lone oriole flutter around outside my window where we have placed bird feeders and hung seeded suet balls. We continually replenish sunflower seed and now and then I impale a withered apple on a bit of grapevine for them. All is graciously received.

Outside, curled into a neat fur ball, is my first, pink-faced possum. He/she sits just outside our front door, pressed against the wall for warmth, a long, similarly pink and quite ratty tail winding round him. An elderly gentleman out for his morning walk says, "Go ahead, pick him up by the tail and fling him into the woods, but be careful because possums are stupid *and* vicious." Not a great combination, we think. And not the prettiest creature in the world, especially with those constantly bared needle-like teeth and his little bulbous eyes. He rather gives me the creeps, so the decision is made to just let him be. Later in the day, we spy a fox scampering across the top of the yard. Amazing sights for former city dwellers.

Valentine's night and every branch is snow-clad; the fresh hush of snow is back. The nights are still, icy and white as white can be. My Valentine prepares an herb and mustard rack of lamb, little red potatoes, roasted parsnips and leeks, and we enjoy it by candle and firelight, along with a bottle of Henry of Pelham 1998 Cabernet-Merlot. For dessert, I make simple little oval-shaped meringues set in a pool of raspberry coulis sided with a few slices of ripe mango. Lovely with Vineland Estates's icewine.

In the last few days of February, the birdsong changes to include the sad yet soothing coo of mourning doves sitting in our black walnut trees. Towards the end of the month, a massive full moon hangs so low it threatens to fall into the trees, shining its eerie light on the now-tired snow and illuminating the spreading forsythia bush by Grasmere's front door. In its light, I see fat, sealed-tight buds, a promise of the yellow and green to come.

In the Vineyard and On the Vine

"There are three components to most wineries: the farm itself or vineyard, the winery, and the shop or hospitality area. At this time of the year, in the vineyard, depending on the weather, we may still be working on picking icewine grapes, finishing off everything through early January. Outside of that we're pruning vines. We're removing excess growth from the year before, shaping the vine to help in the establishment of the crop for the coming season. The whole vineyard has to be pruned and shaped. For us, that means 1,200 vines an acre, with 150 acres in total, so that's a pretty big job. It's a four- to five-month project, which we start in early January and really get into at the outset of the new year.

"In the winery, icewine is fermenting from any picking done in December. We're also really doing a lot of cellar work, getting wines into barrel or out of barrel, filtering, blending. Especially those whites and other wines that don't see oak-aging: Riesling, rosé, Sur Lie Chardonnay, Sauvignon Blanc. All of these will bottle early, because they are not barrel-aged. Nothing much changes in stainless steel! Also, these are wines that are meant to be released a little younger; we think of them as spring wines. We also begin to pull out the top reds from two years ago, because these will be ready for bottling now. For us these would be the Reserve Baco Noir, Cabernet Merlot, Pinot Noir—all the reds that get an extra year in the barrel.

"As for the store, things are generally pretty quiet in the hospitality area right now. Any renovations or upgrading to the winery or other areas is generally done now while it is quiet. This is when we do a lot of planning for the coming season, but our store is open year-round, seven days a week."

Matthew Speck, Henry of Pelham Family Estate Winery

Harvesting Icewine Grapes

A few years ago, while studying for his sommelier certificate (and long before moving to Niagara), my husband, Ted, took part in the annual icewine harvest at Inniskillin Wines. These are hastily scribbled notes he made following the experience.

11:30 A.M. Get the call from Inniskillin asking if I want to pick grapes that night. Leave home about 7:30 p.m. after packing almost every piece of winter clothing I own.

8:45 P.M. Arrive at Inniskillin to find a short line-up outside. Inside, the scene resembles a ski resort, with everyone in suitable winter gear. Later I learn that around 85 people had showed up to pick. The ideal number apparently is 20 to 30 people. I sign in and then the vineyard manager announces we'll have about a half-hour wait. "Just waiting for the temperature of the grapes to drop. Not quite cold enough, we need them down to between -8 and -10°C."

We're invited to view the display upstairs in the loft and help ourselves to coffee and juice.

9:45 P.M. Still waiting, I enjoy a coffee and a viewing of a tape on Niagara wineries.

10:00 P.M. We all get dressed to head outside. Outside? I was quite happy and warm inside! We're shown where to start picking the Vidal grapes under large floodlights. The green protective netting is ripped away and we split up to start harvesting. The grapes are like marbles, with the bunches just breaking off the vine with a snap.

As we work along the row and away from the only light source, it is more difficult to see the grapes. There is no moon and no snow for reflection. Some of the grapes are still soft and turn to mush in your glove. Others are shrivelled, which is fine. A grape is approximately 80 percent water, so once the water is gone, all that is left is pure, naturally sweet concentrated grape nectar.

After picking one or two rows, a gentleman points out that some of the first rows we picked still have grape bunches stuck in the nets, so a second picking of that row is required. Learn later that was Donald Ziraldo, co-founder of Inniskillin. The whole thing is a very labour-intensive operation. Just ask my knees and back! It is very easy to see how this reflects on the final price of $40 to $50 per half-bottle.

1:00 A.M. I get up from my knees and notice there are only three of us left in the vineyard. It must be time for a break! Back inside, the aromas of fresh coffee and hot chili fill my head. Ahh! Just as I am about to dive in, Donald Ziraldo asks for a volunteer—but doesn't say for what. All those old army movies always warned against this sort of thing, but I am curious so I step up. I learn that the LCBO's Michael Fagan (the Matchmaker in their *Food & Drink* magazine) is shooting a video for the LCBO, so off I go back to the vineyard.

After my moment of fame and stardom I finally get my bowl of chili and a fresh bun—man, does it taste good! Then I head off to the winery to see the presses and meet the assistant winemaker. Icewine grapes are pressed outside while still frozen, hence the very low yields. We talk about the grapes and how the crush is going. Everything is good, with a Brix reading of 40 percent. Brix is the approximate measure of concentrated grape sugars. The whole process is monitored very carefully every single step of the way. The temperature has risen, and after conferring with Donald Ziraldo and others, the decision is made to stop the picking for now. This is mostly because Mother Nature is not co-operating, but also because we have too many pickers and the picking is proceeding too fast. We are instructed to wait until 6:00 a.m., when the temperature is expected to drop, before continuing.

For now, I'm done. I really understand more now about the whole icewine process and I'm really glad I had the opportunity to take part.

Ted McIntosh

Everything You Need to Know about Icewine—the Spirit Born of a Canadian Winter

The golden liquid known as icewine is an exceedingly precious commodity. No other Canadian wine receives the recognition and anticipation that Ontario's icewine receives. It regularly garners international awards, all of which attest to the skills required to bring it to the consumer.

Just the facts . . .

- All that glitters is not gold! Authentic icewine is made in only a handful of countries—Germany, Austria and Canada. Some warm-climate countries make icewine using artificial techniques of harvesting the grapes in late fall, placing them in freezers and later pressing the sweet juice. True icewine is made from grapes that have naturally frozen on the vine, are hand-harvested in the winter when temperatures dip to -8°C (18°F) or lower and are immediately pressed while still frozen. The natural method results in an icewine that is more complex in structure and finesse, with subtle layers of honey and tropical fruits.
- Why is it so expensive? The quantity of icewine made from frozen winter grapes is approximately 15 percent compared to the quantity of wine made from grapes picked during the usual fall harvest. Grape growers take big risks leaving fruit on the vine. The sweet grapes can fall prey to hungry birds (most vineyards must be netted), rain can cause bunch rot, and wind and snow can create more loss by stripping grapes from the vine.
- The most widely used grapes for making icewine are Vidal, Riesling and Gewürztraminer. Their slightly thicker skins can withstand the rigours of below-freezing temperatures. Other varieties include red icewines made with Cabernet Franc and Merlot grapes.
- Serve icewine chilled as you would serve white wine. Place a bottle in the refrigerator for up to one hour prior to serving.

- Pour small amounts of icewine—1½ to 2 ounces (50 mL) is the ideal serving portion per person. Serve in a traditional white wine glass to fully experience the rich, full bouquet, or go all out and serve in the Riedel Vinum Extreme Icewine glass.
- When serving icewine with dessert, be sure that the food in question is no sweeter than the icewine. Icewines with desserts like poached pears, an apple or pear tart, fresh figs drizzled with honey and cream, or apricot and nut strudels make memorable partnerships.
- Icewine is an elegant way to begin a meal. Try accompaniments like seared foie gras or rich pâté, especially if served with a fruit reduction or spiced raisin chutney. Blue cheese with tart cranberries in phyllo pastry or an Italian-style squash-stuffed pasta tossed with browned butter also work very well.
- Then there's cheese with icewine. Assertive blues such as Stilton, Roquefort or Cabrales, raw milk cheeses and Ontario's famous Cheddars are great choices. Or serve icewine with soft young cheese, fresh tropical fruits like mango, pineapple and papaya and a handful of fresh-shelled almonds or walnuts.

Simple Seasonal Pleasure

Warm Glazed Pears with Honey, Walnuts & Double Cream

Halve and core 6 ripe pears and brush the cut side with apricot nectar. Roast in a hot oven for about 8 minutes, basting with more of the apricot nectar, until they are beginning to colour and are tender when tested. Serve with a teaspoon of cold double cream in each cavity. Drizzle with warmed honey and toasted walnuts. A natural with icewine.

In Season and On the Table

ROOT VEGETABLES, SMOKED FISH, HAM HOCKS, LAMB, DRIED BEANS,
DUCK, VENISON, PORK, HAZELNUTS, FIGS, PARMESAN

Root Cellar Chowder *12*

Smoked Haddock & Potato Soup *14*

Ham Hock Terrine with Niagara Peach Salsa *16*

Winter Salad of Fennel, Parmigiano & Prosciutto *18*

Mahogany Muscovy Duck Breasts *19*

Arden's Venison Stew in Red Wine *20*

Lamb Shanks in Niagara Olde Jack Strong Ale *22*

Beef in Baco with Porcini *24*

Pork Loin with Crackling & Maple-Spiced Applesauce *26*

Star Anise-Crusted Duck Breast & Noodle Salad
with Pickled Niagara Plums *28*

Butter-Braised Endives with Parsley *31*

Chocolate Fudge Pot Pudding with a Saucy Bottom *32*

Snow Whites with Raspberry Coulis & Sliced Mango *34*

Icewine-Soaked Figs with Hazelnut Strips *36*

Root Cellar Chowder

Recommended: Inniskillin Chardonnay Reserve
Serves 6–8

I've always wanted a root and fruit cellar, a dark and cool section of a cellar in an old house that is devoted to the storage of root vegetables or apples packed in straw, newspapers or sandy soil—and now I have one. Inspired by that philosophy, this satisfying chowder can easily be further embellished with shrimp, mussels, fish or leftover turkey or chicken.

2 Tbsp. (30 mL) butter	2 medium potatoes, peeled and finely
2 Tbsp. (30 mL) olive oil	chopped
2 medium onions, chopped	salt and freshly ground black pepper
2 cloves garlic, minced	to taste
3 Tbsp. (45 mL) flour	3–4 slices lean bacon, finely chopped
½ cup (120 mL) dry white wine	1 cup (240 mL) chopped fresh flat-leaf
5 cups (1.2 L) chicken stock	parsley
½ rutabaga, finely chopped	½ cup (120 mL) walnuts, finely
3 parsnips, peeled and finely chopped	chopped
3 medium carrots, finely chopped	1 cup (240 mL) whipping cream

In a large saucepan or Dutch oven, combine the butter with the olive oil over medium-high heat. Sauté the onions and garlic for 5 minutes, until the vegetables are softened. Whisk in the flour, reduce the heat a little and cook for a further 5 minutes, being careful not to brown the flour.

Whisk the white wine into the flour mixture and increase the heat slightly. Add the chicken stock, rutabaga, parsnips, carrots, potatoes and salt and pepper. Bring to a boil, then reduce the heat and allow the mixture to simmer for about 30 minutes.

Sauté the bacon over medium-high heat for a few minutes, drain off and discard any fat, then add the parsley and walnuts. Continue to sauté over medium heat until the bacon is cooked through, about 5 minutes. Remove from the heat and keep warm.

Stir the whipping cream into the soup and simmer for a further few minutes until heated through. Serve garnished with the bacon mixture.

Henry of Pelham Family Estate Winery

Just like the people responsible for their production, the wines from this premium estate winery up on the Niagara Bench are well-respected, awarded and very popular. The Speck brothers—Paul, Matthew and Daniel—have been seriously involved in the world of wine since they began in 1988. The property that comprises the winery and vineyards was originally deeded to their great, great, great-grandfather in 1794. The crown land was bestowed on him as a reward for being an Empire Loyalist. With the help of winemaker Ron Giesbrecht, the Speck family quietly produce some of the finest wines in the region and the country. And they're nice guys to boot! Their efforts are concentrated on Chardonnay, Riesling, Cabernet Sauvignon, Baco Noir and Riesling icewine.

Smoked Haddock & Potato Soup

Recommended: EastDell Estates Barrel Fermented Chardonnay
Serves 4

EastDell Estates, one of the Beamsville Bench wineries, regularly holds different events throughout the year in their Bench Bistro, where chef Mark Walpole makes the most of local products on his changing menu. One of the regularly scheduled events is EastDell's Robbie Burns Night dinner, complete with haggis that the chef orders from a butcher just outside Hamilton specializing in Scottish foods. The following soup, substantial and warming, is the perfect beginning to any Burns Night feast.

1 ½ lb. (680 g) smoked haddock fillets
2 cups (475 mL) whole milk
1 white onion, finely chopped
3 ½ cups (840 mL) light stock or
    water
2 potatoes, peeled and diced

3 Tbsp. (45 mL) butter
1 cup (240 mL) whipping cream
salt and freshly ground white pepper
    to taste
¼ cup (60 mL) chopped fresh flat-leaf
    parsley

Place the haddock in a large, wide saucepan along with the milk, onion, stock or water. Place over medium-high heat and bring to a gentle boil; reduce the heat and simmer for 5–10 minutes, until the fish is tender. Use a slotted spoon to remove the fish from the liquid and transfer to a plate. Skin and bone the fish, breaking the meat into small chunks as you work.

(continued on page 15)

Winter comes to Inniskillin

Lamb Shanks in Niagara Olde Jack Strong Ale (page 22)

Return the skin and bones to the liquid in the saucepan. Add the potatoes and cook very gently for about an hour. At the end of the cooking time, strain through a sieve set over a bowl. Wipe the saucepan clean and return the liquid to it, along with the reserved fish, butter and cream. Season with salt and pepper and simmer until heated through. Don't allow it to boil. Just before serving, stir in the parsley. Serve in warmed soup plates with plenty of good, crusty bread and butter.

Quackerbox Ducks

Ducks and dogs are the passion of Michelle Seaborn. At any given time Quackerbox Farms, located high above the town of Grimsby on the escarpment, is home to between 3,000 and 5,000 prized Muscovy ducks. On the same property is her golden retriever kennel, Silmaril, which was the reason Michelle and husband, Dr. Richard Stopps, originally moved from their Hamilton home back in 1988. She sells around 50 puppies each year, but thousands and thousands of her ducks go to restaurants and other outlets in the area and beyond. Michelle says, "Half of my duck business goes to the wineries and restaurants, probably because duck is such an excellent meat with wine and fruit, both of which are in abundance out here."

Ham Hock Terrine with Niagara Peach Salsa

Recommended: Peller Estates Winery Founder's Series Late Harvest Vidal
Serves 4–6

Smoked or fresh, ham hocks are a terrific bargain and can be enjoyed in so many ways. At this time of the year, I like to slow-cook them with white beans and tomatoes or I make this chunky, substantial terrine that everybody enjoys with crackers and the award-winning Niagara Peach Salsa from Niagara Presents. It's equally good with mustard pickle or any chutney. Prepare to make this 24 hours in advance.

2 fresh ham hocks, about 4 lb. (1.8 kg) in total
1/4 cup (60 mL) white wine vinegar
1 onion, chopped
1 carrot, chopped
1 stalk celery, chopped
1 small leek, rinsed and chopped
6 whole cloves

4 sprigs fresh thyme
6 cloves garlic, peeled
10 whole black peppercorns
1 large bunch flat-leaf parsley, washed, dried and finely chopped
salt and freshly ground black pepper to taste

Place the ham hocks in a Dutch oven or similar heavy pot, cover with cold water and bring to a boil over high heat. When it has boiled, drain off and discard the water. Add enough cold water to cover the ham hocks. Add the vinegar, chopped vegetables, cloves, thyme, garlic and peppercorns. Return to a boil over high heat, then reduce the heat and simmer for 3–4 hours, until the ham hocks are tender. Make sure the ham hocks are submerged, adding a little additional water if it becomes necessary.

Using tongs, transfer the hocks to a plate or cutting board to cool. Strain the cooking liquid. You will need 2/3 cup/160 mL of the liquid (freeze the rest for soup). As the hocks cool, line a pâté baking dish (or small loaf pan) with plastic wrap, allowing it to overhang slightly.

Using a small paring knife, pull off and discard the ham hock skin. Pull off the meat, discarding all the fat as you work. Using your fingers, tear the meat into rough chunks and cover the bottom of the baking dish with it until you have a substantial layer. Now, scatter the surface generously with chopped parsley and season with salt and pepper. Repeat with another layer of ham until all the ham and parsley are combined. Pour the reserved cooking liquid over the ham. Cover with more plastic wrap and place a weight on top (a large can will do). Refrigerate overnight, or until firm.

Niagara Presents

Niagara Presents is a local, community-based co-operative outlet that develops, sells and distributes specialty food products. Everything from Niagara Presents originates right here in the Peninsula, whether it's the cherries in Very Cherry Chutney, the grapes in Grapes with a Twist or the golden peaches in the award-winning Niagara Peach Salsa. Operating out of Jordan Station, Niagara Presents has just the space for the production of home-style chutneys, preserves, jams, jellies and the like. Besides their own showroom, their products are also available in and around the Niagara Peninsula and farther afield.

Winter Salad of Fennel, Parmigiano & Prosciutto

Recommended: Peninsula Ridge Estates Sauvignon Blanc
Serves 6

Raise the subject of good prosciutto with just about any chef in the Niagara area and the name Mario Pingue will invariably come up. A long-time resident of the region, Mario Pingue regularly produces some of the most authentic-tasting prosciutto and Romano cheese out of his home in St. David's.

2 small fennel bulbs	½ lemon
3 bunches arugula, washed and trimmed	¼ lb. (113 g) prosciutto
⅓ cup (80 mL) extra virgin olive oil	¼ lb. (113 g) Parmigiano-Reggiano cheese
salt and freshly ground black pepper	2 Tbsp. (30 mL) extra virgin olive oil

Trim and discard the bottom of the fennel and any discoloured bits. Cut the fennel bulbs in half lengthwise and then very thinly slice across the width of each bulb. Place the sliced fennel in a large salad bowl along with the arugula. Drizzle with the ⅓ cup (80 mL) olive oil. Add the salt and pepper and a squeeze of fresh lemon juice. Toss well. Distribute the greens among 6 salad plates.

Loosely arrange slices of prosciutto on each, followed by shaved Parmigiano-Reggiano. Drizzle the remaining 2 Tbsp. (30 mL) olive oil over each salad and serve at once with warmed crusty bread.

Mahogany Muscovy Duck Breasts

Recommended: Thirty Bench Wines Riesling Limited Yield Semi-Dry

Serves 4

There are lots of complicated duck preparations, like duck confit and whole duck marinated in good red wine—and I am passionate about all of them. But I really love this one because it is simplicity itself. Serve with simple steamed rice or buttered noodles and sharply dressed greens.

4 boneless duck breasts, trimmed of excess fat

juice of 1 large orange

3 Tbsp. (45 mL) liquid honey

3 Tbsp. (45 mL) soy sauce

½ tsp (2.4 mL) five-spice powder

salt and freshly ground black pepper

Lay the duck breasts on a baking tray. Squeeze the orange juice over the breasts. In a small bowl, combine the honey, soy sauce, five-spice powder, a little salt and a good bit of black pepper. Whisk this mixture together and brush over each of the duck breasts. Let the breasts sit for about ½ hour, then brush again with the remaining mixture.

Preheat the oven to 450°F (230°C). Place a piece of parchment paper on the bottom of a roasting pan (this will keep the duck from scorching and ease clean-up later). Place a rack in the pan and lay the breasts on the rack skin side up. Place in the preheated oven and roast for 10–12 minutes. Check during this time to see that the breasts are not browning too fast; if the glaze looks as though it is, cover loosely with foil. Remove from the oven and let sit for a few minutes, keeping them warm. Slice on the diagonal to serve.

Arden's Venison Stew in Red Wine

Recommended: Hernder Estates Baco Noir
Serves 6–8

From Arden Vaughn at Lake Land Game Meats, this is a true cold-weather dish, rich, fragrant and very satisfying. From Arden: "Venison stewing meat is generally cut from the shoulder. You could make it with leg meat if you wished, but leg cuts cost more and the stewing process tenderizes the shoulder cuts well enough. I like to use Hernder's Baco Noir when I make this. It gives the stew a rich, full flavour." Serve with mounds of mashed potato or buttered egg noodles.

3 lb. (1.35 kg) boneless venison stewing meat, cut into 2-inch (5-cm) chunks
salt and freshly ground black pepper to taste
5 Tbsp. (75 mL) olive oil
4 slices bacon, cut into strips
1 tsp. (5 mL) dried thyme
10 juniper berries
2 bay leaves

2 Tbsp. (30 mL) tomato paste
4 Tbsp. (60 mL) all-purpose flour
2 Tbsp. (30 mL) red wine vinegar
1 cup (240 mL) Hernder Estates Baco Noir
2 large carrots, diced
1 large onion, diced
1 cup (240 mL) beef broth
3 Tbsp. (45 mL) cranberry or red currant jelly

Pat the meat dry and season with salt and pepper. Heat the olive oil in a large, heavy saucepan or Dutch oven over medium-high heat. Working in batches, sear the venison on all sides, removing it with a slotted spoon as it browns. When all the venison has been browned, reduce the heat and add the bacon and sauté for a few minutes, until softened. Add the thyme, juniper berries, bay leaves, tomato paste and flour and cook the mixture, stirring, for a few minutes more. Add the vinegar and the red wine, stirring with a wooden spoon and scraping up any bits clinging to the bottom of the pan. Add the carrots, onion, beef broth and the browned meat with its accumulated juices to the pan, give it a good stir and bring it to a boil. Reduce the heat, loosely cover and simmer for 2 hours, or until the meat is tender. Stir the stew occasionally and add a little more wine or water if necessary. Add the jelly and stir it into the stew. Taste and adjust the seasoning if necessary before serving.

Niagara Brewing Company

The 13-year-old Niagara Brewing Company is the area's only micro brewery. Producing great beer in traditional wine country is not that odd when you consider that NBC is owned and operated by the Criveller family, whose Criveller Company has manufactured equipment for wineries for some time. Gritstone Premium Ale is, perhaps, NBC's most popular brew, but they also have the distinction of producing North America's only true ice beer made in the style of the best German *bock*, whereby the beer is frozen and water extracted during the brewing process. A few years after Eisbock achieved overnight success, the big-boy breweries, Labatt and then Molson, introduced their own "ice beer," each one laying claim to its creation.

Lamb Shanks in Niagara Olde Jack Strong Ale

Recommended: Niagara Brewing Co. Olde Jack Strong Ale
Serves 6–8

When slow-cooked in dark beer, the meat on lamb shanks becomes tender, moist and flavourful. This is a simple, rustic dish that begs to be served with a mound of your best mashed potatoes and oven-roasted root vegetables. If you can't easily obtain lamb shanks, thick-cut shoulder lamb chops will work well. And if you can't find Niagara Brewing's Olde Jack Strong Ale at your local outlet, raise a fuss!

8 lamb shanks
salt and freshly ground black pepper
    to taste
½ cup (120 mL) all-purpose flour
⅓ cup (80 mL) olive oil
8 large cloves garlic, peeled
1 bay leaf
2 sprigs fresh thyme

2 branches fresh rosemary
1 large carrot, finely chopped
1 large onion, finely chopped
2 bottles (341 mL each) Niagara
    Brewing Olde Jack Strong Ale
2 cups (475 mL) beef stock
¼ cup (60 mL) chopped fresh parsley

Preheat the oven to 350°F (180°C). Season the lamb shanks with salt and pepper and then dust lightly with some of the flour, shaking off the excess. Heat half the oil in a Dutch oven or flameproof casserole and brown the shanks in batches over medium heat for about 15 minutes, turning them as they brown and adding the remaining oil as needed. Transfer the shanks to a plate as they are browned.

    Add the garlic, bay leaf, thyme, rosemary, carrot and onion to the pan and cook until the vegetables are slightly softened, about 3 minutes. Sprinkle the remaining flour over the vegetables and stir in well, cooking for another minute. Add the beer, stirring it in well. Bring to a boil and scrape up any bits on the bottom of the pan. Let boil for 5 minutes or so, covered.

Remove the lid and add the beef stock, stirring it into the mixture. Return the lamb shanks to the pot, cover and place in the preheated oven. Cook for about 2 hours, basting the meat every half hour or so. When the shanks are very tender, carefully transfer them and the whole garlic cloves to a plate and keep warm. Strain the liquid and return it to the pan along with the shanks and the garlic. Reheat slightly and serve garnished with the parsley.

Chef Stephen Treadwell of Queen's Landing

"The secret is that food must satisfy not just the physical pangs of hunger but also the nourishment of memory. For eating is at the heart of the art of living." That quote is uncredited but it hangs in the little office of Stephen Treadwell, the talented British-born chef at Tiara restaurant in Niagara-on-the-Lake's Queen's Landing Hotel. It neatly sums up Treadwell's culinary philosophy. Treadwell has helped to spawn other industries and businesses in the area, like Wyndym Farm, which supplies him with more than 16 varieties of lettuce, heirloom tomatoes and unique Asian-influenced food products. One of the nicest things about the restaurant is its close proximity to the lakeshore. "During the summer boaters moor their sailboats and walk up to dine on our outdoor barbecue patio. Where else in Ontario can you do this?" asks Treadwell.

Beef in Baco with Porcini

Recommended: Henry of Pelham Family Estate Baco Noir Reserve
Serves 6

We are big fans of Henry of Pelham's Baco Noir, especially their Baco Noir Reserve 1999, which was ranked second overall out of all red wines at Cuvée 2001. Their Baco Noir 2000 is also rich, concentrated and balanced, making it the perfect choice for this rustic dish. This preparation is even better when made a day ahead. Serve with good, crusty bread. Beef marrow bones are available in the meat department at supermarkets or at butcher shops. If you don't see them, inquire, and make sure they are filled with marrow.

⅓ cup (80 mL) olive oil
1 large onion, chopped
3 lb. (1.35 kg) stewing beef, excess
    fat trimmed and cut into 1-inch
    (2.5-cm) pieces
2 good-sized beef marrow bones
4 bay leaves, preferably fresh, or
    2 dried
2 whole cloves

salt and freshly ground black pepper
    to taste
2 cups (475 mL) Henry of Pelham Baco
    Noir
1 Tbsp. (15 mL) tomato paste
1 oz. (25 g) dried porcini mushrooms,
    soaked for 15 minutes and then
    strained (reserve soaking liquid)
2½ cups (600 mL) beef stock

Warm the oil in a Dutch oven or flameproof casserole over medium-high heat. Sauté the onion for 5 minutes or so, until softened. Brown the beef on all sides in two batches. Add the beef marrow bones, bay leaves, cloves and a good grinding of salt and pepper. Continue to cook and stir for another 10 minutes, turning the meat and bones over frequently. Splash in the red wine, increase the heat to high and cook for about 10 minutes, until the wine has reduced slightly and the mixture has thickened. Reduce the heat.

Blend the tomato paste into the porcini soaking liquid and add it and the porcini to the meat. Pour in half the beef stock, increase the heat and bring to a gentle boil. Reduce the heat to a simmer, cover loosely and cook slowly for about 2 hours, checking occasionally and adding additional stock during the cooking time. Cook until the sauce is nicely thickened and the meat is tender. Use a small spoon to remove the marrow from the bones and add it to the sauce. Discard the bones and bay leaves and serve immediately.

Strewn Winery & Wine Country Cooking School

Owners Jane Langdon and Joe Will might have named their winery Cannery Row as Strewn is housed in a refurbished canning factory just outside the Old Town of Niagara-on-the-Lake. Inspired by experiences they enjoyed in California's Napa Valley, the couple decided to make a cooking school part of the package, because, as Jane puts it, "food and wine naturally go together." Known for their award-winning Rieslings and Chardonnays, Strewn is also home to Terroir La Cachette, a pretty Provence-inspired dining room featuring the best of seasonal Niagara foods.

Pork Loin with Crackling & Maple-Spiced Applesauce

Recommended: Cave Spring Cellars Gamay Reserve Estate Bottled

Serves 6

When we first arrived in Niagara, I chatted with chef Michael Olson, who had just switched his focus from that of chef at Cave Spring's Inn on the Twenty restaurant to teaching at the Niagara Culinary Institute at Niagara College. Michael spent about an hour telling me where to go in the area to get the best of everything food-wise—from Italian food products to schnitzel. When I told him I was planning an old-fashioned pork loin with crackling for Christmas dinner, he said, "Call Dougherty's Meats in Allanburg and order one. Tell them I sent you." So I did, and what a magnificent piece of pork we had for Christmas dinner—moist, juicy and full of flavour. Crackling—the pig's fatty skin—is totally unfashionable these days, but this is a classic component of a dinner that comes but once a year. You'll probably have to order a pork loin with crackling ahead of time. Any good butcher can prepare it for you by scoring it deeply with a sharp knife. This allows the fat just beneath the skin to melt and bubble up when in the oven—making the top layer ultra-crispy and crackly. The crackle chorus can get pretty loud around the table when everyone digs in! Make the applesauce ahead of time, but warm it gently before serving.

For the applesauce:

2 lb. (900 g) tart apples, peeled, cored and thickly sliced

juice of 1 lemon

3 Tbsp. (45 mL) dark brown sugar

½ tsp. (2.5 mL) ground cinnamon

¼ tsp. (1.2 mL) ground nutmeg

¼ tsp. (1.2 mL) ground cloves

2 Tbsp. (30 mL) water

3 Tbsp. (45 mL) dark rum

⅓ cup (80 mL) pure maple syrup

Preheat the oven to 350°F (180°C). Lightly butter a baking dish. Toss the apples with the lemon juice, half the sugar and the cinnamon, nutmeg and cloves. Place in the baking dish, add the water and bake until soft, about 35 minutes or until the apples are tender. Remove from the oven.

Turn on the oven broiler. Sprinkle the rum over the apples and drizzle the maple syrup over the tops; don't mix the syrup in. Sprinkle with the last bit of sugar and place beneath the broiler to caramelize. It should just take a few minutes.

For the pork:
1 boneless pork loin complete with
    scored skin, 3 ½ lb. (1.6 kg),
    rolled and tied
salt

Place the rack in the centre of the oven and preheat the oven to 500°F (260°C). Dry the surface of the roast, if necessary, and rub salt over the meat surface. Place in a roasting pan and roast for about 20 minutes. Lower the temperature to 375°F (190°C) and continue to roast the pork for just under an hour, or to an internal temperature of about 160°F (70°C). Transfer the pork to a cutting board and let rest for 15 minutes before carving. Untie the pork loin. The crackling should come off in one piece quite easily; set it to one side as you carve the meat. Serve each portion of pork with some of the crackling and the apple sauce. (If you find it easier, instead of a knife cut the crackling into serving pieces with kitchen shears.)

Star Anise-Crusted Duck Breast & Noodle Salad with Pickled Niagara Plums

Recommended: Marynissen Estates Cabernet Sauvignon/Merlot
Serves 4 as an appetizer

This presentation celebrates Chinese New Year. Chef Stephen Treadwell of Queen's Landing designed it for Si Wai Lai, the owner and operator of the spectacular chain of properties in Niagara-on-the-Lake known collectively as the Vintage Inns. I have to point out that the pickled plums in question are made by the chef during the summer season and are stored for at least six months before using. You may be able to find pickled plums at specialty food shops or substitute fresh poached plums and plan to make your own pickled plums when prune plums are available. Don't be intimidated by the length of this recipe. The chef has simplified the steps to make this a very doable, yet utterly impressive, dish. Note that the plums need at least a week or so to give them a chance to ripen in the pickling liquid.

For the pickled plums:

1 cup (240 mL) sugar	2 star anise seeds
1 cup (240 mL) water	2 lb. (900 g) prune plums, rinsed
¼ cup (60 mL) rice wine vinegar	

Combine the sugar and water in a saucepan. Place over high heat and boil for 8-10 minutes to make a clear syrup. Add the vinegar and star anise seeds and boil for another 5 minutes. Place the plums in a sterilized preserving jar. Pour the boiling mixture over the plums and seal according to the jar manufacturer's directions.

For the orange curry dressing:

8 cups (2 L) good-quality orange juice (not from concentrate)

2 Tbsp. (30 mL) hot curry powder

3 Tbsp. (45 mL) plum sauce

¼ cup (60 mL) rice wine vinegar

½ cup (120 mL) mirin (rice wine)

salt and freshly ground black pepper to taste

Place the orange juice in a stainless saucepot; cook over medium-high heat until it is reduced by 90 percent to about a cup (240 mL), and quite thick. Transfer to a blender and add the curry powder, plum sauce, rice wine vinegar and mirin. Process until well blended; season with salt and pepper and set aside until you are ready to use it.

For the noodle salad:

2 bunches asparagus, rinsed and trimmed

1 package Asian thin egg noodles

2 bunches leaf spinach, rinsed and chopped

1 bunch basil, chopped

¼ bunch mint, chopped

1 bunch chives, finely chopped

1 bunch green onions, diagonally chopped

Blanch the asparagus in hot water for 30 seconds. Cool in ice water, then drain. Bring a large pot of water (6 L) to a boil, then remove from the heat. Add the dried noodles and let soak until the noodles are just tender; rinse beneath cold running water and drain well. Place all the ingredients in a bowl and mix with most of the orange curry dressing, reserving a little to garnish the plate. Refrigerate for up to 2 hours.

For the duck breast:

1 large Muscovy duck breast
   (boneless)
1 Tbsp. (15 mL) five-spice powder

Trim the excess fat from the duck breast. Score the skin with a sharp knife in a criss-cross pattern. Sear the duck breast in a hot pan, skin side down, for 3–4 minutes or until the skin is golden brown and a layer of fat has been rendered (dissolved). The resulting fat layer should be ⅛ inch (.3 cm) thick. Let cool slightly and then rub the breast with the five-spice powder. Place the breast skin side up in a 9 x 13-inch (23 x 33-cm) pan and place an identical pan on top. Place a weight (like a heavy can) on top of the pan and allow to press the duck breast for up to 3 hours, refrigerated.

When ready to proceed, preheat the oven to 400°F (200°C). Sear the duck breast in a hot ovenproof pan for a minute or so, then transfer to the oven for approximately 10–12 minutes, or until medium-rare. Let rest for 10 minutes before slicing.

To serve, place a good portion of the noodle salad in the centre of a plate. Slice the duck breast and place a portion on the noodles. Garnish with pickled plums and a little chervil or cilantro. Spoon the reserved dressing decoratively around each plate and serve.

Butter-Braised Belgian Endives with Parsley

Recommended: Harbour Estates Winery Sauvignon Blanc
Serves 6

Like the pork with crackling, this side dish is old-fashioned and very good. We've also enjoyed it with roast goose, duck and lamb. If you tend to eat Belgian endives chopped fresh in salads or use their leaves as an hors d'oeuvre vehicle, you are in for a treat. When cooked, endive becomes silky smooth, with a subtle character and delicate flavour.

12 Belgian endives, trimmed and washed
salt and freshly ground black pepper to taste
³⁄₄ cup (180 mL) beef stock

1 Tbsp. (15 mL) lemon juice
4 Tbsp. (60 mL) butter
¹⁄₄ cup (60 mL) chopped fresh flat-leaf parsley

Preheat the oven to 325°F (165°C). Arrange the endives in a Dutch oven or flameproof casserole large enough to accommodate them in one layer, if possible. Season with salt and pepper, add the beef stock and lemon juice and dot with the butter. Cut a round of parchment or waxed paper and use it to cover the endives as they cook (this keeps them moist). Cover the pot and bring to a boil over medium-high heat; cook at a gentle boil for about 20 minutes or until they are tender. Transfer the Dutch oven to the preheated oven and continue to cook the endives for about 1¹⁄₂ hours, until they are very soft and almost all the liquid has evaporated. Carefully transfer to a serving dish, pour over any remaining liquid and scatter the chopped parsley over them before serving.

Chocolate Fudge Pot Pudding
with a Saucy Bottom

Recommended: Niagara Brewing Limited Edition Eisbock
Serves 4–6

At some point over a long winter, a warm chocolate dessert is definitely in order, especially one—like this—that, as it bakes, makes its own dark chocolate sauce on the bottom. This is wonderful for a special dinner at the start of a new year. Of course, it is also the ideal way to please your Valentine at the close of a romantic dinner. Serve it quite warm with cream. Make sure the Eisbock is ice cold and serve it in elegant flutes.

2 Tbsp. (30 mL) quality cocoa powder	1 tsp. (5 mL) pure vanilla extract
1 cup (240 mL) self-rising flour	2 Tbsp. (30 mL) milk
¼ lb. (113 g) butter, softened	1 cup (240 mL) dark brown sugar
1 cup (240 mL) granulated sugar	2 Tbsp. (30 mL) quality cocoa powder
2 large eggs	1 cup (240 mL) hot water

Preheat the oven to 375°F (190°C). Lightly butter a deep 7-cup (1.75-L) round or oval baking dish. Sift the 2 Tbsp. (30 mL) cocoa and flour onto a sheet of waxed or parchment paper and set it to one side. In a mixing bowl, cream the butter and granulated sugar until light and fluffy. In another mixing bowl, lightly beat the eggs with the vanilla extract. Gradually add the beaten egg mixture to the butter and sugar mixture, then fold in the sifted flour mixture and the milk. When well incorporated with no traces of flour remaining, scrape the mixture into the baking dish and smooth the surface to make it level. In a little mixing bowl, whisk together the dark brown sugar, remaining 2 Tbsp. (30 mL) cocoa and hot water until well blended. Pour this over the top of the batter in the baking dish. Place the baking dish on a baking sheet covered with parchment paper (in case the batter overflows) and bake for about 40 minutes. Let sit for a few minutes before serving.

Creekside Estate Winery

Located in the village of Jordan Station, Creekside Estate Winery has as its slogan "out of the ordinary" and, indeed, this expanding winery has a stylishly casual feel to it. Owners Peter and Laura McCain Jensen are originally from Nova Scotia, where they operate two vineyards and a winery. On board are two young Australians, winemaker Marcus Ansems and Tyrene Newman, who acts as retail sales manager and conducts tastings. The winery main house with retail outlet has a large deck, picnic pavilion and underground barrel cellar. A premium winery called Paragon, located outside of Niagara-on-the-Lake, will feature Bordeaux-style reds with limited availability.

Snow Whites with Raspberry Coulis & Sliced Mango

Recommended: Inniskillin Cabernet Franc Icewine
Serves 2–4

This is a very simple sweet that I made for our Valentine's Day dinner by the fire. The meringues are poached, rather than baked, and are paired with a straightforward raspberry sauce and sided with slices of fresh mango. Very pretty and very easy. Have the mango ready so last minute assembly will go smoothly.

For the raspberry coulis:
½ cup (120 mL) frozen raspberries,
    thawed
2 Tbsp. (30 mL) sugar

Purée the raspberries and sugar together in a blender or food processor. Pour through a fine sieve to remove the seeds. Set to one side.

For the meringues:
6 egg whites, at room temperature
1½ cups (360 mL) sugar

Fill a wide, shallow saucepan with boiling water to about 3–4 inches (8–10 cm). Keep it at a gentle simmer. Line a baking sheet with paper towels. In a large bowl, whisk the egg whites until they form soft peaks. Add half the sugar and continue to whisk, gradually adding the rest of the sugar. Whisk until the mixture is quite stiff.

Use a large dessert spoon to shape the meringues into ovals and very carefully place them in the simmering water to poach for just a minute. Use the spoon to nudge the meringue over and poach on the other side for another minute. Use a slotted spoon to transfer the meringues from the water to the paper towels to drain.

To serve:
2 ripe mangoes, peeled, thinly sliced
2 Tbsp. (30 mL) whipping cream

Pour a little of the raspberry coulis onto a dessert plate. Overlap a few slices of mango in the centre. Carefully place three of the meringues on the coulis. Finally, dot the surface of the coulis in three or four places with a bit of cream, then draw a toothpick or skewer through the dot of cream so it resembles a heart. Serve immediately.

Thirty Bench Vineyard & Winery

The trio of partners who make up Thirty Bench are each responsible for particular wines: Frank Zeritsch is involved in the icewine and Vidal-Riesling, Dr. Tom Muckle focusses on the Rieslings, while McMaster professor Yorgos Papageorgiou is devoted to working on Chardonnays, Cabernets and Merlots. Located on an especially ideal section of the Beamsville Bench, near the Thirty Mile Creek, the vineyards and winery of Thirty Bench enjoy a microclimate that is supremely favourable to premium viticulture. Established in 1980, the thirty-five acres of vinifera grapes produces about 10,000 cases of wine annually.

Icewine-Soaked Figs with Hazelnut Strips

Recommended: Inniskillin Riesling Icewine
Serves 4

Trained at La Varenne in Paris, chef Izabela Kalabis has been associated with the Inniskillin winery for about 13 years. She regularly presents seasonal menus and specific dishes to complement Inniskillin's family of wines. This recipe is inspired by a dessert Izabela designed that featured a hazelnut crust filled with white chocolate mousse, sided with fresh figs macerated in icewine and an icewine sabayon. Serve this with good-quality vanilla ice cream or crème fraîche.

For the figs:
1 Tbsp. (15 mL) butter
4 ripe figs
½ cup (120 mL) Inniskillin Icewine

Melt the butter in a saucepan. Place the figs in the saucepan and cook gently, turning the figs as they cook, for a few minutes. Add the icewine and continue cooking until the wine evaporates and the figs are slightly caramelized.

For the hazelnut strips:

1 cup (240 mL) sugar	1 Tbsp. (15 mL) water
1 cup (240 mL) butter	½ cup (120 mL) finely chopped
1 egg, separated	hazelnuts
2 cups (475 mL) all-purpose flour	

Preheat the oven to 350°F (175°C). In a mixing bowl, cream together the sugar and butter until creamy. Add the egg yolk and mix to blend well. Stir in the flour gradually, mixing well after each addition. Press this mixture onto a lightly buttered jelly roll pan (15 ½ x 10 ½ x ¾-inch/39 x 27 x 2-cm). Whisk the egg white with the water until foamy. Brush over the dough. Sprinkle with the hazelnuts and bake for 20–25 minutes, until pale brown. Immediately cut into 3 x 1-inch (7.5 x 2.5-cm) strips. Let cool before serving. Serve one split fig per person and add a dollop of vanilla ice cream or crème fraîche and two or three hazelnut strips. Store any remaining strips in an airtight container.

Hillebrand Estates Winery

Award-winning wines are just one of the reasons to visit Hillebrand Estates Winery, based in Niagara-on-the-Lake and founded in 1982. The winery features one of the loveliest dining rooms in the region. Regional cuisine has long been the focus of chef Tony de Luca's menu at Hillebrand's Vineyard Café thanks to his knowledge of local growers and producers, many of whom are brought to his attention through "forager" John Laidman. There are daily winery tours and anticipated events like Springtime in the Vineyard, a guided viticulture tour of their Stone Road Vineyard, and their two popular jazz and blues concerts held in July and August respectively.

Green Shoots & First Leaves

The beginning of March and the annual gala wine event, Cuvée 2001, is held at the lovely Queen's Landing inn in Niagara-on-the-Lake. This is the evening when many of the Ontario wineries and the best chefs in the region strut their stuff. In the weeks prior to this, all the winemakers involved gather for a special blind tasting to select their favourites, then the awards themselves are presented at the gala. For a few days following the event, wineries hold special Cuvée-related events throughout the weekend. Cuvée En Route involves tastings, wine and food pairings, and the like.

MARCH 11. We knew there were hidden delights waiting to show themselves in the garden surrounding the house and now, bit by bit, the unveiling begins. At the base of the horse chestnut trees there are the beginnings of hyacinths and up the driveway masses of brilliant daffodils and lovely narcissus, the latter the colour of thick double cream. Crocuses and snowdrops, and so many things showing promise, especially heartwarming during some typically grey spring days. The very early shoots of orange lilies are pushing up through the soil everywhere. Nearby, we witness the field, orchard and farm workers trimming, pruning, tying up vines—the work that never ends goes on.

I discover that the former owners planted chives, oregano, thyme, mint and tarragon, right by my kitchen door, and all of these are beginning to emerge by mid-March. Our indoor greenhouse is thriving, tomatoes, eggplants, morning glories, fava beans, herbs all competing for light and window warmth.

A massive winged creature nearly strikes the side of the car as I drive up our road one morning. Out of the corner of my eye at first I think it is one of my Canadian geese, but looking back in the rear-view mirror I see the tell-tale red gobble of a wild turkey! It is enormous, ungainly as it struggles to become airborne. Bird-dog Casey hangs out the car window, silent in astonishment.

Mornings are often deeply foggy, misty, moist. There is still the odd soft snowfall overnight, just enough to coat the branches and all but bury the nodding snowdrops. It is soon gone, though.

MARCH 24. We attend the Showcase of Chefs Gala, an annual event put on by the Niagara Culinary Institute, where a number of local chefs are playfully honoured for specific dishes they have created. It's done in a sort of Oscar Night style—Best Salad, Best Entrée, etc.—and each dish is presented for guests to taste. Chef Roberto Fracchioni of Cave Spring's Inn on the Twenty won Best Pasta Course for his St. Anne Venison on Cabernet Shiitake Risotto and Fried Leeks. Another winning plate was the Best Fish Course: Baked Arctic Char with Lobster Mashed Potatoes and Sage Hollandaise from Paul Pennock and Barry Burton, two chefs from the Niagara Parks Commission. As we enjoy dinner, a substantial snowstorm rages outside. Spring is doubtless delayed, but how beautifully.

APRIL 3. The birds are never-ending—especially the geese. Seasonally early though it may seem, the first week of April, late at night I hear crickets and croaky, squeaky frogs . . . summer night sounds. Seems so early for those calls.

Everything is bursting with a new wet warmth. We sell the huge decorative windmill set behind the house and, when it is dismantled, we discover a new mother raccoon and her four brand-new babies, eyes still shut tight, tiny little bodies squirming and wriggling. The Dutch-born windmill buyers are not impressed and offer to dispose of the lot in a bucket of water! "Do you know how much corn an adult raccoon eats in a season?" they ask. Casey chases the mother off into the woods and we are left to worry about her offspring. We decide the best course of action is to put them in a box by the edge of the wood and wait for her return. She does. After a few days, one baby is gone, then one more until she has finally removed them all to safety. At least, that's what I choose to believe. Living in the wooded areas surrounding us there are coyotes, foxes and phantom-like creatures called "coy-dogs"—the odd hybrid offspring of stray dogs and coyotes. A neighbour tells me she has heard about them hungrily snatching toy poodles and chihuahuas out of the arms of their owners and tearing off into the woods with them clutched in their jaws. Good thing our cats are fleet of paw.

The first three days of April have been unremittingly grey and damp, then brilliant sun and mild temperatures coax the snowdrops to lift their lovely heads up and away from the melting snow. Our tomato seedlings have taken over every sunny window in the house. We continue to plan our vegetable garden: I want yellow corn (not peaches & cream) and every variety of tomato I read about. Ted brings me red tulips in a European-styled bouquet from the Watering Can, a lovely little shop he found in St. Catharines. That night we go to Casa Mia, in Niagara Falls, and have a lovely Italian dinner. Especially good: the arugula and and prosciutto with warmed pear filled with melted gorgonzola.

Mid-April, and my daughters, Alysa and Jenna, and little grandson, Colsen, come for Easter weekend. Walking near our house we spy a poor limp brown rabbit lying in the middle of the road. Clearly this is a big moment and a chance for me to do some serious grandmothering. I tell Cole the bunny must have strayed too far from his family and the cars on our road go too fast. His four-year-old face becomes very grave, furrowed brow, serious and thoughtful, and lots of "why Gwan" as I try to explain life and death the simplest way I know. We had just read Peter Rabbit that morning—useful comparisons there. We decide to come back in the lawn tractor to this spot, scoop up the ex-bunny and bring him/her back for a proper burial at the edge of the woods behind the house. This goes over very well, especially when we gather round the little mound and sing "there goes Peter Cottontail . . . hopping down the bunny trail." Much discussion, too, to ensure that this particular bunny was neither Peter Rabbit, Peter Cottontail or the Easter Bunny—just poor old Brown Bunny. Months after this, whenever we are in the car and Cole spies some road kill remnant, an unfortunate raccoon or squirrel, he wants very much to repeat the burial experience.

First week after Easter, a damp, cold night and a dusting of snow drifts across the top of the daffodils. It coats my fat forsythia buds but the morning sun ensures it is gone by noon.

Towards the end of April we spend an entire weekend involved in our first serious gardening. It is unseasonably warm, really extra warm, and there is such a lovely feeling of renewal and discovery. There is much to tend to, pull out and discard, but much to enjoy, too. Ted has to stop me from buying more seeds each time I spy some. He's right, it's best to go slow this first season, see what we have and what we can handle before going over the top. From early morning to night, we are inundated with beautiful birdsong.

In the Vineyard and On the Vine

"In the vineyard, we're still pruning, we're usually working on the hardier varieties in January and February. The more sensitive varieties, like Cabernet Sauvignon, Merlot, Pinot Noir and some Chardonnay, we do now. We are also starting to tie, because the canes are pliable now. Anyway, when it's colder you need gloves and you can't tie with gloves on. Time is crucial now, there is not such a window of time as for pruning in January and February, so there is a big rush to finish before the buds open. You have four to five months to prune but only two months to tie, so you have to work at more than twice the speed, twice as fast as when you are pruning. April is when the farm really gets busy—we tend to have not much of a spring up here on the Bench. Usually, weather-wise, we get right into summer. So, while we will have 3 or 4 people pruning, we'll have 10 to prune and tie.

"In the winery, again we are heavy into cellar work in the spring, even busier as the push is on to get a lot of those wines in bottle, get those whites that are in barrel out, like our Chardonnay Reserve. The cellar work for sweet wines involves preparing, settling and filtering the wine prior to bottling, and we blend and define whites that have seen barrel and get them ready for bottling.

"Bottling is really continuous from January right through to July. Some early whites that don't see oak, whites that see barrel (Reserve Chardonnay), also bigger reds from two years ago, like our Pinot Noir, Cabernet-Merlot and Reserve Baco Noir, will be bottled now.

"As for other events, we are involved in Cuvée at this time of the year and may conduct focus tastings. We might build a series around the wines that are to be featured at Cuvée, or sometimes hold barrel tastings or the occasional dinner. We take part in the Toronto Wine & Cheese show as well at this time."

Matthew Speck, Henry of Pelham Family Estate Winery

Simple Seasonal Pleasure

Mum's Lemon Curd

Combine 1½ cups (360 mL) sugar, the juice and finely minced zest of 5 lemons, 5 lightly beaten eggs and ½ lb. (225 g) unsalted butter in a good-sized saucepan. Mix well and place over a larger pot of boiling water on relatively high heat. Cook for ½ hour, or until thick, making sure to stir frequently. Pour into prepared jars and keep refrigerated until ready to use. Use it to fill small tart shells, to sandwich a sponge cake or as the filling for a jellyroll or trifle. Or just spread it on hot, buttered toast.

In Season and On the Table

OYSTERS, ONIONS, CHEDDAR, ASPARAGUS, LOBSTER, SEA BASS,
CHICKEN, LAMB, RABBIT, QUAIL, RHUBARB, LEMON, MAPLE SYRUP

Romano Bean & Pasta Soup
with Morningstar Mill Whole-Wheat Scones *46*
Oyster & Leaf Spinach Soup *48*
Asparagus with Mustard Hollandaise & Prosciutto *49*
Real Cheddar & Ale Rarebit with Red Onion Confit *51*
Asparagus & Lobster Flan *54*
Sea Bass with Cilantro Cream *56*
Chicken & Spinach Crêpes *58*
Rabbit Rillettes with Niagara Presents Grapes with a Twist *60*
Quail Braised in Cabernet with Garlic & Rosemary *62*
Lamb with Rhubarb & Mint *64*
Quail Stuffed with Truffled White Beans *66*
Spring Chicken in Riesling with Southern Biscuits *68*
April's Rhubarb Fool *71*
Lemon Cream Pots *72*
White Meadows Farms Maple Raisin Muffins *73*
Oranges & Lemons Tea Cake *74*

Romano Bean & Pasta Soup
with Morningstar Mill Whole-Wheat Scones

Recommended: Thomas & Vaughan Vintners Marechal Foch Old Vine
Serves 4–6

Romano, white kidney beans, navy beans or even black-eyed peas can all be used with success in this popular soup. As the recipe calls for precooked pasta, this is a good time to use leftover pasta, if it is not overcooked. You can expand on this soup as you wish, adding carrot, celery, leek or tomato to make it a complete meal. If you are not a heat-seeker, omit the dried chili. The recipe for the scones follows.

2 Tbsp. (30 mL) olive oil
1 large onion, finely chopped
2 cloves garlic, minced
2 19-oz. (540-mL) cans romano beans,
    rinsed and drained
6 cups (1.5 L) chicken stock
2 Tbsp. (30 mL) red wine vinegar
salt and freshly ground black pepper
    to taste

2 cups (475 mL) cooked short tubular
    pasta (ditali, tubetti, rotelle)
4 Tbsp. (60 mL) freshly grated
    Parmesan cheese
4 Tbsp. (60 mL) chopped fresh flat-
    leaf parsley

In a large, heavy saucepan, warm the oil over medium heat. Add the onion and sauté, stirring, for a few minutes until softened. Add the garlic and continue to cook, stirring for another minute. Add the beans and stock and bring to a boil. Use a potato masher to mash about half the beans (do this in the saucepan) until the soup is thickened somewhat. Stir in the vinegar and seasoning. Add the cooked pasta and simmer for another 2–3 minutes. Ladle into warm bowls and sprinkle a little of the Parmesan cheese and parsley over each serving. Serve immediately with the scones.

Spring begins in the vineyard

Sea Bass with Cilantro Cream (page 56)

Morningstar Mill Whole-Wheat Scones

Makes 12 scones

I first made these lovely scones with freshly milled whole-wheat flour from Morningstar Mill, the beautiful, historic and now refurbished mill near Decew Falls, just down the road from our home. Besides the soup, they are wonderful with smoked salmon and cream cheese. Make sure to serve them warm.

2 cups (475 mL) whole-wheat flour
2½ tsp. (12.5 mL) baking powder
½ tsp. (2.5 mL) salt
6 Tbsp. (90 mL) cold unsalted butter

1 large egg
1 tsp. (5 mL) white vinegar
½ cup (120 mL) whole milk

Preheat the oven to 425°F (220°C). Lightly butter a baking sheet. In a mixing bowl, sift the flour, baking powder and salt together. Add any whole-wheat flakes that don't pass through the sifter into the bowl. Add the butter and work into the flour mixture with your fingertips until the mixture is crumbly.

Whisk together the egg, vinegar and milk in a little bowl and add all at once to the flour mixture. Stir to blend all the ingredients. Turn out onto a lightly floured surface and knead for a minute or two or until smooth. Pat or roll the dough into a circle about ¾ inch (1.9 cm) thick. Using a sharp knife, cut into 12 equal wedges. Transfer to the baking sheet and bake in the centre of the preheated oven for 15 minutes, or until lightly browned.

Oyster & Leaf Spinach Soup

Recommended: Creekside Estates Sauvignon Blanc
Serves 4–6

At least once during the early spring, a warming soup is called for. This delicate, satiny soup is quick to prepare and features barely cooked oysters in a lustrous base just touched with Pernod. A perfect prelude to St. Patrick's Day dinners. Oysters need very little encouragement to cook, so be gentle with them. Make a batch of toast using thinly sliced baguette to accompany this soup.

4 Tbsp. (60 mL) butter
1 clove garlic, minced
1 leek, trimmed, rinsed and thinly
    sliced (use all of the white part
    and half of the green)
2 cups (475 mL) leaf spinach, washed
2 Tbsp. (30 mL) Pernod

24 oysters, shucked and the liquour
    reserved
3 cups (720 mL) whole milk
1 cup (240 mL) whipping cream
salt and freshly ground white pepper
    to taste

In a large saucepan, melt the butter over medium heat. Add the garlic and leek and sauté for about 3–4 minutes until softened; don't allow to brown. Add the spinach and sauté, stirring, for another 2–3 minutes until it is wilted. Stir in the Pernod, oyster liquour, milk, cream and seasoning. Bring the mixture very carefully to a gentle boil, then lower the heat immediately and let simmer for about 5 minutes.

Carefully slip the oysters into the cream mixture. Remove the pan from the heat, cover and let stand for about 8 minutes, or just until the edges of the oysters are beginning to curl. Serve immediately in warmed soup plates.

Asparagus with Mustard Hollandaise & Prosciutto

Recommended: Cilento Wines Sauvignon Blanc Reserve
Serves 4–6

Here is a lovely appetizer to serve at spring suppers or as part of a Sunday after-noon buffet. The slightly piquant mustard hollandaise is equally good with poached eggs, cooked ham or cauliflower.

1 lb. (455 g) fresh asparagus, trimmed	3 egg yolks
½ lb. (225 g) thinly sliced Italian prosciutto	1 Tbsp. (15 mL) boiling water
	2 Tbsp. (30 mL) Dijon mustard
½ cup (120 mL) butter	

Pare the bottom 2 inches (5 cm) of each asparagus stalk. Place the aspara-gus in a shallow pan and cover with boiling water. Add a little salt and cook until tender-crisp, about 3–5 minutes, depending on the thickness. Drain and refresh under cold running water; drain again.

Loosely arrange the prosciutto attractively on a large oval serving plat-ter. Arrange the asparagus over the prosciutto. Set to one side as you pre-pare the hollandaise.

Melt the butter in a small saucepan and keep warm. In another small saucepan (or using the top of a double boiler) combine the egg yolks with the boiling water, whisking continuously over low heat until the yolks begin to thicken. (Don't allow the water in the double boiler to boil or it will cook the yolks.)

Add the mustard to the yolks and whisk it in well. Gradually add the warm melted butter and continue to whisk over low heat for a few minutes until the sauce is nicely thickened and smooth. Add a little white pepper, if you wish, or a bit of chopped fresh herbs like parsley or chives.

Pour the sauce over the plated asparagus and serve immediately.

The Good Earth Cooking School

Visitors to Nicolette Novak's Good Earth Cooking School & Food Company will find it hard not to be envious. The Beamsville Bench Eden-like setting of her school, placed among lush gardens on a 55-acre fruit farm is one of the loveliest spots in Niagara. Classes are limited to 12 and, in the summer months, take place in the school's outdoor classroom beneath a white cloth canopy. The hands-on classes feature resident chefs Lenny Karmiol, a graduate of the Stratford Chef School, and Lisa Rollo. The demonstration classes are hosted by many of the region's best chefs, such as Roberto Fracchioni of Inn on the Twenty, pastry chef Anna Olson, also of Inn on the Twenty, Mark Picone of Vineland Estates Restaurant and Hillebrand's Tony de Luca. The Good Earth delights in all the best that the region has to offer in the way of food and wine.

Real Cheddar & Ale Rarebit
with Red Onion Confit

Recommended: Niagara Brewing Pale Ale or Henry of Pelham Family Estate Zweigelt-Gamay
Serves 8

I used to live near Cheddar, Somerset, so I like to think I know a thing or two about great Cheddar cheese. But I have never tasted any Cheddar anywhere as wonderfully rich and balanced as that made by Jim and Rosemary Thompson. The first time we visited the farmer's market in St. Catharines we had the pleasure of discovering the cheese that they sell out of the back of a little van parked at the market. They're easy to find—just look for the longest lineup. While we could eat it every day just as it comes, it is sensational when used to make this traditional cheese rarebit (or rabbit, as purists call it) that includes another great product from our region: Niagara Pale Ale. If you have any left-over cheese rarebit, it keeps for up to a week covered and stored in the refriger-ator. It also freezes well. Serve this dish alongside a peppery green salad. The onion relish is fabulous with pork, ham, sausages, cold meats, burgers or eggs—in short, anything!

For the red onion confit:
2 Tbsp. (30 mL) butter

2 Tbsp. (30 mL) olive oil

$\frac{1}{2}$ cup (120 mL) sugar

1$\frac{1}{2}$ lb. (680 g) medium red onions,
  thinly sliced

$\frac{3}{4}$ cup (180 mL) Henry of Pelham
  Zweigelt-Gamay

$\frac{1}{3}$ cup + 1 Tbsp. (95 mL) sherry
  vinegar

salt and freshly ground black pepper
  to taste

In a large saucepan, melt the butter with the oil over low heat. Add the sugar and stir to dissolve completely. Add the onions all at once and stir to coat with the butter and sugar mixture. Cover loosely and cook for about 30 minutes, stirring occasionally.

Stir in the wine and vinegar and increase the heat. When it has come to a boil, reduce the heat and simmer gently, uncovered, for another 30 minutes or until the liquid has evaporated and the onions are tender. Season with salt and pepper. The mixture should be thick and jam-like. Remove from the heat and cool. Transfer to a bowl, cover with plastic wrap and refrigerate until ready to use.

For the rarebit:

1 lb. (455 g) extra old Cheddar cheese, grated

⅔ cup (160 mL) Niagara Pale Ale

2 Tbsp. (30 mL) all-purpose flour

4 Tbsp. (60 mL) fresh, fine white breadcrumbs

1 Tbsp. (15 mL) English mustard powder

2 tsp. (10 mL) Worcestershire sauce

salt and freshly ground white pepper to taste

2 eggs

2 egg yolks

1 loaf rustic country-style bread, thickly sliced

In a large saucepan, combine the grated Cheddar with the ale. Stir over low heat until the cheese is melted. Do not allow to boil or the cheese will separate. One by one, add the flour, breadcrumbs and mustard powder, using a whisk to incorporate each ingredient well before adding the next. Continue to stir and cook until the mixture starts to pull away from the sides of the pan and forms a ball. Remove the pan from the heat and whisk in the Worcestershire sauce and seasoning. Set to one side to cool.

When it has cooled slightly, use a whisk to blend in the eggs and then the egg yolks. Use immediately, or transfer the mixture to a bowl, cover with plastic wrap and refrigerate.

Preheat the broiler and grill the slices of bread on both sides. (Or toast the bread if you prefer.) Keep the broiler on.

Gently reheat the onion confit and pile a good bit on each of the toasts. Spoon out a generous portion of the cheese mixture on top of the onion, place on a non-stick baking sheet and slip beneath the preheated broiler. When the rarebit is bubbling and beginning to brown in places, remove from the oven.

Philip Dowell of Inniskillin

Inniskillin's general manager and winemaker, Philip Dowell, brings a little bit of Australia to Niagara. He honed his craft at Wirra Wirra Vineyards, in McLaren Vale and Coldstream Hills in Victoria, where he also worked with renowned wine writer James Halliday. Dowell joined Inniskillin in 1998, just as Canada's best wines began to receive serious recognition internationally.

Asparagus & Lobster Flan

Recommended: Peller Estates Winery Private Reserve Sauvignon Blanc Barrel Aged
Serves 6–8

The gala for Cuvée 2001 was held at Queen's Landing inn in Niagara-on-the-Lake where a number of the area's best chefs put together some spectacular dishes for the event. Stephen Treadwell has headed up the kitchen at Queen's Landing since 1995 and in that time has helped to bring cuisine with the "world-class" moniker to the town and the area. This recipe is inspired by one Stephen made for Cuvée 2001 in which individual tart shells were filled with a mixture of asparagus, corn, chorizo and lobster. Shrimp, crab, scallops or salmon can also be used here. Use your own pastry recipe for this or substitute half a dozen layers of phyllo dough, making sure to follow the directions on the package for working with phyllo.

pastry for a 9-inch (23-cm) single-crust pie

½ lb. (225 g) chorizo (or other hard, spicy sausage), sliced and cubed

4 spears asparagus, trimmed and chopped

2 large shallots, finely chopped

¼ cup (60 mL) chopped fresh chives

1 lb. (455 g) cooked lobster meat, roughly chopped

1 cup (240 mL) grated Gruyère cheese

6 eggs

salt and freshly ground pepper to taste

½ tsp. (2.5 mL) freshly grated nutmeg

1 cup (240 mL) whipping cream

½ cup (120 mL) whole milk

Preheat the oven to 350°F (175°C). Line the pie dish with pastry, leaving a substantial overhang of about 1 inch (2.5 cm). Scatter half the chorizo, asparagus, shallots, chives, lobster and cheese over the bottom of the pastry shell.

In a large mixing bowl, whisk together the eggs, salt and pepper, nutmeg, cream and milk. Add the remaining chorizo, asparagus, shallots, chives, lobster and cheese to the egg mixture, combining well. Place the pie dish on a baking sheet, open the oven and pull out the rack. Place the pan on the rack and pour the filling into the pastry shell. Carefully slide the rack into the oven and bake for about 50–55 minutes, until it is puffed and golden brown and a tester inserted in the centre emerges clean. Let sit for 15 minutes before serving.

Niagara College's Niagara Culinary Institute

What could be more appropriate than a state-of-the-art culinary facility in wine country? Niagara College's Niagara Culinary Institute regularly receives applications from an international assortment of would-be chefs and those interested in pursuing a career in hospitality and tourism. And who better to teach, instruct and inform than experienced chefs—like Michael Olson and J. Mark Hand—who now make teaching these hopefuls their full-time occupation.

Sea Bass with Cilantro Cream

Recommended: Reif Estate Winery Sauvignon Blanc
Serves 4

Until recently, British-born chef Lee Parsons presided over the kitchen at Niagara-on-the-Lake's Prince of Wales Hotel. For Cuvée 2001, he created an intricate marinated sea bass preparation served with bundled matchstick-sized vegetables and a lovely coriander cream, all of which led me to this dish. The contrast of delicate, warm fish with the flavourful fresh herb cream is lovely for spring suppers. Nice accompanied with small boiled potatoes tossed with a little butter and thin green beans or asparagus.

4 6-oz. (170-g) sea bass fillets (or halibut, salmon, tuna)
salt and freshly ground black pepper to taste
3–4 Tbsp. (45–60 mL) all-purpose flour
1 Tbsp. (15 mL) butter
1 Tbsp. (15 mL) olive oil
2 cloves garlic, chopped
½ leek, white part only, rinsed and finely chopped
juice of 1 lemon
¾ cup (180 mL) whipping cream
½ cup (120 mL) yogurt
½ bunch cilantro, leaves only
2–3 Tbsp. (30–45 mL) olive oil

Pat the fillets dry and season with a little salt and pepper. Lightly dust with the flour, shaking off any excess. Set aside.

In a medium-sized skillet, melt the butter along with the 1 Tbsp. (15 mL) olive oil over medium heat. Sauté the garlic and leek for about 3 minutes. Stir in the lemon juice, reduce the heat and simmer for a couple of minutes to reduce the juice. Add the cream and yogurt and return to a boil. Reduce the heat and allow the mixture to simmer for 3–4 minutes, or until the liquid is reduced and thickened. Scrape the mixture into a blender or food processor, add the cilantro and purée until smooth.

Transfer to a small saucepan and keep warm over the lowest heat possible while you prepare the fish.

In a large skillet, warm the 2–3 Tbsp. (30–45 mL) oil over medium heat. Add the fish fillets and cook for about 4–5 minutes per side, longer if you prefer it well done. Serve the fish with the sauce spooned over it.

Cuvée

Held each year in early spring, Cuvée is a three-day event billed as "a celebration of excellence in Ontario wine-making." It begins with a strictly supervised blind tasting restricted to winemakers, who select the winners in categories such as Best Red, Best White, Best Dessert Wine, Best Sparkling Wine and others. A few weeks later, at the Cuvée Gala at the Queen's Landing inn in Niagara-the-Lake, ticket holders gather to enjoy the handiwork of some of the region's best chefs, taste the award-winning wines and take part in the festivities as the winners are announced. Following the gala, ticket holders may also take part in Cuvée En Route, as participating wineries present featured events especially arranged for the Cuvée weekend.

Chicken & Spinach Crêpes

Recommended: Vineland Estates Chardonnay Reserve
Serves 6

These savoury crêpes are the perfect comfort food for an early spring supper. Satisfying and nice enough to serve to guests, you can vary the filling by using cooked turkey, salmon, tuna or haddock.

For the crêpes:

2 eggs

1 cup (240 mL) whole milk

½ tsp. (2.5 mL) salt

1 cup (240 mL) all-purpose flour

2 Tbsp. (30 mL) butter, melted

Combine all the crêpe ingredients in a food processor or blender and mix until smooth. Cover and let stand for 30 minutes or so.

Place a pan or skillet with a 6- to 7-inch (15- to 18-cm) base over medium-high heat. Melt a little extra butter and use a pastry brush to lightly film the pan. Add 2 Tbsp. (30 mL) of batter to the pan and swirl it around to cover the bottom of the pan evenly. Don't use too much batter or the crêpe will be too thick. Cook for a few minutes until the bottom is lightly browned and the edges lift away from the pan easily. The crêpe should move freely and loosely in the pan. Use a metal spatula to lift and flip (or use your fingers if that is easier). Cook the other side for just a minute or less. Remove to a plate and continue with the remaining batter. Place a sheet of waxed or parchment paper between each crêpe to keep them from sticking together. You should get at least 12 crêpes from this batter.

For the filling:

4 Tbsp. (60 mL) butter	8 oz. (225 g) spinach, rinsed, dried,
1 large green onion, trimmed and	trimmed and chopped
finely chopped	3 Tbsp. (45 mL) grated Parmesan
2 cloves garlic, minced	cheese
$\frac{1}{4}$ cup (60 mL) all-purpose flour	salt and freshly ground pepper to
$1\frac{1}{4}$ cups (300 mL) light cream	taste
$\frac{3}{4}$ cup (180 mL) chicken stock	2 cups (475 mL) cooked chicken,
$\frac{1}{4}$ cup (60 mL) dry white wine	roughly chopped

Melt the butter over medium-high heat in a medium-sized saucepan and sauté the green onions for a few minutes. Add the garlic and sauté for another 2 minutes or so, being careful not to let the garlic brown. Add the flour and stir to blend it into the butter mixture. Gradually add 1 cup (240 mL) of cream, stirring as you blend. Add the stock, wine, spinach and 1 Tbsp. (15 mL) of the cheese, blending well. Simmer for about 5 minutes, then taste for seasoning.

Remove from the heat. Place the cooked chicken in a bowl and cover with half the sauce, folding it together. Reserve the other half of the sauce.

Preheat the oven to 350°F (175°C). Lightly butter a 13 x 9 x 2-inch (33 x 23 x 5-cm) baking dish. Fill each crêpe with a serving spoonful of the mixture, roll up and place seam side down in the baking dish. Repeat with the remaining crêpes and filling. Add the remaining $\frac{1}{4}$ cup (60 mL) of cream to the remaining half of the sauce and pour over the crêpes. Sprinkle with the remaining 2 Tbsp. (30 mL) of cheese. Bake for 20–25 minutes, until the sauce is bubbling around the edges of the crêpes and the surface is golden brown.

Rabbit Rillettes with Niagara Presents Grapes with a Twist

Recommended: Southbrook Winery Merlot
Serves 6–8

Rillettes (ree-YEHT) is a flavourful French meat paste, what they call potted meat in England. Pork, duck and rabbit, or combinations thereof, may all be used. The meat is cooked in fat until extremely tender, then shredded and packed into little crocks or ramekins and sealed with melted lard or clarified butter. Rillettes make a lovely appetizer or accompaniment to soups. For more formal occasions, serve as a first course with lots of sliced baguette and a good green salad dressed in a mustard vinaigrette. I especially like this rich meat paired with Grapes With a Twist or Inferno Red Pepper Jelly, both from Niagara Presents. A good butcher (and even many supermarkets) can provide you with the pork belly and the fatback, which, by the way, is not salt pork. Fatback is unsmoked and unsalted fat from a pig's back. Start preparation for this early in the day; it is a bit fiddly, but well worth it.

2-lb. (900-g) young farm-raised rabbit, cut into 6 pieces	5 large cloves garlic, crushed
1½ lb. (680 g) pork belly	1 tsp. (5 mL) ground cinnamon
¾ lb. (340 g) pork fatback	½ tsp. (2.5 mL) ground nutmeg
2 sprigs fresh thyme	salt and freshly ground black pepper to taste
10 juniper berries	

Place the rabbit pieces in a Dutch oven or similar heavy pot. Cut the pork belly and fatback into 1½-inch (3.8-cm) cubes and add to the rabbit. Add the thyme, juniper berries, garlic and just enough cold water to cover. Bring to a boil over high heat, then lower the heat to a simmer and cook for 2 hours, longer if necessary, until the meat is falling off the bone.

Strain the mixture and reserve the cooking liquid. Skim the fat from the cooking liquid and reserve both the fat and the liquid.

Remove the meat, any skin and fat from the bones, discarding the fat and bones and transferring the meat to a bowl. Shred the meat with your fingers, or use two forks to pull it apart. Add about ¾ cup (180 mL) of the cooking liquid, or just enough to moisten the meat. Season with the cinnamon, nutmeg and plenty of salt and pepper. Transfer the mixture to a 6-cup (1.5-L) ceramic dish or individual ramekins or crocks. Use a large spoon to ladle a little of the reserved fat over the surface to seal. Cover with plastic wrap and refrigerate for at least 1 day or up to 2 weeks.

Magnotta

In 1989 Gabe & Rossanna Magnotta started their winery, selling directly to consumers exclusively from their own five retail outlets, an approach that is becoming more common among a handful of regional Ontario wineries these days. Bests include their award-winning Chardonnays and unique sparkling icewine.

Quail Braised in Cabernet
with Garlic & Rosemary

Recommended: Henry of Pelham Family Estate Cabernet-Merlot
Serves 6

Lake Land Game Meats has the most terrifically plump little quail I have ever encountered. As robust as they may appear though, quail are delicate, with very little fat. Don't overcook them as we did once when I dispatched my husband, Ted, to smoke a batch of them in our outdoor stone smoker. I had visions of smoked quail on wild mushroom risotto. To say we miscalculated the time it took to smoke them is putting it gently; let's just say we had crispy-critter quail chips for dinner that night. Try this recipe instead, which results in lovely, moist little birds in an unforgettably good sauce. Serve them with creamy polenta or boiled potatoes. Be sure to serve the garlic cloves as an accompaniment. Nutty, smooth, sweet and delicious they can be squeezed out of their skin onto crusty bread.

3 Tbsp. (45 mL) olive oil
12 plump quail
10 plum tomatoes, peeled, seeded
   and chopped (or canned plum
   tomatoes, drained and chopped)
2 cups (475 mL) Henry of Pelham
   Cabernet-Merlot

1 cup (240 mL) water
2 heads fresh garlic, separated,
   unpeeled
3 branches fresh rosemary
salt and freshly ground black pepper
   to taste

Warm the oil in a large skillet placed over medium-high heat. Brown the quail on all sides, turning often. Add the chopped tomatoes and cook a few more minutes.

Pour in the wine and water; add the garlic cloves, rosemary, salt and pepper. Give it a bit of a stir and cook, loosely covered, for about 20–25 minutes until the quail are cooked. Using tongs, transfer the quail and garlic cloves to a plate or bowl. Pass the contents of the skillet through a sieve placed over a bowl, making sure to rub the contents through to extract all the flavour. Return the cooking liquid to the skillet, replace the quail and garlic cloves and reheat gently for a moment or two before serving.

Crown Bench Estates Winery

"I will remember the land," is the credo of this Bench winery located in an especially scenic bit of the Niagara Escarpment. It offers vineyard tours and tastings and encourages visitors to investigate the winery's special "entrance" to the adjacent Bruce Trail.

Lamb with Rhubarb & Mint

Recommended: Malivoire Wine Co. Old Vine Foch
Serves 4

Inspired by a healthy patch of rhubarb, I decided to use it in something other than sweets and desserts. As good as lamb is with its traditional partner, fresh mint, I really love the sharp contrast provided by rhubarb, my other favourite harbinger of spring. Serve it with basmati rice tossed with a few cashews and a bit of finely chopped parsley.

2 lb. (900 g) boneless lamb (shoulder preferably)
2 Tbsp. (30 mL) unsalted butter
2 Tbsp. (30 mL) olive oil
2 white onions, sliced
1 tsp. (5 mL) ground coriander
1 tsp. (5 mL) ground cumin
salt and freshly ground black pepper to taste
$\frac{1}{2}$ cup (120 mL) chopped fresh flat-leaf parsley
$\frac{1}{4}$ cup (60 mL) chopped fresh mint
1$\frac{1}{2}$ lb. (680 g) rhubarb, trimmed and chopped

Prepare the lamb by cutting it into 2-inch (5-cm) chunks. In a Dutch oven or similar heavy saucepan with a lid, melt the butter with the olive oil over medium-high heat. Sauté the onion until it is just beginning to colour (don't let it brown), about 4 minutes. Using a slotted spoon, transfer the cooked onion to a plate. Return the pan to the heat, increase the heat to high and brown the lamb in batches, adding a little more oil if necessary.

When all the lamb has been browned, return the meat and onion to the pan along with the coriander and cumin. Stir to combine well and add just enough water to cover. Bring to a gentle boil, reduce the heat immediately to a simmer, cover and cook very gently for about 1$\frac{1}{2}$ hours, stirring occasionally. Season to taste with salt and pepper.

Half an hour before the end of the cooking time, add the parsley and mint. Stir to combine well and cook for another 15 minutes, loosely covered, stirring once or twice. In the last 15 minutes, stir in the rhubarb and continue to cook just until the rhubarb is softened. Adjust the seasoning once more, and serve immediately.

Brock University's Cool Climate Oenology and Viticulture Institute (CCOVI)

Established in 1996 in partnership with the Wine Council of Ontario and the Ontario Grape Growers Marketing Board, the Cool Climate Oenology and Viticulture Institute (CCOVI) at Brock University has grown in size and reputation in the last six years. An impressive program dedicated to the study of wines and grape-growing in cool climates, the facilities include biotechnology and viticulture labs, sensory evaluation facilities, a pilot winery and a 43,000-bottle wine cellar with an enviable Canadian wine library.

Quail Stuffed with Truffled White Beans

Recommended: Cave Spring Cellars Gamay Reserve Estate Bottled
Serves 6 as an appetizer

Chef Roberto Fracchioni of Inn on the Twenty carries on the tradition estab-
lished by his predecessor, chef Michael Olson, of using the best of local ingredi-
ents. He bones plump quail, then fills them with a fragrant stuffing based on
white beans cooked with fresh thyme and serves the finished birds on local baby
greens drizzled with his own chive oil. Lovely for early spring. Look for the
truffle oil at specialty food shops or just use good extra virgin olive oil.

3 cups (720 mL) dried white kidney
    beans, soaked overnight in water
    to cover
1 bay leaf
1½ Tbsp. (22.5 mL) chopped fresh
    thyme leaves
1 shallot, diced
1½ Tbsp. (22.5 mL) minced garlic

½ tsp. (2.5 mL) extra virgin olive oil
    infused with truffle
salt and freshly ground black pepper
    to taste
6 boneless quail
3 Tbsp. (45 mL) butter

Drain the beans and place them with the bay leaf in a large pot. Cover with
12 cups (3 L) of cold water. Place over high heat and bring to a boil.
Reduce the heat and cook the beans until tender, about 1½ hours, skimming off any foam that rises to the surface. With a slotted spoon, transfer
¼ of the beans to a bowl and set aside.

Mash the remaining beans with the thyme, shallot, garlic and truffle
oil. Season with salt and pepper. Mix in the reserved beans. Divide the
mixture into 6 even portions, patting them into a round shape. Preheat the
oven to 375°F (190°C).

Place a quail on a cutting board, skin side down. Season lightly with salt and pepper and place one portion of beans on top of the quail. Wrap the quail around the stuffing, making sure the stuffing is completely covered. If it is difficult to keep closed, fasten with a toothpick or tie with a bit of kitchen string. Place ½ Tbsp. (7.5 mL) butter on top of the quail and transfer to a roasting pan. Repeat with the remaining quail. Place the pan in the oven and roast for 20 minutes, basting with melted butter every 5 minutes. Serve hot over greens drizzled with a little oil.

Kittling Ridge Winery & Spirits

In the same neck of the woods as Andrés Wines, Kittling Ridge Estate Winery & Spirits—the third largest winery in the province of Ontario—has the distinction of being the nation's only winery/distillery. It takes its name from a particular segment of the Escarpment and also offers dining and accommodation at the adjacent Kittling Ridge Winery Inn.

Spring Chicken in Riesling
with Southern Biscuits

Recommended: Cave Spring Cellars Dry Riesling
Serves 4

When is a coq au vin not a coq au vin? When it is made with Riesling and cream. This is a lovely variation on France's beloved chicken in wine. The addition of a little cream gives it a slight edge over other, more traditional versions. I like to use thighs and drumsticks for this because they are never dry, are full of flavour and are always a bargain. But any cut of chicken will serve you well. Serve with hot rice and lengths of steamed rapini or broccoli. The recipe for the Southern Biscuits follows.

For the chicken:
2 Tbsp. (30 mL) butter
1 Tbsp. (15 mL) olive oil
¼ lb. (113 g) pancetta (unsmoked bacon), finely chopped
2 onions, chopped
2 cloves garlic, chopped
4 chicken thighs, trimmed of excess fat and skin
4 chicken drumsticks
½ lb. (225 g) small button mushrooms, wiped clean

¼ cup (60 mL) brandy or cognac
2 cups (475 mL) Cave Spring Cellars Dry Riesling
1¼ cups (300 mL) whipping cream
3 Tbsp. (45 mL) chopped fresh tarragon
3 Tbsp. (45 mL) chopped fresh flat-leaf parsley
salt and freshly ground black pepper to taste

In a Dutch oven or similar heavy saucepan, combine the butter with the olive oil over medium-high heat. Add the pancetta and cook for a minute or two until softened, then add the onion and garlic. Cook, stirring, for about 4 minutes, or until the onion has softened. Use a slotted spoon to transfer the bacon and onion mixture to a bowl, retaining the cooking fat in the pan. Return the pan to the heat and brown the chicken pieces, a few at a time, on all sides. If necessary, add a little more oil. Add the mushrooms, using a wooden spoon to distribute them under and around the chicken pieces. Cook for a minute or two, then return the bacon and onion mixture to the pan.

Increase the heat slightly, then add the brandy or cognac and shake the pan back and forth a bit to settle it throughout. Cook for a minute, then add the wine. Allow the mixture to come to a boil, then turn it down to a simmer. Leave it to cook for about 30–40 minutes, uncovered. Check it now and then, turning the chicken pieces over and adding a little more wine or water if necessary. When the chicken is cooked through (check to see if juices run clear when it is pierced with the tip of a paring knife), use tongs to remove the chicken pieces to a plate.

Add the cream, tarragon and parsley to the pan, stirring well. Season with salt and pepper. Bring mixture to a gentle boil and return the chicken to the pan. When all is heated through and the sauce is thickened, serve.

Stoney Ridge Cellars

Vineland is home to a number of prestigious wineries, and Stoney Ridge is one. Winemaker Jim Warren is renowned for his hand-crafted wines and is something of a legend in Ontario and Canadian amateur winemaking circles as he has grown and developed his considerable skills producing classic vinifera wines, limited edition varieties, interesting blends and fruit wines. Stoney Ridge boasts the largest selection of VQA (Vintners Quality Alliance) wines of such consistently high quality that demand for them often surpasses the supply.

Southern Biscuits

Makes 10–12 biscuits

These are the real thing and, for this recipe, that means lard—a four-letter word for some, I know. There are those who maintain bacon fat must be used to lightly grease your baking sheet. Not exactly what you'd call spa food, but we all fall off the wagon now and then where food is concerned; just make sure when you do it is for something really good, like these hefty, mouthwatering biscuits. Self-rising flour is generally widely available in supermarkets right alongside all the other flours, but if you can't find it or want to make your own, use this equation: 1 cup (240 mL) all-purpose flour, $1\frac{1}{4}$ tsp. (7.2 mL) baking powder and a pinch of salt for every 1 cup (240 mL) of self-rising flour.

    4 cups (950 mL) self-rising flour (plus
        additional for shaping)
    $\frac{1}{2}$ cup (120 mL) lard
    $1\frac{3}{4}$–2 cups (420–475 mL) buttermilk

Preheat the oven to 450°F (230°C). Lightly grease a baking sheet. Sift the flour into a mixing bowl and work in the lard with your fingers until crumbly. Make a well in the centre of the flour mixture and add the buttermilk a little at a time until you get a slightly wet dough. You may not need it all. Be careful to work the dough as little as possible. Scrape the dough from your fingers and sift a fine layer of flour over the dough. Lightly dust your hands with flour and scoop up a portion of the dough with your hands. Work it into a squarish biscuit shape, plopping the dough lightly from palm to palm. It should be about 2–3 inches (5–7.5 cm) in diameter and fairly thick. Lay it on the baking sheet and repeat with the remaining dough, sifting additional flour over the surface as needed. Allow the biscuits to nudge each other slightly on the baking sheet. Bake them for about 15–20 minutes. Serve warm.

April's Rhubarb Fool

Recommended: Thirty Bench Winery Special Select Late Harvest Riesling
Serves 4

Fools are lovely old-fashioned sweets that are simple to make. They can be based on just about any fruit you can think of. What better time to enjoy one than during the month that kick-starts a bit of tom foolery—April. This version is a little less rich than most because of the addition of yogurt. If you use forced greenhouse rhubarb, decrease the amount of sugar slightly. Serve it with crisp butter biscuits or biscotti.

1½ lb. (680 g) rhubarb, trimmed and
    chopped
½ cup (120 mL) soft brown sugar,
    packed
2-inch (5-cm) piece of fresh ginger,
    finely chopped

½ cup (120 mL) whipping cream
¼ cup (60 mL) plain yogurt
2 tsp. (10 mL) pure vanilla extract

Preheat the oven to 350°F (175°C). Combine the rhubarb, sugar and ginger in a shallow baking dish. Bake for about 30 minutes, stirring occasionally. When cooked through and tender, transfer to a large bowl to cool.

Whip the cream until thick, then whip in the yogurt and vanilla until well blended. Fold the cream mixture into the cooled rhubarb. Spoon into parfait glasses.

Lemon Cream Pots

Serves 8

Sort of a cross between a parfait, a custard and panna cotta, this lovely, lemony sweet is perfect after a spring lamb or chicken dinner. It's especially good when sided with a little bit of rich, dark chocolate. Or use cooked rhubarb to serve as a topping or a base. Use traditional custard cups or ceramic ramekins for this recipe.

½ cup (120 mL) fresh lemon juice
½ cup (120 mL) sugar
6 egg yolks
1½ cups (360 mL) whipping cream

1 Tbsp. (15 mL) very finely grated
    lemon zest
fresh mint leaves for garnish

Preheat the oven to 325°F (165°C). Combine the lemon juice and sugar in a small mixing bowl and whisk to completely dissolve the sugar. Set to one side. Whisk the egg yolks in a large mixing bowl. Gradually whisk in the cream, then the lemon juice mixture, making sure to thoroughly combine all the ingredients. Carefully pour the mixture through a fine sieve into another bowl. Stir in the lemon zest and let the mixture stand for a couple of minutes. While the mixture is resting, place custard cups or ceramic ramekins in a baking pan. Use a ladle to half-fill each cup with the cream mixture. Carefully pour enough hot (not boiling) water into the pan to come halfway up the sides of the cups. Lay a large piece of parchment paper or foil loosely on top of the cups and place in the centre of the oven. Bake for 30 minutes, or until the custard is set. Remove from the oven and transfer the cups to a baking tray. Let cool, then loosely cover with plastic wrap and refrigerate for at least 3 hours or overnight. Serve in the cups, garnished with a leaf of mint.

White Meadows Farms Maple Raisin Muffins

Makes 12 large muffins

White Meadows Farms is a third-generation family farm not far from St. Catharines. Besides dairy and grape production, Murray and Ann Bering have over 2,100 maple syrup taps in operation. On March weekends, visitors can take part in guided tours to the sugar bush to learn more about the craft of sugaring, then head back to the Pancake Hut for pancakes and sausages or giant muffins made with the farm's maple syrup.

2 cups (475 mL) bran	2 tsp. (10 mL) baking powder
1¼ cups (300 mL) buttermilk	2 tsp. (10 mL) baking soda
1 egg, beaten	1 tsp. (5 mL) ground cinnamon
1¼ cups (300 mL) pure maple syrup	½ cup (120 mL) vegetable oil
1 cup (240 mL) all-purpose flour	1 cup (240 mL) raisins

Preheat the oven to 350°F (175°C). In a mixing bowl, combine the bran, buttermilk and egg. Mix well, add the maple syrup and mix again. Let stand for 5 minutes.

In another bowl, sift together the flour, baking powder, baking soda and cinnamon. Gradually add the dry ingredients to the wet mixture. Stir in the oil and raisins and mix until just blended. Fill large muffin tins ¾ full with the mixture and bake for 20–25 minutes. Do not overbake.

Oranges & Lemons Tea Cake

Recommended: Vineland Estates Riesling Icewine
Serves 8–12

Just like the bells of St. Clemens, this cake says oranges and lemons. It is simple to prepare and even travels well if transported in the tube pan in which it is baked. Serve with unsweetened whipped cream and a dollop of Mum's Lemon Curd (page 11).

For the cake:

½ lb. (225 g) butter, softened

2 cups (475 mL) granulated sugar

3 eggs

3 cups (720 mL) sifted all-purpose
    flour

1 tsp. (5 mL) baking soda

½ tsp. (2.5 mL) salt

1 cup (240 mL) sour cream

¼ cup (60 mL) whole milk

2 Tbsp. (30 mL) grated lemon zest

2 Tbsp. (30 mL) grated orange zest

2 Tbsp. (30 mL) lemon juice

2 Tbsp. (30 mL) orange juice

Preheat the oven to 325°F (165°C). Generously butter a two-piece, 10-inch (25-cm) tube or Bundt pan. In a mixing bowl, cream the softened butter and sugar until light. Carefully beat in the eggs, blending well after each one. Sift the flour, baking soda and salt together. Combine the sour cream and milk. Add the flour mixture to the egg mixture alternately with the sour cream mixture. Add the lemon and orange zest and juices and blend well. Pour into the prepared pan and bake for about an hour, or until a cake tester inserted in the centre comes out clean. Cool for about 10 minutes.

For the glaze:
juice of 2 lemons
4 Tbsp. (60 mL) icing sugar

Remove the outer portion of the pan, but keep the cake on the tubular base. As it cools slightly, whisk the juice of two lemons with the icing sugar. While the cake is still hot, drizzle the icing mixture over it, allowing it to drip down the inside and outer edge of the cake.

Vineland Estates Winery

Vineland is often described as the region's most picturesque winery. A former Mennonite homestead, the property dates back to 1845 and now houses visitor and production facilities, while the original barn has been converted into a wine boutique, the exclusive outlet for most of its premium and reserve wines. Its well-run restaurant has one of the best menus (and views) in the area. A lovely cottage on the property is ideal for honeymooners. Vineland is renowned for full Chardonnays, Rieslings, Merlots and Cabernets.

May

Darling Buds to Bountiful Blossoms

The last of the winter has gone and the area is readying itself for the lush, heady green season to come. Today's grey, rainy morning has an indefinable sweetness in the air as every growing thing sends forth its own particular perfume, some floral, some the very definition of green. The generous branches of the huge horse chestnut trees that front our house bob and weave beneath the downpour, graciously holding the extra weight of big creamy pink blossoms, like extravagant pale strawberry ripple ice cream cones. On closer inspection, it is the pink-tendrilled centres that give the overall pink hue as the petals themselves are a warm white. Unlike the fragile and short-lived little apple and cherry blossoms, these sumptuous blooms last and last. City people come to the Niagara Blossom Festival and visit our surrounding countryside, to take in the absolute beauty of the apple, cherry and peach blossoms. A sea of delicate colour.

Fat bobbing robins hop across the lawn in an effort to be the first to get the emerging worms. There is thunder and sweet-scented rain drenches the grapevine outside my window. The vine shares the arbour with an old climbing rose. They seem to like each other and the heavy, almost impenetrable clay soil in which both are firmly rooted. The rain ends and a new spring sun breaks through, beaming on the broad green drop-spattered leaves of the trees. We find a nest in one, beautifully built. What a lovely place to be born, nestled in the groove of a fat, black bough, sheltered by shimmering green leaf, swaying slightly with the breeze.

MAY 2. This weekend we will plant the tomatoes, fava beans and morning glories, all of which are threatening to take over the sunny family room. The morning glories twine up the curtain tie and around the window, having attached themselves to a blind pull.

Old Molly, our portly, matronly feline, has made friends with two feral cats, one the colour of milk, the other mottled grey and white. Driven by hunger, they gingerly approach the house and wolf down a dish of proffered food. Jean, next door, who has lived on this road more than 70 years, says that all of her three cats were strays. "People drive up from the city and just let them go out here," she says.

MAY 8. Oregano, mint, garlic chives and tarragon have been growing by our kitchen door since late last month. Such a treasure this early in the year. I crave *arrabiata* sauce and lengths of pasta to wind round my fork, so I gather handfuls of the fresh herbs. I chop them quickly and throw them into a simple sauce based on canned plum tomatoes, garlic, onions, chilies and good olive oil and use it to dress lengths of sturdy bucatini.

I've dubbed the massive, ominous-looking bees "the 747s." They soar impossibly high all around our house; I've never seen anything like them. Ted chooses the huge rectangular space for our fledgling vegetables and lays railway ties. We fill in the space with topsoil and cow dung we have had delivered. A warm soft rain falls as our cats, Molly and Cider, give it all a good sniffing. This will be our vegetable garden.

MAY 11. A picture-perfect mid-May day, cloudless blue sky, constant sun, temperate climate. This would be a lovely time for a wedding in our front garden. The horse chestnuts thoughtfully scattering their pale pink breeze-borne blossoms with the slightest gust, like floral confetti. The next few days are glorious, then quite rainy, but the soil so needs it, cracking as it is with dryness. We have planted tomatoes, eggplant, fava beans and scarlet runner beans, seed Yukon Golds, strawberries, mixed lettuces and more rhubarb. Most of the clematis sold in Ontario originates with a grower in Fonthill, we learn; in honour of that discovery we plant one. The lovely old guy at Niagara Nursery also tells us that the deep-purple one we have chosen—Polish Spirit—is a variety resistant to clematis wilt. There is so much to learn. Apparently tomatoes and peppers like a spoonful of Epsom salts when they begin to flower, as the salts contain magnesium.

The day after planting, I discover information about planting and weeding using the lunar cycles as guide. Fascinating to read that the moon's gravitational pull has an influence on plant energy and how nutrients move above and below the ground. Ideally, tubers, bulbs, biennials and perennials (plants with underground storage systems) should be planted from a full moon to the last quarter or waning moon. Conversely, plants whose growth is mostly aboveground should be planted from a new moon to a full or waxing moon. My down-to-earth Ted finds this all just a little too intense. But I tell him women have long felt an association with the moon, the tides, the stars. Oh well, hope my spuds thrive even though I didn't check to see if we were in the midst of a waning full moon cycle.

My eldest daughter, Alysa, gave me a delicate white polyanthus rose for Mother's Day and I have planted it by the sunny kitchen door. Planted rosemary, too. Oregano, mint, garlic chives are thriving and I have just noticed thyme from last year creeping up. The mass of lovely, bending greenery growing along the driveway has been identified as Solomon's seal. They will be beautiful in full bloom.

Had an urge for potato salad as Alysa likes to make it, with handfuls of garlic, chopped mint and other fresh herbs, but didn't have waxy potatoes. Had huge amounts of baking potatoes, so chunked and roasted them with olive oil, salt and pepper. Then, while still warm, tossed them with fresh chopped garlic, and a handful of chopped mint, oregano, chives and more good olive oil. Lovely with chicken breasts pounded thin, seared and squirted with a bit of fresh lemon.

MAY 17. Because we have decided to keep the grass "off drugs," a few dandelions prevail. Well, quite a few, actually, about as far as the eye can see. We joke that if we lived in the city, neighbours would be complaining—loudly. Weeding, serious weeding, is in order as dandelions pop up overnight after a mowing. Every cliché about weeds I've ever heard runs through my head as I yank them out. Then we think, why? What harm can there be—we have so much land here, so much lovely green space, we can live with them. I'll use some of the leaves for salad greens, like the resourceful Italians. If you can't beat 'em, eat 'em. The larger outside leaves are rather hairy and can be quite bitter, so I pick as many of the tiny, inner leaves as I can find—quantity is not a problem, believe me—and add them to a bowl of mixed greens. I feel good about eating them. I'll try sautéeing them, too, with a bit of bacon and throw in a handful of homemade croutons to make a sort of warm wilted salad. They'd also make a great addition to my herb-laden frittatine, the thin version of frittata. I've been reading about dandelions and have learned that the leaves, the buds, the roots *and* the blossoms are edible. We may never go hungry.

MAY 20. Have now learned more than I really want to about those enormous black bees. They are carpenter bees and they use their incredibly efficient nose drills to make perfect circular holes in our lovely old wood house, the better in which to lay their eggs. We call pest control and learn that we will have to spray or rebuild our house of a non-wood material. Not really an option, so he's hired. In the front yard, we dig up dozens of old horse chestnuts (called conkers in England) that have not fallen far from the tree. They are already starting to send out strong, little unwavering roots, surprisingly substantial. The beginning of tiny trees. Other, less-threatening bees hover and visit the pink, cone-shaped blossoms. I guess the bees are mad at us because we removed a number of red shutters from our house and discovered their old nests behind each one.

Between the two main horse chestnut trees we have slung our hammock. As I hang suspended between these two sentinels, gazing up through their green canopy to glimpse the cloudless blue sky, a bit of a breeze drifts the hammock gently back and forth. It is easy to get lost.

MAY 29. The end of the month brings lots of rain, light drizzles, heavy downpours and everything in between. Everything is ultra-green. Our many and varied peonies are about to pop. The horse chestnut blooms are almost, but not quite, gone. They have been so pretty for so long, I'll miss them. Amidst the usual evensong of geese, crickets and frogs, we hear an owl late one night.

In the Vineyard and On the Vine

"In the vineyard, this is what we call bud break; it should be happening from the end of April to mid-May and is a most stressful time. We may still be finishing up pruning and tying, and, as always, we are most concerned with the possibility of spring frost. We haven't really had that as a problem yet, but there is always the chance. When vines are dormant they are protected from the cold and frost; in the middle of winter they can take a lot and still pull through. But by May, once the buds are open, one good frost could eliminate the crop. If it happens, you've pruned, you've tied; there is really nothing you can do to correct it. Over the last few years, we've had early springs and they have been a mixed blessing. You'll have a longer growing season so it takes some of the pressure off the fall, but you also run the risk of that late frost damage, so you have to rely on better weather from that early start on. At this time we are also starting to cultivate on the farm and any fertilizing is done now.

"In the winery in May and June we are starting to bottle sweet wines. Wines with residual sugar need to be bottled as they run the risk of re-fermenting. There is no benefit to keeping them unbottled. We begin to do barrel work with the reds from the previous vintage and we'll start to look at barrel blends. Also the blending of our Mosaic wine, which is a blend of Gamay and Zweigelt.

"In the store area, the long weekend in May is generally the date by which we want to have everything up and running and any renovations to property completed, as this is the time the visitors really start to show up.

"All the area fruit trees are in blossom now, so there is a lot of activity. Everything happens very quickly at this time of year. If there is any spring at all it is in May, but it goes by fast and dissolves into summer."

Matthew Speck, Henry of Pelham Family Estates Winery

Simple Seasonal Pleasure

True Hollandaise

The lusty month of May is when real hollandaise comes into its own. Just the thing for asparagus, poached eggs, salmon and smoked fish. There is no need to be intimidated by the preparation of this simple emulsion. Just remember to keep the egg yolks at a minimally even heat as you add the melted butter. If you suddenly find yourself heading towards the horrors of curdle town, remain calm, add a big fat ice cube and keep whisking until it has melted. Or throw the lot in the blender and whiz it around a bit. Lastly, you might want to remember that it's a good idea not to attempt any of this on a particularly humid day. To begin, slowly melt ½ cup (120 mL) unsalted butter in a small saucepan. Remove from the heat and keep warm. Have a small amount of hot water at the ready in a separate small saucepan (or your kettle). Now, ever so slightly, heat 1½ Tbsp. (22.5 mL) of lemon juice. Place 3 egg yolks in the top of a double boiler over hot water and beat with a whisk until they begin to thicken. Add exactly one tablespoon (15 mL) of the hot water and keep beating as the mixture thickens. Repeat this procedure until you have added 3 more tablespoons (45 mL) of hot water. Make sure your reserved lemon juice is still warm and beat it into the mixture. Remove the pot from the heat and keep beating while—with excruciating slowness—you add the melted butter. Add a little salt and a smidge of cayenne. Beat until thick. This will make about 1 cup (240 mL) of heavenly hollandaise.

In Season and On the Table

FRESH PEAS, MINT, YOUNG VEGETABLES, EGGS, CHEESE, FIDDLEHEADS, MORELS,
SALMON, NEW POTATOES, VEAL, CHICKEN, RHUBARB

Fresh Pea Soup with Mint & Curry *86*

Primavera Soup with Gruyère Toasts *88*

Warm Asparagus Salad with Watercress & Radishes
in Rhubarb Riesling Dressing *90*

Frittatine with the First Fresh Herbs *92*

Three-Cheese & Herb Cakes with Tomato Jam *94*

Fresh Noodles with Asparagus, Fiddleheads & Morels *96*

Asparagus Ravioli with Basil Butter *98*

Spring Spinach & Ricotta Gnocchi
with Sweet Peppers & Lemon Cream *100*

Lobster & Pea Sprout Salad with Roasted Garlic Aïoli *102*

Seared Salmon on Fiddleheads & New Potatoes *104*

Fragrant Spiced Chicken with Rhubarb Chutney *106*

Duck Breast with the Great Canadian Sweet
& Sour Sauce & Onion Spaetzle *108*

Pan-fried Veal Chops with Gremolata *111*

Leek & Lemon Focaccia *112*

Chocolate Cheesecake with Butter Toffee Topping *114*

Fresh Pea Soup with Mint & Curry

Recommended: Château des Charmes Estate Winery Pinot Gris
Serves 6

You owe it to yourself to make this at least once a year with the season's first fresh peas. I like to add a big dollop of thick yogurt cheese (yogurt thickened to a crème fraîche or soft cream cheese consistency) to each serving. Plan to make the yogurt cheese that finishes the dish the day before. Line a colander or sieve with several layers of dampened cheesecloth or a coffee filter. Place this over a bowl and pour in a container of plain yogurt (not low-fat) of good quality. Allow the yogurt to drain for at least 8 hours or as long as 12 if you want the resulting mixture to be really thick. You don't have to refrigerate it while it is draining, but the finished yogurt cheese should be covered and stored in the refrigerator where it will keep for about a week. Great as a spread, especially when combined with fresh chopped herbs, as a topping for baked potatoes, as the base for a creamy dressing and perfect as a soft, creamy garnish for this soup.

3 Tbsp. (45 mL) butter
1 large Spanish onion, thinly sliced
2 Tbsp. (30 mL) curry powder
4 cups (950 mL) chicken stock
2 cups (475 mL) shelled fresh peas
3 Tbsp. (45 mL) chopped fresh mint leaves

salt and freshly ground white pepper to taste
½ cup (120 mL) yogurt cheese (see above) or sour cream
6 or 8 whole mint leaves

Melt the butter in a good-sized saucepan over medium-high heat and cook the onion until quite soft, about 15 minutes, stirring now and then (do not allow it to brown). Work in the curry powder and let cook for another 2 minutes. Whisk in the chicken stock and bring the mixture to a boil. Add the peas and cook for 1 or 2 minutes. Have ready a large bowl half-filled with ice water and another bowl set atop it.

Remove the pan from the heat. Pour the soup mixture into the empty bowl sitting in ice water and stir the mixture to cool for about 3 minutes. (This will retain the bright green colour of the soup.) Purée the mixture in a blender or food processor (in batches if necessary), adding some of the mint to each batch. Wipe the saucepan clean, set a sieve over it and pour the purée through it. Reheat very gently over low heat. Season with salt and pepper. Serve garnished with a dollop of yogurt cheese and a fresh mint leaf.

Chef Anna Olson

If, like so many visitors to Cave Spring Cellars Inn on the Twenty restaurant, you have swooned over the creative desserts and house-made breads and baked goods, it is Anna Olson you can thank. Anna has been in charge of this area of the kitchen since she made the transition from "the savoury" side in 1997, reversing the order in which many women rise to prominence in the cooking profession. Breakfast pastries, breads, sweets and accompanying sauces are her beat and, like her husband, Michael Olson, it is local foods that make her creations really sing.

Primavera Soup with Gruyère Toasts

Recommended: Cave Spring Cellars Sauvignon Blanc
Serves 6

Chef Roberto Fracchioni of Cave Spring's Inn on the Twenty restaurant is passionate about wild things—especially wild leeks, asparagus and morels. I'm happy to opt for the first young leeks and onions from our garden to make this light and pretty spring soup. Vary the vegetables as you wish, just make sure they are young and tender.

For the soup:

4 Tbsp. (60 mL) butter

4 young, slim leeks, trimmed, rinsed and thinly sliced

4 thin green onions, trimmed and thinly sliced

4 cups (950 mL) chicken stock

6 small, waxy potatoes, scrubbed and diced

1 cup (240 mL) shelled fresh peas

2 cups (475 mL) baby spinach leaves (rinsed, if necessary)

salt and freshly ground pepper to taste

3 Tbsp. (45 mL) chopped fresh chives

Melt the butter in a large saucepan over medium-high heat Add the leek and green onion, reduce the heat and allow the vegetables to cook very slowly for about 10 minutes, stirring occasionally. Pour the chicken stock over the vegetables, then add the potatoes. Increase the heat slightly and cook for about 10 minutes. Add the peas and cook for a further few minutes until the vegetables are tender. Stack the spinach leaves and shred them with a sharp knife. Add the leaves to the soup and cook for just a minute longer. Season with salt and pepper, sprinkle with chives and serve immediately with the toasts.

For the toasts:

¼ lb. (113 g) Gruyère cheese, grated

2 Tbsp. (30 mL) butter, softened

½ tsp. (2.5 mL) cayenne (or to taste)

12 thin slices baguette

Preheat the oven broiler. Arrange the baguette slices on a baking sheet. Combine the grated cheese with the butter and cayenne in a small mixing bowl. Use the back of a large spoon to work the ingredients together until smooth and well blended.

Toast the baguette slices on one side, then remove from the oven. Turn them over and spread the cheese mixture on each slice, pressing it down onto each. Return to the oven until bubbling and golden brown. Serve with the soup.

Chef Roberto Fracchioni

Inn on the Twenty's Grimsby-born chef with Italian roots, Roberto Fracchioni ("Frac" to his buddies) has effortlessly taken over the reins from his predecessor, Michael Olson. Rob is one of those chefs that you can talk to, really talk to, about food—for hours. Visits to Italy were many when he was growing up and he tells me about the influence of both his grandmother (his Nona) and his mother.

Rob says everyone expected him to "cook Italian" at the restaurant when he assumed the mantle of chef, so he fights it a bit. But when a supplier told him he had a great deal on a couple of boxes of veal, he couldn't help but make veal scallopine, breaded with black truffle. He also ages montasio cheese—his favourite after-school snack as a boy—at the Inn on the Twenty.

Warm Asparagus Salad
with Watercress & Radishes
in Rhubarb Riesling Dressing

Recommended: Cave Spring Cellars Off-Dry Riesling
Serves 4

During his many years as chef at Inn on the Twenty, Michael Olson was known for his insistence on using the best local ingredients. This recipe is his tribute to spring in wine country. From the chef: "Cooks in Niagara get 'antsy' in the spring as they can almost hear the produce growing, but many of the local gems aren't ready until July. We tend to grab onto early season items like delicate lettuces, crunchy icicle radishes and lip-puckering rhubarb. This salad is an excellent starter to enjoy on your deck on a warm spring day with a glass of Riesling, or serve it as a side to grilled fish or chicken."

1 lb. (455 g) fresh asparagus
1 bunch watercress
1 cup (240 mL) radishes
salt
4 Tbsp. (60 mL) olive oil
½ cup (120 mL) rhubarb cut into
    ¼-inch (.6-cm) dice

¼ cup (60 mL) sugar
½ cup (120 mL) Cave Spring Cellars
    Off-Dry Riesling
juice of 1 lemon

Wash the asparagus and peel the bottom half of the spears. Cut into 2-inch (5-cm) lengths. Wash the watercress and trim off dry stems and brown leaves. Slice the radishes and sprinkle lightly with salt.

Cook the asparagus for 2 minutes in boiling salted water. Drain and toss with 2 Tbsp. (30 mL) of the olive oil. Cook the rhubarb with the sugar and wine over medium heat until tender, about 15 minutes.

Toss the watercress and radishes with the remaining 2 Tbsp. (30 mL) olive oil and the lemon juice. Arrange the watercress and radishes loosely on plates. Top with the warm asparagus. Place a dollop of rhubarb over the asparagus.

Chef Tony de Luca

Tony de Luca, chef of Hillebrand's Vineyard Café, brought with him a wealth of culinary experience gleaned from high-profile restaurants like Toronto's Four Seasons Hotel, Bistro 990, Jump, Canoe and Auberge du Pommier. Tony uses produce from at least 40 growers in the Niagara Peninsula including items like pineapple sage, blue banana squash, specialty tomatoes and heirloom vegetables. While the chef revels in the wealth of seasonal foods available during the growing season, he maintains that "one of the best times to visit Niagara is during the winter months. We have wonderful hydroponic and cellared vegetables and fruits that we have preserved and a terrific five-course tasting menu."

Frittatine with the First Fresh Herbs

Recommended: Strewn Wines Pinot Blanc
Serves 4–6

Frittatine is a thinner version of frittata, the open-faced Italian omelette. Like its heftier sibling, it can be made with any manner of fillings. Using a larger skillet or pan results in a thinner, more delicate dish that is cut into thin strips, tossed with a light vinaigrette and served over salad greens. Versatile and portable, you can also use it to fill small, crusty rolls and take along on a cycling or hiking picnic. Use a large ovenproof skillet or pan for this; the larger the pan, the thinner the finished frittatine will be.

For the vinaigrette:

⅓ cup (80 mL) extra virgin olive oil

4 tsp. (20 mL) fresh lemon juice

1 Tbsp. (15 mL) Dijon mustard

pinch sugar

salt and freshly ground black pepper
to taste

In a mixing bowl, whisk the oil and lemon juice until well blended. Whisk in the mustard, sugar, salt and pepper. Adjust the seasoning to taste, adding more oil or lemon as desired.

For the frittatine:

3 Tbsp. (45 mL) olive oil

1 onion, finely chopped

1¼ cups (300 mL) chopped mixed
 fresh herbs (use parsley, mint,
 chives, oregano, basil, tarragon)

8 eggs

3 Tbsp. (45 mL) fresh, fine
 breadcrumbs

3 Tbsp. (45 mL) grated Parmesan
 cheese

2 tsp. (10 mL) whole milk

½ tsp. (2.5 mL) salt

¼ tsp. (1.2 mL) freshly ground black
 pepper

In a large ovenproof skillet, warm half of the olive oil over medium heat. Add the onion and sauté for about 5 minutes, until softened. Transfer the onion mixture to a bowl and add the chopped herbs, mixing to blend well. Set to one side. Wipe the skillet clean with a paper towel.

In a mixing bowl, whisk together the eggs, breadcrumbs, cheese, milk, salt and pepper. Gently fold in the cooled onion and herb mixture.

Preheat the oven broiler. Return the skillet to medium heat. Add the remaining olive oil, swirling to coat the surface of the skillet. Pour the egg mixture into the skillet; cook, gently running a narrow metal spatula around the edges to lift the cooked egg up and allow the uncooked egg to run beneath. Continue cooking for about 5 minutes, or until the mixture is set and cooked on the bottom.

Place the skillet 6 inches (15 cm) beneath the broiler element. Cook for about 2 minutes, or until the top is set and golden brown. Remove from the oven and let cool to room temperature before cutting into thin strips and tossing with the vinaigrette.

Catherine O'Donnell, Pastry Chef

Toronto born and raised Catherine O'Donnell, the pastry and dessert chef at Hillebrand's Vineyard Café, studied chocolate making at the Callebaut Chocolate Institute in Belgium before joining the King Edward Hotel. She also worked for the prestigious Oliver's chain of restaurants and was pastry chef for Vintage Inns of Niagara-on-the-Lake before joining chef Tony de Luca's culinary team at Hillebrand. Catherine is also involved in sharing her knowledge with aspiring pastry chef students at George Brown and Niagara Colleges.

Three-Cheese & Herb Cakes
with Tomato Jam

Recommended: Peller Estates Winery Gamay Noir Founder's Series
Serves 4

This makes a nice little savoury for lunch on its own, or use it as a first course for dinner with chicken or fish to follow. In the summertime, when fresh tomatoes are ours for the picking, I use them to make the dark, buttery tomato spread that accompanies these crispy little fritters. At the beginning of the growing season, if I can't find good hydroponically grown tomatoes, I rely on quality, canned plum tomatoes for this. Great for using up assorted bits of cheese. The accompanying greens are undressed as there is enough richness in the cheese cakes.

For the tomato jam:

1 Tbsp. (15 mL) olive oil	1 Tbsp. (15 mL) sherry or red wine
1 small red onion finely chopped	vinegar
1 clove garlic, peeled and crushed	1 tsp. (5 mL) dark brown sugar
2 cups (240 mL) chopped ripe	salt and freshly ground black pepper
tomatoes	to taste

Heat the olive oil in a saucepan over medium-high heat. Add the onion and garlic and cook until softened, about 5 minutes. Add the tomatoes, vinegar, sugar, salt and pepper. Stir to mix the ingredients well. Simmer the mixture, stirring occasionally, for about 30 minutes, or until the liquid has evaporated and the mixture is thick and jam-like. Set to one side.

For the cheese herb cakes:

⅓ cup (80 mL) all-purpose flour

½ tsp. (2.5 mL) cayenne

salt and freshly ground black pepper
    to taste

2 large eggs

2 Tbsp. (30 mL) whole milk

¼ lb. (113 g) old Cheddar cheese,
    grated

¼ lb. (113 g) fontina cheese, grated

¼ lb. (113 g) Gruyère cheese, grated

¼ cup (60 mL) finely chopped mixed
    fresh herbs (use parsley, chives,
    rosemary, oregano)

3 Tbsp. (45 mL) olive oil

4 cups (950 mL) arugula, rinsed and
    dried

Combine the flour, cayenne, salt and pepper in a large mixing bowl. Make a well in the centre and break the eggs into it. Using a whisk, blend the mixture until well mixed. Whisk in the milk until you have a smooth batter. Stir in the three cheeses and the chopped herbs. Cover with plastic wrap and set to one side for about an hour.

Lightly dust your hands with a little flour. Using about 1 Tbsp. (15 mL) of the mixture at a time, shape into 12 patties and transfer them as you work to a lightly floured baking sheet. Turn them over once or twice to lightly coat them with flour. Preheat the oven to 275°F (135°C).

When they have all been shaped, heat the olive oil in a heavy frying pan or skillet and fry them a few at a time, for about 1 minute on each side. Transfer them to a paper towel-lined baking sheet to keep warm in the oven.

Arrange the arugula on individual serving plates. Place two cakes on each plate and mound the tomato jam alongside each serving.

Fresh Noodles with Asparagus, Fiddleheads & Morels

Recommended: Henry of Pelham Family Estate Pinot Noir
Serves 4

Three harbingers of spring in Niagara—asparagus, fiddleheads and morels—combine with fresh pasta and a light, butter-herb sauce. Fiddleheads are grown commercially very close to our home, in a section of forest in the Effingham hills, near Pelham. Use a vegetable peeler to peel the asparagus stems, holding the asparagus by the tip end and peeling down the stalk.

½ lb. (225 g) small asparagus, peeled (reserve peels)
1 cup (240 mL) whipping cream
¼ lb. (113 g) cold butter, cubed
salt and freshly ground black pepper to taste
1 cup (240 mL) fiddleheads, rinsed
2 shallots, minced

1 cup (240 mL) morel mushrooms, sliced
1 lb. (455 g) fresh noodles (fettuccine, linguine or other)
2 Tbsp. (30 mL) chopped mixed fresh herbs (such as parsley, chervil, tarragon, chives)
finely grated zest of 1 lemon

Place the reserved asparagus peels in a saucepan and cover with the cream. Gently bring to a boil over medium-high heat, then immediately turn off the heat and allow the peels to steep in the hot cream for 30 minutes. Bring the cream back to a boil and strain through a sieve. Return to the saucepan and whisk in half of the cold butter. Season with salt and pepper and set aside.

Blanch the asparagus and fiddleheads in lightly salted boiling water until just tender, about 5–7 minutes. Transfer to a bowl of ice water and let chill for 2–3 minutes. Drain the vegetables. Using a vegetable peeler, peel the asparagus stems lengthwise to get fettuccine-like strips. Set the fiddleheads and all the asparagus to one side.

Melt the remaining butter in a large skillet or sauté pan over medium-high heat. Add the shallots and sauté for about 3 minutes. Add the morels and cook for about 5 minutes. Add the fiddleheads and all the asparagus to the skillet, tossing the ingredients together until warmed through. Remove from the heat.

Bring a large pot of salted water to a boil. Add the pasta and cook until just tender; fresh pasta should only take 2–3 minutes. As it is cooking, simmer the reserved cream with the vegetables in the skillet. When the noodles are cooked, drain and add them to the skillet. Add the chopped herbs and lemon zest and toss quickly together. Serve immediately.

Chef Jason Rosso

Chef de cuisine Jason Rosso is a relative newcomer to Niagara, joining the Peller Estates Winery Restaurant when it opened in the summer of 2001. Born and raised in Toronto, Jason has worked at more than one bustling city hotel dining room and other upscale urban restaurants in Toronto and Calgary. Working in one of the most modern, state-of-the-art culinary facilities in Niagara is inspiring enough; coupled with the beauty of the region itself and all that it has to offer—including Peller's family of premium VQA wines—Jason is creating his own brand of creative wine country cuisine.

Asparagus Ravioli with Basil Butter

Recommended: Peninsula Ridge Estates Sauvignon Blanc
Serves 4–6

You can vary this pasta preparation by using fiddleheads in place of the aspara-gus or make some of each vegetable in separate ravioli wrappers. This dish can be made a little more substantial by topping each serving with a few pan-seared shrimp or scallops.

¾ lb. (340 g) asparagus, washed and trimmed
4 Tbsp. (60 mL) butter
1 clove garlic, chopped
1 green onion, chopped
salt and freshly ground black pepper to taste
3 Tbsp. (45 mL) finely chopped fresh basil

¼ cup (60 mL) water
1 Tbsp. (15 mL) all-purpose flour
10 egg roll wrappers (or won ton wrappers about 3 inches (7.5 cm square)
½ cup (120 mL) freshly grated Parmesan cheese

Cut the asparagus stalks into 2-inch (5-cm) lengths; reserve the tips for garnish. In a large skillet, heat 1 Tbsp. (15 mL) of the butter over medium-high heat. Add the asparagus stalks, garlic and green onion. Season with salt and pepper, then add half the basil and 2 Tbsp. (30 mL) of the water. Cover and cook for 3–5 minutes, or until the asparagus is tender. Transfer to a blender or food processor and purée until fairly smooth. Let cool, cover and refrigerate for at least an hour or overnight.

In a little bowl, blend the flour with the remaining 2 Tbsp. (30 mL) water to make a smooth paste. Place an egg roll wrapper on a dry work sur-face. Mound a heaping teaspoonful of asparagus purée near each corner of wrapper. Brush the flour paste around the mounds of purée. Position a sec-ond wrapper on top so that the edges are even; press down around the mounds to force out air and seal well all around the mounds. Using a sharp cookie cutter or paring knife, cut around each mound to make four ravioli. (If using won ton wrappers, place one mound of purée in the centre of each.) Transfer to a baking sheet lined with parchment paper and cover with a tea towel. Repeat with the remaining wrappers and filling, covering the finished ravioli with the tea towel as you work. (Ravioli can be prepared up to 1 hour before cooking.)

Bring a large pot of water to a boil, add a little salt and cook the ravioli in batches for about 2 minutes, or until they rise to the top and are tender. Drain on a clean tea towel and transfer to heated plates. Keep warm in a 275ºF (135ºC) oven. When cooking the last batch of ravioli, add the asparagus tips and cook for 2–3 minutes, or until tender, then drain well. In a small pan, melt the remaining 3 Tbsp. (45 mL) butter and stir in the remaining basil. Drizzle the butter over each serving and sprinkle with Parmesan. Garnish each with asparagus tips and serve immediately.

Cave Spring Cellars

Founded in 1986 in the very heart of the Beamsville Bench in the wee town of Jordan, Cave Spring Cellars has long been at the forefront of excellence in winemaking. Cave Springs vineyards feature some of the province's first plantings of vinifera grapes, established in 1978. Company founder Leonard Pennachetti has always held fast to his philosophy that great wines are grown, not made, a truism that visitors happily attest to whether they visit the winery shop for tastings or enjoy lunch or dinner at the Inn on the Twenty, the first critically acclaimed restaurant in wine country. In 1993, they opened The Vintner's Inn, adjacent to the winery, an artfully conceived and designed operation that is the work of Helen Young, Leonard's wife.

Spring Spinach & Ricotta Gnocchi with Sweet Peppers & Lemon Cream

Recommended: Vineland Estates Winery Sauvignon Blanc

Serves 6

Jan-Willem Stulp is the chef de cuisine at the Vineland Estates Winery restaurant. This is his recipe for a fitting first course for spring. From the chef: "The secret to this recipe is to work quickly, use just enough flour to bind the pasta and have plenty of salted, boiling water ready."

For the gnocchi:

1 lb. (455 g) ricotta cheese

1 cup (240 mL) blanched spinach, squeezed dry and finely chopped

1 egg

3 egg yolks

¼ cup (60 mL) grated Parmesan cheese

salt and freshly ground black pepper to taste

1–1½ cups (240–360 mL) all-purpose flour

½ tsp. (2.5 mL) nutmeg

Place the ricotta in a sieve set over a bowl. Let stand for a few minutes if the ricotta is quite wet. Discard the liquid and wipe the bowl clean. In the bowl combine the ricotta, spinach, egg, yolks, Parmesan, salt and pepper. Stir together with a wooden spoon just until well mixed. Combine the flour and nutmeg in another bowl. Stir in the flour, ¼ cup (60 mL) at a time, adding more as needed to form a workable dough that is still moist. Take a small ball of dough and roll it into a long, cylindrical shape, about ½ inch (1.2 cm) thick. Repeat this until you have about 5 or 6 long lengths of dough, using a little flour for your hands if necessary. Cut the lengths diagonally into 1-inch (2.5-cm) pieces. Dust very lightly with flour and transfer to a baking sheet lightly dusted with flour or lined with parchment paper. Let rest while you bring a large pot of salted water to a boil.

As it comes to a boil, start to prepare the sauce.

For the sauce:

2 Tbsp. (30 mL) olive oil

1 large red bell pepper, seeded and
   thinly sliced

1 large yellow bell pepper, seeded
   and thinly sliced

1 red onion, thinly sliced

finely grated zest of 1 lemon

3 Tbsp. (45 mL) chopped fresh herbs
   (thyme, rosemary, parsley)

$\frac{1}{4}$ cup (60 mL) Vineland Estates
   Winery Sauvignon Blanc

$\frac{1}{2}$ cup (120 mL) chicken stock

1 cup (240 mL) whipping cream

juice of 1 lemon

salt and freshly ground black pepper
   to taste

Warm the olive oil in a sauté pan over medium-high heat. Add the peppers, onion, lemon zest and herbs and sauté until softened and fragrant, about 6 minutes. Add the wine, scraping up any bits that are clinging to the pan, then add the chicken stock, cream and lemon juice. Adjust the seasoning with salt and pepper. Reduce the heat to quite low and simmer for about 10–12 minutes, until slightly thickened.

Cook the gnocchi, in batches of a dozen or so, for 5 minutes, or until they bob to the surface. Remove them with a slotted spoon. Add the cooked gnocchi to the sauce to heat through briefly, then serve.

Lobster & Pea Sprout Salad
with Roasted Garlic Aïoli

Recommended: Peller Estates Winery Gewürztraminer Vineyard Series
Serves 2–4

"The most popular item on the summer menu," is how chef Jason Rosso of Peller Estates Winery Restaurant describes his elegant lobster salad, one of the first recipes the young chef devised for the restaurant. Surely one of the reasons for the dish's popularity—apart from its obvious elegance and good taste—is the sheer luxury of enjoying lobster out of the shell. No work for the eater, just complete hedonistic pleasure. Chef Rosso recommends that you save the lobster shells to make a bisque. This is truly wonderful paired with one of Peller's finest wines, their Gewürztraminer Vineyard Series.

2 large eggs
1 tsp. (5 mL) dry mustard
1½ cups (360 mL) vegetable oil
1 Tbsp. (15 mL) cider vinegar
1 Tbsp. (15 mL) roasted garlic purée
salt and freshly ground black pepper
   to taste
2 lobsters, 1½ lbs. (680 g) each,
   cooked and meat extracted

1 cup (240 mL) pea sprouts (or other
   delicate greens)
1 yellow bell pepper, seeded and
   finely diced
1 red bell pepper, seeded and finely
   diced
1 small red onion, finely diced
1 Tbsp. (15 mL) capers, drained

Combine the eggs and mustard in a blender or food processor. With the motor running, gradually add the oil until a thick mayonnaise forms. Add the vinegar and the garlic purée and continue to blend until creamy and smooth. Season with salt and pepper. (Cover and refrigerate if not using straight away.)

Cut the lobster meat into large, bite-sized chunks. Place in a large stainless steel bowl along with the sprouts, bell peppers, onion and capers. Add the aïoli and toss to combine well. Serve with fresh baguette or rye bread.

Lobster—Taking the Plunge

It's not a fun job ending a lobster's brief life, but someone's got to do it—that is, if you want to make this recipe. The easiest method (and the only one I can manage) is to just plunge a live lobster into a pot of boiling water and clamp on a lid. If you follow this method, make sure you have at least a gallon (4 L) of water on the boil for each lobster and cook them one at a time. A 1½-lb. (680-g) lobster should take about 6–8 minutes (add 2 minutes more for each additional pound/455 g). Now, you don't want the lobster to really boil, as that will result in tough, rubbery flesh. The water should be at a good brisk boil when your lobster takes the plunge, but as soon as the water starts to return to a boil, turn the heat down to allow the lobster to poach slowly. Have an ice bath ready and place the boiled lobster in it to chill for a few minutes before removing the meat from the shell.

Roasting Garlic

This makes more than you will need for the aïoli, but there is no end of uses for it—spread it on good bread, use it as an omelette filling, or add it to soups, salads or sandwiches. Preheat the oven to quite high, about 450°F (230°C). Slice about ½ inch (1.2 cm) from the stem end of each of two heads of garlic, just enough to expose the "meat" of the cloves. Trim a little off each root end, but make sure the cloves stay attached. Rub off any papery outer skin. Pour about 1 Tbsp. (15 mL) of olive oil in a little gratin dish. Rub the garlic heads all over with the oil. Add about ¼ cup (60 mL) of vegetable or chicken stock to the dish and roast for about 25–30 minutes. Allow to cool before handling. Transfer the heads to a cutting board and use the back of a broad knife to push the soft cloves from their skins into a little bowl. Mash the cloves with a fork, adding a little of their roasting liquid if desired.

Seared Salmon on Fiddleheads
& New Potatoes

Recommended: Pillitteri Estates Winery Chardonnay Family Reserve
Serves 4

To my mind, pan-searing fresh salmon fillets is the best way to enjoy one of the world's greatest fish. Grilling salmon over too high a heat does nothing for the fish's naturally delicate flavour. Too often it emerges overcooked, masked with a harsh grill taste. I really prefer this method, which treats olive oil-rubbed salmon fillets to a searing in a very hot pan. The cooking time given here will produce salmon with a wet heart, as I call it. It will be like a steak cooked to medium rare. If you prefer your salmon well done, extend the cooking time. By the way, the roasted garlic aïoli in the Lobster & Pea Sprout Salad (page 102) works wonderfully well with this salmon.

4 6-oz (170-g) salmon fillets, with skin
2 Tbsp. (30 mL) olive oil
salt and freshly ground black pepper
    to taste
16 small new potatoes, lightly
    scrubbed and left whole
2 cups (475 mL) fiddleheads
⅓ cup (80 mL) chopped fresh chives

2 Tbsp. (30 mL) chopped fresh basil
2 Tbsp. (30 mL) chopped fresh flat-
    leaf parsley
½ cup (120 mL) extra virgin olive oil
2 tsp. (10 mL) Dijon mustard
salt and freshly ground black pepper
    to taste
juice of 1 lemon

Rub the salmon all over with the 2 Tbsp. (30 mL) olive oil and season with salt and pepper. Set aside.

Place the potatoes in a large saucepan and just cover with boiling water. Add a little salt and cook until tender, about 20 minutes. During the last 5 minutes of cooking time, place the fiddleheads in a steamer (or sieve) and set over the potatoes. Drain the potatoes and the fiddleheads, then plunge quickly and briefly in cold water. Drain again and let sit for a minute. Halve each potato lengthwise. Place the potatoes and fiddleheads in a bowl with the chives, basil and parsley, the ½ cup (120 mL) olive oil, mustard and seasoning. Toss together to thoroughly coat the vegetables and cover the bowl loosely with a tea towel while you finish the salmon.

Preheat the oven to low, about 275°F (135°C), and place a baking sheet on the centre rack. Heat a large heavy frying pan (cast iron is good) until it is searingly hot (the hotter the better). Working with 2 fillets at a time, add the salmon to the hot pan, cut side down. Cook for about a minute, until seared brown. Brush the skin with a little more oil and turn over. Continue to cook for a further 2–3 minutes until the skin is crispy and brown. Remove from the pan and transfer to the oven to keep warm while you cook the remaining salmon.

To serve, place a portion of the fiddlehead and potato mixture in the centre of a warmed plate. Top with salmon, add a drizzle of lemon juice and serve immediately.

De Sousa Wine Cellars

In 1987 De Sousa Wine Cellars became the first traditional Portuguese-style winery in Canada. Through a combination of Portuguese tradition and Vitis vinifera with French hybrid grapes and just the right microclimate and soil, John De Sousa and his son, John De Sousa, Jr., carry on the wine styles beloved by Portuguese-born Canadians. Beamsville-based De Sousa is also home to a historic museum featuring antique Portuguese winemaking artifacts, including a horse-drawn buggy that would have been used to carry wine to the markets and an eighteenth century wine press. Their retail outlet offers a full selection of their wines.

Fragrant Spiced Chicken
with Rhubarb Chutney

Recommended: Daniel Lenko Estate Winery Gewürztraminer
Serves 4

Be they ever so humble, chicken thighs are nevertheless the cook's best friend. They are inexpensive, versatile, unfailingly tender and moist and always full of flavour—especially when treated to an aromatic spiced marinade like this one. The rhubarb chutney is a snap to make (makes a nice gift, too) and is very good with grilled sausages or any pork. Serve this with basmati rice tossed with a few toasted cashews.

For the rhubarb chutney:

½ tsp. (2.5 mL) whole allspice
½ tsp. (2.5 mL) whole cloves
1-inch (2.5-cm) piece cinnamon
1 tsp. (5 mL) mustard seeds
¼ tsp. (1.2 mL) celery seeds
1 ⅓ cups (320 mL) dark brown sugar
1 ¼ cups (300 mL) cider vinegar

½ cup (120 mL) water
½ tsp. (2.5 mL) salt
2 onions, chopped
1 lb. (455 g) rhubarb, trimmed and cut
    into small chunks
2 cups (475 mL) golden raisins

Tie the allspice, cloves, cinnamon, mustard seeds and celery seeds together in a small piece of cheesecloth with kitchen string. Combine the spice bag with the sugar, vinegar, water and salt in a large, heavy, non-reactive saucepan and bring to a boil over high heat. Boil for about 5 minutes, stirring now and then. Add the onions and rhubarb, cover, reduce the heat and let simmer for about 30 minutes. Add the raisins and continue to cook for another hour until the mixture is thick. Remove the spice bag, transfer to a bowl and cool. Refrigerate, covered, until needed.

For the chicken:

1 large onion, chopped
3 cloves garlic, peeled and crushed
2 tsp. (10 mL) cumin seeds
2 Tbsp. (30 mL) coriander seeds
1 tsp. (5 mL) salt
2 tsp. (10 mL) ground ginger
2 tsp. (10 mL) ground cinnamon

2 tsp. (10 mL) turmeric
juice of 1 lemon
1 Tbsp. (15 mL) olive oil
1 cup (240 mL) plain yogurt
1½ lb. (680 g) boneless, skinless
    chicken thighs, each one cut
    lengthwise into thirds

In a food processor, combine the onion, garlic, cumin and coriander seeds, salt, ginger, cinnamon and turmeric. Pulse to achieve a fine paste. Scrape this mixture out into a small bowl and blend in the lemon juice, olive oil and yogurt. Mix together well. Arrange the chicken pieces in a glass baking dish and cover with the marinade. Cover with plastic wrap, refrigerate and let marinate for at least 2 hours or overnight.

Preheat the oven to 350°F (175°C). Remove the plastic wrap and bake the chicken, loosely covered with foil, for about 35–40 minutes (although if you cook it longer it will still be moist). Serve with the rhubarb chutney.

Duck Breast with the Great Canadian Sweet & Sour Sauce & Onion Spaetzle

Recommended: Hillebrand Estates Cabernet Sauvignon Glenlake Vineyard Unfiltered
Serves 4

It's no secret that chefs in Niagara love to cook with fresh duck—it lends itself to so many different preparations and is a naturally great "wine" meat. Chef Tony de Luca of Hillebrand's Vineyard Café has adapted one of his favourite dishes to make it more accessible for the home cook. While you can invest in a special spaetzle press, I rather like the method that the chef uses to make the fresh pasta dumplings: simply transfer the spaetzle batter to a colander with large holes and use a pastry scraper to rub the batter through the holes directly into the boiling water. It will help, time-wise, if you prepare the basic spaetzle ahead, then make the sauce and combine to keep warm.

1 Tbsp. (15 mL) butter
2 Tbsp. (30 mL) olive oil
2 shallots, finely diced
1 clove garlic, minced
½ cup (120 mL) Hillebrand Estates Cabernet Sauvignon Glenlake Vineyard Unfiltered

½ cup (120 mL) veal, chicken or duck stock
¼ cup (60 mL) red wine vinegar
2 sprigs fresh thyme, leaves only, finely chopped
1 Tbsp. (15 mL) honey

In a very small saucepan, heat the butter and olive oil over medium-high heat until frothy. Add the shallots and stir for a few minutes; add the garlic and continue to sauté for a few seconds longer. Add the wine and cook until the mixture is thickened and reduced to 1 Tbsp. (15 mL). Add the stock and reduce again until 3 Tbsp. (45 mL) remain. Add the vinegar and cook until the mixture is reduced and thickened. Pass the mixture through a fine sieve and return to the saucepan. Allow to come to a simmer. Add the chopped thyme and honey and stir until dissolved. Set the sauce aside and keep it warm.

For the spaetzle:

¼ cup (60 mL) olive oil	1 large onion, thinly sliced
2 cups (475 mL) all-purpose flour	2 cloves garlic, finely chopped
½ cup (120 mL) whole milk	salt and freshly ground black pepper
¼ cup (60 mL) water	to taste
2 Tbsp. (30 mL) butter	

Bring a large pot of water to a rapid boil. Add a pinch of salt and the olive oil. In a mixing bowl, combine the flour, milk and water and stir to a paste. Fill a large bowl with ice water and set to one side. Place a colander with large holes over the boiling water and use a pastry scraper to push the spaetzle batter through the colander holes directly into the boiling water. Cook for a few minutes, stirring frequently. When the spaetzle float to the surface, use a slotted spoon to transfer them to the bowl of ice water. When they have chilled thoroughly, remove them from the ice water and drain.

Melt the butter in a large sauté pan over medium-high heat. Add the onion and garlic and sauté until golden brown, about 6 minutes or so. Stir in the spaetzle and season with salt and pepper. Keep the spaetzle warm as you prepare the duck.

For the duck:

2 Tbsp. (30 mL) olive oil	salt and freshly ground black pepper
2 Tbsp. (30 mL) butter	to taste
2 boneless duck breasts	fresh thyme sprigs for garnish

Preheat the oven to 400°F (200°C). Heat the olive oil and butter in an ovenproof sauté pan over medium-high heat. Season the duck with salt and pepper. When the butter is frothy, add the duck, skin side down. Place the pan in the oven and roast for 15 minutes. Using tongs, turn the duck over and cook for another 5 minutes. Remove the pan from the oven and transfer the duck to a cutting board. Let it rest for a few minutes before slicing (use half a duck breast per main dish serving).

To assemble, place a few spoonfuls of spaetzle in the centre of each dinner plate. Arrange the duck slices on top of the spaetzle. Spoon the sweet and sour sauce around the plate and garnish with fresh thyme.

Lakeview Cellars Estate Winery

Another of the Beamsville Bench wineries, Lakeview was founded some 10 years ago and is one of Niagara's first cottage wineries. Award-winning amateur winemaker Eddy Gurinksas decided to seriously pursue his passion for producing wine after retiring when he and his wife, Lorraine, bought a small—by winery standards—13-acre vineyard. Today, even as it grows, Lakeview maintains its modest approach, with most of their wines produced from their own grapes. A patio bar is open throughout the summer where Wine Route visitors may enjoy a glass of wine and a bite to eat.

Beamsville in blossom

Asparagus Ravioli with Basil Butter (page 98)

Pan-fried Veal Chops with Gremolata

Recommended: Inniskillin Pinot Noir Founders' Reserve
Serves 4

Sumptuous, succulent veal chops need little in the way of embellishment. However, the gremolata adds a refreshing accent to complement the delicate flavour of the meat. Capers are not a traditional ingredient in gremolata, but I like the extra flavour lift they provide. Serve with a creamy potato gratin and sautéed wild mushrooms.

4 cloves garlic, finely minced
4 Tbsp. (60 mL) chopped fresh flat-
  leaf parsley
3 Tbsp. (45 mL) capers, drained and
  roughly chopped
zest of 1 large lemon, finely minced

4 Tbsp. (60 mL) extra virgin olive oil
4 veal rib or loin chops, cut $\frac{3}{4}$ to
  1 inch (2 to 2.5 cm) thick
salt and freshly ground black pepper
  to taste

Combine the garlic, parsley, capers and lemon zest in a small bowl and toss together. Set to one side.

Drizzle olive oil over both sides of the chops and season well with salt and pepper. Heat a skillet over high heat (add a little more oil if desired) and sear the chops quickly on both sides. Reduce the heat to medium-high and fry the chops until slightly crusted and golden brown on each side, turning once or twice. Cook for about 12 minutes in total, or to desired doneness. Just before serving, pat a generous portion of gremolata onto the top of each chop.

Leek & Lemon Focaccia

Recommended: Cave Spring Cellars Chardonnay Musque
Makes 1 18 x 10-inch (45 x 25-cm) bread

This recipe is from Anna Olson of Cave Spring's Inn on the Twenty restaurant, renowned for its good breads and creative desserts. Anna says: "Focaccia is a delicious and convenient style of bread to make. It doesn't require skill in shaping, but instead is spread with a rolling pin and gently dimpled with the tips of your fingers. The shape and soft texture of this bread, with its lemon fragrance and soft, green leek accents, lends itself well to sandwiches, especially grilled chicken or roast pork."

5 Tbsp. (75 mL) olive oil (plus some for brushing)
2 leeks, white and light green parts only, washed and chopped
2 cups (475 mL) warm water (110°F/43°C)
1 Tbsp. (15 mL) active dry yeast
1 Tbsp. (15 mL) honey
2 Tbsp. (30 mL) lemon zest
¼ cup (60 mL) cornmeal
5 cups (1.2 L) all-purpose flour
1 Tbsp. (15 mL) salt
coarse salt or grated Parmesan cheese (optional)

Heat the oil in a sauté pan over medium heat, add the leek and sauté until tender, about 5 minutes. Remove from the heat and allow to cool.

In an electric mixer fitted with the dough hook attachment, combine the water, yeast, honey, lemon zest and cornmeal. Process on low speed for 1 minute. Add the flour, salt and cooled leek to the mixer and blend on low speed for 1 minute, then on medium speed for 8 minutes. The dough should just come away from the sides of the bowl while adhering to the bottom. If necessary, add a touch of water or flour as needed to achieve this. Place the dough in a lightly oiled bowl and cover with plastic wrap. Let rise for 1 hour in a warm, draught-free place.

Grease a baking sheet or line it with parchment paper. Turn the dough onto a floured surface and roll it out to an inch (2.5 cm) in thickness. Lift it gently and place onto the baking sheet. Cover the dough with a tea towel and let rest for 20 minutes.

Preheat the oven to 350°F (175°C). Dimple the dough with the tips of your fingers. Bake for 30–40 minutes, until golden brown in colour. While warm, brush the focaccia with olive oil. For an added kick, sprinkle with coarse salt or grated Parmesan cheese.

EastDell Estates

Formerly Walter Estates, EastDell Estates is owned by Susan O'Dell and Michael East and is blessed with one of the loveliest of settings. Built entirely of wood and stone harvested from the property, this winery is perched on the Beamsville Bench and, on the right clear day, offers views of the Escarpment, Lake Ontario and the recognizable skyline of Toronto on the far side. There are more than 60 acres of vineyard, hiking trails through the adjacent wooded area and a cabin in a woodland setting available for a romantic rendezvous. Chef Mark Walpole heads up the kitchen of the winery's Bench Bistro, that features many of his preserves, chutneys and the like available for purchase.

Chocolate Cheesecake
with Butter Toffee Topping

Makes 15–20 servings

Chef Catherine O'Donnell, in charge of pastries and desserts for both Hillebrand's Vineyard Café and the new dining room at Peller Estates Winery, is one busy woman. This is her recipe for a rich, seriously good—and big—cheesecake. (You will need a 10-inch/25-cm springform pan for this recipe.) Crush the cookies for the base in a food processor.

For the cookie crust base:
1½ cups (360 mL) ground Oreo
    cookies
4½ Tbsp. (67 mL) melted butter

Preheat the oven to 350°F (175°C). Blend the ground cookies with the melted butter in a bowl. Mix together well, then press onto the bottom and a little way up the sides of the springform pan. Bake in the preheated oven for about 5 minutes to set. Remove from the oven and set to one side to cool.

For the butter toffee topping:
1 14 oz. can (1¼ cups/300 mL)
    condensed milk
¾ cup (180 mL) butter

3 Tbsp. (45 mL) corn syrup
¾ cup (180 mL) brown sugar

Choose a medium-sized saucepan with a heavy base and combine all the topping ingredients. Place over medium-high heat and stir the mixture constantly as it comes to a boil. Still stirring, let the mixture boil for 5 minutes to thicken. Once it is thickened, remove from the heat. Pour half of the mixture on the prepared cookie crust, smoothing it to cover the surface. Set aside the remaining mixture.

For the filling:

2¼ lbs. (1 kg) cream cheese,
    softened

¾ cup (180 mL) sugar

6 oz. (170 g) semi-sweet chocolate,
    melted

5 eggs

Increase the oven temperature to 400°F (200°C). In the bowl of an electric mixer, blend the cheese, sugar and melted chocolate. When smooth and well blended, add the eggs, one at a time, mixing well after each addition. Pour this mixture on top of the toffee topping in the base, smoothing the surface.

Bake for 15 minutes, then reduce the heat to 300°F (150°C) and continue to bake for 45 minutes to 1 hour. The cake will have a firm centre and will be just beginning to brown when it is done. Turn off the oven, open the oven door and allow the cake to cool slowly in the oven for an additional hour. Remove from the oven, cool to room temperature and chill well before serving. To serve, slice the cheesecake, wiping the knife clean between slices. Drizzle each slice with the remaining butter toffee topping.

June

The Summer Table Beneath the Trees

June inspires clichés, I guess, but the truth is that it really is busting out all over, especially if you judge by the grass that really is greener over our septic tank. We are overwhelmed by the magnificence, the magnitude of our massive peonies, white tinged with burgundy, magenta and pink. In the city, I longed for a garden with even one or two peony bushes and here are more than a dozen. What riches. The two venerable climbing roses hold dark scarlet blooms, like vintage Victorian velvet, and the arboured grapevine is thriving and vibrant. The trumpet vine, with its thick, twisty base, seems well on its way to becoming a full-fledged tree. It is as invasive as we have heard; bits of it are popping up throughout the lawn and flagstones. It seems to grow as I look at it, but so beautiful with its long, nodding floral heads. Hummingbirds hover daily, inserting their made-to-measure beaks down the length of the prominent coral-orange blossoms.

There are snails galore, sleeping on the underside of peony blossoms and nestled amid the dark green foliage. Ted says we have to open a "snail pub"—put out pans of beer to attract and, ultimately, trap them. Not the worst way to go, I guess. I think I'll leave it to Ted to arrange as I have an aversion to (live) snails. Years ago in southwest England, with a cook's plan for homemade *escargots à la Bourguignonne* in mind, I captured dozens of garden-variety snails. I had heard some well-meaning BBC radio host claim that if you captured them and fed them white flour for a few days (to clean their digestive tracts), then changed their diet to include a mixture of flour and fresh herbs, a bit of garlic—thereby effectively stuffing them—you could cook them in the best French bistro style, bathed in a garlicky butter sauce. Escargot—gratis! Well, no one told me to put a weight on the pot lid. The morning after an evening of collecting, I entered my kitchen to find it completely hung with trailing, trawling snails. They dangled from the airing rack, the kitchen counter, the kettle's handle. They edged up windows, in and out of the sink drain, across the floor and up my little fridge like movable magnets. Stephen King or David Cronenberg could not have written a more lurid scene.

After dinner each evening, we sit in the gazebo with a glass of wine and take great delight in feasting our eyes on the burgeoning vegetable garden. Performed a bit of mental arithmetic and calculated that, what with the railway ties, truckloads of soil and compost (well, a lot of dirt anyway), cages to keep things upright, other cages to keep creatures out, special little Velcro thingies to secure slender stalks, bamboo tripods (artfully constructed by Ted) for the beans to run happily, environmentally friendly soap rinses to keep baddies at bay, special no-fail fertilizers and so on, these are bound to be the world's most expensive vegetables. By my estimate, the first tomato we eat will be worth about $43.

JUNE 5. I lie in bed at night, listening to the summer night sounds, and read about horned green tomato worms (the pictures!), cutworms, potato bugs, rot of all description and wonder how anyone ever gets anything they can actually eat by growing it themselves. I have enormous respect for anyone who does this in an effort to make a living. For every food there is an eater who will doubtless get there long before us. Last night we surprised a family of brown rabbits as they were preparing to tear towards the vegetable patch, no doubt to nibble at my fetal fava beans. I felt like Mr. McGregor. If I spy them, I will pie them.

JUNE 13. Our first salad from the garden, dressed with Sicilian olive oil, fresh herbs and peppery-tasting chive blossoms. From garden to table in minutes—sensational. I will soon be able to add the pepperiness of nasturtiums. Planted not so long ago, they are coming up quickly as well as my new bay plant, the oregano, mint, chives, tarragon, rosemary, parsley and basil. Scarlet runner beans emerging, Swiss chard and carrots, rhubarb, tomatoes, fava beans all looking beautiful in our framed vegetable garden. Beautiful days, yesterday and today, quite warm, full sun. Diminutive horse chestnuts emerging on our two big trees, collecting in healthy little brilliant green bunches, ready to pop later in the summer. The tiny maple seed pods—helicopters, Ted calls them—root everywhere, in my basil pot and throughout the garden. Everything grows here with a brilliant green vengeance. I'm astonished to learn that the peanuts we buy at Picards, wonderfully great big fat redskins, grow nearby. They are without a doubt the best peanuts I have ever tasted. This is indeed the Carolinian Zone.

There are strawberries as of last week (June 7) at Whitty Farms—and they are perfect. We have them at almost every meal. Before the harvest is over, I will make jam.

JUNE 16. Visitors to Grasmere include my cousin Anne from Wales, assorted relatives from the city and good friends Peter and Katrin visiting from Austria. We take them along the Bruce Trail and stop in at Morningstar Mill to pick up a little bag of all-Canadian whole-wheat flour for them to take home. Dropped in to Vineland Estates Winery so they could taste their Riesling and picked up a couple of bottles of their wonderful bubbly, Vineland Estates Winery Riesling Cuve Close, then on to Henry of Pelham. Can't resist their Baco Noir Reserve, an absolutely big, luscious wine that we will savour with our rib-eyes for dinner. Ted smokes some peppers in the old stone smoker and we side everything with local asparagus and corn (not ours, yet), tomatoes and salad greens from our garden. Fresh strawberries and cream for dessert. This is Katrin's first visit to Canada and she is enchanted with everything. And Devon-born Peter, who left Canada to live in Tobago for a number of years, loves it. We feel blessed, proud to share all of this beauty, good food and wine with good friends.

JUNE 24. We have discovered sour cherries on the edge of our property, there for the picking and the pie-making! Almost ready. Very exciting. The fragrance of the catalpa trees with their beautiful, tiny orchid-like white blossoms is so subtle, so attractive it pulls me to it as I walk by. My herb garden is awash in mint, must make lots of mint sauce and juleps.

The wild berries we are trying to identify—like blackberries, but longer, slimmer—I find out later are mulberries, of course. Too many of them have been lost to the birds. Next year I will be ready for them and make jam. These were the berries my Mum used to tell me about in England. Her grandmother made mulberry wine, Mum drank too much and had a deep purple experience on the way home.

Our old established Concord grapevine is like a monitor or bellwether of the others in our region, albeit a happily untended one. I check it every few days and think about the acres and acres of grapevines so near to us. It has masses of teeny, brilliant green grapes. Even for all its foliage it musters enough energy to issue them. The red velvet roses climb and nod round my window.

Canada Day weekend, coolish on the Saturday, very windy and a bit grey, then all the clouds blown away, bright clear sunlight and no humidity. Ted dug a fire pit (at the site of the sold windmill) and we had the last of our post-dinner wine (Henry of Pelham Zweigelt-Gamay) around a roaring fire, while enjoying the beautiful blue-pink-mauve strata sunset. The first fava bean pods are showing and the first red peppers. Tomatoes are in flower, Yukon Gold greenery tall and showy. Salad greens every night now—so far we've kept the bunnies at bay. We had veal burgers with Morbier cheese, first of the season corn, asparagus (still lots available) and home fries from local spuds. Ted caught a firefly in a jar for me, its light going on and off like a tiny switch, and I am reminded of the line from one of my favourite Joni Mitchell songs. Magical here now.

Alysa came at the beginning of the weekend and we had rib-eyes in the gazebo with new peas and new spuds. A handful of spice-grilled shrimp and wonderful Creekside Estates Winery Laura's Blend. I made focaccia strewn with dressed salad greens from our garden. Fresh local strawberries and cherries with mascarpone.

Saturday, and Jenna and I made 12 jars of strawberry jam and a sour cherry pie with crumble top, the cherries gleaned from the tree on our property. What a thrill. They weren't large and they weren't many, but they were enough. Went looking for the wild raspberries I spotted earlier, but either the birds or hikers got to them before me.

We see a bridal party at Morningstar Mill readying themselves for photos. So pretty.

Every day we remind ourselves of where we are, and how lucky we are. People drive here to cycle and walk where we live.

In the Vineyard and On the Vine

"In the vineyard, things are really starting to grow—everything explodes in June. Vines experience very quick vegetative growth now, gaining a couple of inches overnight. All the energy stored from the previous year is pushed out now as the vines grow and begin to take shape, and it really begins to look like a vineyard. It is the end of the flowering period, approximately, which is also a very important time. Flowering is when the berries are formed; they're like clusters in May, each berry begins as a flower that has to be pollinated. Vines are self-pollinating but the weather has a huge impact on how well that pollination will go. What we want are warm, dry days with light breezes, not cold, wet or damp, as that encourages everything to stick together. We also want the warmth so the plants will continue to grow. This is the next stage, the flowering. Once the flowering is complete, we know there is a distinct number of days to harvest. From this period between bud break and flowering, we can predict the harvest, obviously taking into consideration that not all vines have the same growing period. Some, like Baco Noir and Pinot Noir and some Chardonnay, are early, but generally speaking, from flowering to harvest is between 110 and 120 days. Riesling and Cabernet Sauvignon, for example, are late season.

"Flowering is critical; if it happens late in July we're in trouble because it means we will be picking well into November and everything gets pushed back. In the year 2000, we had a late flowering period. The ideal is to have flowering completed by the end of June to early July.

"The winery in June sees us full into bottling; the biggest months for bottling are June and July. Our goal is to have a shutdown for most of August to give everyone a break before September, when we are incredibly busy.

"In the hospitality and store area, everything is quite busy. By now our café will be up and running."

Matthew Speck, Henry of Pelham Family Estate Winery

Simple Seasonal Pleasure

Crème Fraîche

For strawberries! Warm 1 cup (240 mL) of whipping cream gently. Remove from the heat and combine with 2 Tbsp. (30 mL) buttermilk or sour cream in a glass bowl. Mix well, cover and let stand at room temperature overnight. Give the mixture a good stir once it has thickened, then cover and refrigerate. It will thicken even more once chilled and keeps well for up to 10 days in the refrigerator.

In Season and On the Table

FRESH HERBS, CHÈVRE, CUCUMBER, STRAWBERRIES, SOUR CHERRIES, RADISHES, LEAFY GREENS, SMOKED TROUT, WATERCRESS, LAVENDER, SALMON, LAMB TENDERLOINS, FLANK STEAK, MUSHROOMS

Summer Vegetable Soup with Fresh Basil Pesto

Recommended: Southbrook Winery Triomphe Sauvignon Blanc
Serves 4

Inspired by the season, our burgeoning vegetable and herb garden and local produce, this soup became a warm weather favourite. Paired with good cheese and bread and followed by fresh sour cherry pie, it becomes the perfect early summer supper. I added one of my favourite canned beans to this recipe—the small French kidney beans known as flageolet. Substitute any canned small bean (like cannellini) if you wish. Make sure all the vegetables are tender and young. You'll receive more pleasure if you make your basil paste by hand via a mortar and pestle, but it can be accomplished in a blender or food processor, too. I don't add Parmesan cheese to this pesto because I want it to taste only of the basil and oil. If you wish a heartier pesto, add ½ cup (120 mL) freshly grated Parmesan cheese to the final paste.

2 sprigs each, parsley, thyme
1 bay leaf
14-oz. (398-mL) can flageolet beans, rinsed and drained
6 cups (1.5 L) water
salt and freshly ground black pepper to taste
4–5 large leaves celery, rinsed and roughly chopped
3 slim leeks, trimmed, rinsed and thinly sliced
4 slim carrots, trimmed and diced
5 small new potatoes, scrubbed and diced

½ cup (120 mL) fresh shelled peas
3–4 stalks red or green Swiss chard, rinsed, trimmed and shredded
3 cloves garlic
1 tsp. (5 mL) coarse sea salt
2 cups (475 mL) fresh basil leaves
⅓–½ cup (80–120 mL) extra virgin olive oil
2 cups (475 mL) assorted peppery greens (arugula, mustard greens or other), rinsed, drained and shredded

Tie the parsley, thyme and the bay leaf together and combine in a large pot with the beans, water, salt and pepper. Bring this mixture to a boil over high heat, add the celery leaves, leeks, carrots and potatoes. Return to a boil, reduce the heat slightly and cook for about 10 minutes. Add the peas and Swiss chard, give it a good stir and return to a boil. Reduce the heat and simmer for 5–10 minutes, until the vegetables are tender; don't overcook.

Meanwhile, make the basil paste. Mash the garlic cloves and salt to a paste with a mortar and pestle. Adding a few leaves of basil at a time, use the pestle to drag the leaves against the rough sides of the mortar to incorporate them into the paste. When all the basil has been ground in, start adding the olive oil a bit at a time, until it becomes sauce-like and thin enough to pour.

Remove the bunch of herbs from the soup. Add the assorted greens to the pot and bring it back to a boil. Stir in the basil paste and let the soup bubble for a minute or two before serving.

The Good Earth Potato Focaccia
with Fines Herbes

Recommended: Thirteenth St. Winery G.H. Funk Vineyards Sauvignon Blanc
Makes 2 focaccia

From the Good Earth Cooking School in Beamsville comes this authentic focaccia that features potatoes as the central ingredient within the dough itself, not as a topping. This is in the style of focaccia made in the south of Italy. Boil the potatoes first, reserve the cooking water and use it to make the dough instead of plain water. I have embellished their recipe somewhat by adding a summery selection of fresh herbs. Serve this at lunch with lots of fresh tomatoes or as an accompaniment to summer grills of chicken or fish.

For the fines herbes:

4 Tbsp. (60 mL) chopped fresh flat-leaf parsley

1 Tbsp. (15 mL) chopped fresh basil

1 Tbsp. (15 mL) chopped fresh chives

1 Tbsp. (15 mL) chopped fresh tarragon

1 large clove garlic, minced

Combine all the ingredients in a small bowl and set to one side.

For the potato focaccia:

1½ cups (360 mL) warm potato cooking water

2 tsp. (10 mL) dry yeast

4–5 cups (950–1.2 L) hard wheat bread flour

2 cups (475 mL) cooked potatoes, chopped

½ cup (120 mL) potato cooking water

2 tsp. (10 mL) salt

1 tsp. (5 mL) olive oil

olive oil and coarse sea salt for the top

Place the 1 ½ cups (360 mL) warm potato cooking water in a large mixing bowl. Add the yeast and 2 cups (475 mL) of the flour. Stir 100 times to develop the gluten. Let the sponge stand, covered with plastic wrap, for 30 minutes to 2 hours.

Purée the potatoes in a blender along with the ½ cup (120 mL) potato cooking water. Transfer to another large mixing bowl and add the salt and the fines herbes mixture (at this point you can also add other ingredients to flavour the focaccia, such as chopped black olives or sun-dried tomatoes, if you wish).

Add ½ cup (120 mL) of the flour to the sponge and stir well. Add the potato mixture and stir well. Add the remaining 1–2 cups (240–475 mL) of flour until it is no longer sticky. Knead well for 10 minutes. Clean the bread bowl and oil lightly. Transfer the finished dough to the bowl and cover with plastic wrap. Let rise 2–3 hours or until doubled in bulk.

Turn the dough onto a lightly floured surface. Divide it into 2 pieces. Form into rounds and press them into lightly oiled 12-inch (30-cm) cast-iron skillets or springform pans. Let the dough rest for 5 minutes, then press it down gently to ensure it reaches the edges of the pans. Cover and let rise for 30 minutes.

Preheat the oven to 400°F (200°C). When the dough has risen, brush the tops with the olive oil and sprinkle generously with coarse salt. Dimple the dough with your fingers. Bake for 10 minutes, then reduce the heat to 375°F (190°C). Bake for another 12 minutes, or until the bread is golden and it sounds hollow when tapped on the bottom.

Let the bread cool in the pans on a rack for 10 minutes. Remove from the pans and finish cooling on the racks. Serve warm with extra virgin olive oil alongside for dipping.

Lemon Thyme Marinated Chèvre

Recommended: Peninsula Ridge Estates Sauvignon Blanc
Serves 4–6

Either chèvre or feta (made from sheep, cow or goat's milk) can be used in this recipe that combines the mellow qualities of creamy cheese with quality olive oil and flavourful lemon thyme. These cheeses will keep for 1–2 weeks in a cool place. Serve on a bed of mixed salad greens accompanied by toasted or grilled baguette slices or the Good Earth Potato Focaccia (page 128). If you use feta in place of chèvre, omit the salting.

1 lb. (500 g) round chèvre
sea salt as needed
6 sprigs of fresh lemon thyme, bruised
    slightly
1 bay leaf (fresh, if possible)

2–3 fresh red chiles
zest of ½ lemon
12 small black olives
3 cups (720 mL) extra virgin olive oil

Slice the cheese into rounds and salt lightly. Place in a sieve set over a bowl. Cover with plastic wrap and let drain overnight in the refrigerator. Scrape off any remaining salt, then place the cheese in a sterile wide-mouthed jar. Add the remaining ingredients and cover with olive oil. Allow to marinate for a day or two before using.

Pickled Sour Cherries

Recommended (to accompany antipasto): Inniskillin Pinot Grigio
Makes about 4 1-pint jars (2 cups/475 mL)

These make a lovely addition to antipasto platters, with prosciutto and other cold meats, with cheese courses or with good pâtés, in place of the usual gherkins or silverskin onions. You don't have to pit them.

2 lb. (900 g) sour cherries
2 cups (475 mL) white wine vinegar
2 cups (475 mL) red wine vinegar
2¼ cups (535 mL) light brown sugar,
    lightly packed
1 heaping Tbsp. (17 mL) pickling salt

6 cloves
6 juniper berries, crushed
zest of 1 lemon, cut into fine strips
2-inch (5-cm) piece cinnamon, broken
    into pieces

Sort through the cherries, discarding any that are bruised or otherwise damaged. Trim the stems to about ¼ inch (.6 cm). Rinse and dry thoroughly. Have ready 4 sterilized pint jars. Using a needle, prick the cherries several times, then pack them into jars, filling the jars to about an inch (2.5 cm) below the rim.

In a stainless steel saucepan, combine the vinegars, sugar, salt, cloves, juniper berries, lemon zest and cinnamon. Bring to a boil over high heat, stirring to help dissolve the sugar and salt. Reduce the heat and simmer for 10 minutes.

Pour the hot vinegar mixture over the cherries, making sure each jar gets a bit of lemon, cloves, cinnamon and juniper berries. Wipe the rims clean and fix the lids. Place in a dry, dark cupboard for about a month before using. Use within three months. (Alternatively, seal the jars according to jar manufacturer's directions and process in a boiling water bath for 10 minutes.)

Shrimp & Pea Sprout Spring Rolls

Recommended: Vineland Estates Winery Gewürztraminer
Makes about 20 spring rolls

Perfect fare to enjoy when dining beneath the trees on a hot summer day, these rice paper wraps with their accompanying sauce are closely related to a Vietnamese or Thai spring roll, the sprouts taking the place of the usual rice vermicelli noodle. They are fresh-tasting, simple to prepare and quite satisfying. If you wish, use leftover cooked chicken or pork in place of the shrimp and any sprout at all in place of the pea sprouts. Have all the ingredients prepared and ready to be assembled. Quite the elegant company fare and a great prelude to summer grills.

For the dipping sauce:

2 Tbsp. (30 mL) Asian fish sauce
2 Tbsp. (30 mL) hoisin sauce
juice of 1 lime
1 large clove garlic, minced

1 tsp. (5 mL) fresh ginger, minced
1–2 Tbsp. (15–30 mL) hot Chinese
chile sauce (or any hot sauce)

In a small bowl, whisk all the ingredients together until well blended. Cover and let sit at room temperature while you prepare the rolls.

For the spring rolls:

20 dried rice paper wrappers, about 6–8 inches (15–20 cm) in diameter

1 head red oak leaf lettuce, separated into about 20 pieces, washed and dried

20 jumbo shrimp, cooked

1 cup (240 mL) pea sprouts

1 large red bell pepper, seeded and thinly sliced

½ seedless cucumber, thinly sliced (peeled, if you wish)

20 fresh mint leaves

Work with one rice paper wrapper at a time. Dip the wrapper into a small bowl of warm water to soften, which should just take a few seconds. As soon as it is pliable, remove from the water and place on the work surface; dab with paper towel. Lay a piece of lettuce on the wrapper, top with one shrimp, a few sprouts, a slice or two of red pepper and cucumber. Add a mint leaf and roll it up. Place it seam side down on a serving platter and continue with the remaining ingredients. Serve with the dipping sauce.

Grilled Tuna
with Sweet Peppers & Arugula Herb Salad
with Sun-dried Tomato Tapenade

Recommended: Peninsula Ridge Estates Winery Barrel Aged Merlot
Serves 4

Ray Poitras, chef of The Restaurant at Peninsula Ridge, likes to serve this main course with small new potatoes that are halved and tossed with olive oil, then seasoned with chopped fresh thyme and rosemary and a little salt and pepper before roasting. If you don't want to use the oven, parboil them slightly, season, transfer to a grill basket and grill until cooked through.

For the sun-dried tomato tapenade:

2 cups (475 mL) oil-packed sun-dried tomatoes

½ cup (120 mL) loosely packed fresh basil leaves

1 shallot, chopped

1 clove garlic, chopped

¼ cup (60 mL) pitted kalamata olives

2 Tbsp. (30 mL) pine nuts

1 cup (240 mL) olive oil

¼ cup (60 mL) freshly grated Parmesan cheese

salt and freshly ground black pepper to taste

Cover the tomatoes in boiling water and let stand for 15 minutes to soften. Drain and pat dry.

In a food processor, combine the tomatoes, basil, shallot, garlic, olives and pine nuts; process until chopped. Add the oil in a stream, using just enough to make a smooth, sauce-like mixture. Add the Parmesan and season with salt and pepper.

For the tuna and salad:

2 red bell peppers, seeded and
quartered

2 yellow bell peppers, seeded and
quartered

4 thick tuna loin steaks (5 oz./140 g
each)

1 tsp. (5 mL) crushed fennel seeds

1 tsp. (5 mL) paprika

1 bunch arugula, torn into bite-sized
pieces

2 cups (475 mL) lightly packed fresh
flat-leaf parsley sprigs

1 cup (240 mL) lightly packed fresh dill
sprigs

3 Tbsp. (45 mL) extra virgin olive oil

juice of ½ lemon

salt and freshly ground black pepper
to taste

Preheat the grill to medium-high. Brush the pepper quarters lightly with olive oil and season with salt and pepper. Grill, turning often, until they are just tender and the skins are lightly charred.

Brush the tuna with the olive oil and season with the fennel, paprika, salt and pepper. Grill for 3–4 minutes per side to medium rare.

Combine the arugula, parsley and dill in a bowl. In another bowl, whisk together the olive oil and lemon juice. Season with salt and pepper. Pour the dressing over the greens and toss. Divide the greens among 4 serving plates. Arrange the tuna in the centre of each and surround with the grilled peppers. Spoon sun-dried tomato tapenade over the tuna and drizzle a little more tapenade around the edges of the plate. Serve immediately.

Exotic Mushroom Salad
with Wyndym Farm Micro-seedlings

Recommended: Willow Heights Winery Sauvignon Blanc
Serves 4

Some of the most innovative and beautifully wrought dishes in the Niagara Peninsula emanate from the kitchens at the Queen's Landing Hotel in Niagara-on-the-Lake. This is chef Stephen Treadwell's recipe that has as its focus the produce that is the specialty of Dave Perkins' Wyndym Farms. Micro-seedlings are extremely young, delicate and tiny greens. If you can't obtain these, substitute your favourite sprouts, or young watercress or a combination. The chef serves this with a gaufrette potato wafer or chip cradling the softened goat's cheese. These are easily made using a mandoline. You could substitute good quality potato chips or make your own by slicing a large baking potato as thinly as possible and frying quickly in hot fat. Or improvise further by making an ultra-thin potato cake with shredded potato.

1 Tbsp. (15 mL) butter
2 shallots, finely chopped
1¼ cups (300 mL) Willow Heights
   Winery Sauvignon Blanc
2 tsp. (5 mL) tarragon vinegar
6 oz. (170 g) fresh chanterelles (or
   other specialty mushroom), wiped
   clean, left whole

salt and freshly ground white pepper
   to taste
3 oz. (85 g) goat cheese, softened
4 large gaufrette chips (see note
   above)
2 cups (475 mL) tiny new greens (see
   note above)
truffle oil for drizzling (optional)

Melt the butter in a large skillet over medium heat. Add the shallot and sauté for a few minutes until softened. Add the white wine and vinegar and cook until the mixture is reduced and thickened, about 15 minutes. Stir the chanterelles into the reduction, then cover and cook for 1 minute. Season with salt and pepper and keep warm.

Shape the goat cheese into four egg-shaped ovals (quenelles). To serve, use tongs to place a portion of the mushroom mixture in the centre of a shallow pasta bowl. Top with a chip, then nestle one of the cheeses in the chip and top with a small portion of baby greens. Spoon a little of the mushroom cooking reduction around the salad and drizzle with truffle oil, if using.

Morningstar Mill

Within walking distance of our home, the grand old Morningstar Mill at Decew Falls was originally constructed in 1872 by Robert Chappel and was one of the first in Canada to be powered by a turbine rather than a waterwheel. The mill that stands today is not the original; it was destroyed by fire in 1895, leaving only the stone structure. At that time the owner, Wilson Morningstar, who operated the mill until his death in 1933, rebuilt the mill and much of the existing equipment inside. Morningstar was a busy man; he also built a sawmill across the stream from the mill (which is being reconstructed today), a blacksmith and carpentry shop, a cider mill, an observation staircase to the bottom of the gorge and a lovely house positioned at the top of a hill at the rear of the mill. Morningstar Mill was sold to Ontario Hydro following his death and eventually resold to the City of St. Catharines. It was the city's intention to restore the mill to working order, but funds ran dry. The restoration came about through the combined efforts of community volunteers. The Friends of Morningstar Mill, formed in 1992, have dedicated themselves to restoring the historic site to its original condition. The "friends" of the mill can be found working onsite most Tuesdays, Thursdays and Saturdays. Special events are held throughout the summer season; at the Annual Grist & Chopping Show in August, visitors can meet the people responsible for the mill's restoration, tour the site and buy a bag of authentic stone-ground whole-wheat flour.

Cucumber & Strawberry Salad

Recommended: Henry of Pelham Family Estate Winery Rosé
Serves 6

I know this may sound a strange combination to some, but it is actually an old-fashioned English preparation that works well on a warm June day. Great for a picnic, but make sure to chill it well beforehand. Serve with cold ham or chicken.

1 small seedless cucumber, peeled
and thinly sliced
12 large strawberries, hulled and
thinly sliced
½ bunch watercress, rinsed, dried
and chopped

2–3 Tbsp. (30–45 mL) raspberry
vinegar
1 heaping Tbsp. (17 mL) sugar
salt and freshly ground black pepper
to taste

Place the cucumber and strawberry slices in a large bowl. Whisk the remaining ingredients in a separate bowl, making sure the sugar is completely dissolved. Pour over the strawberries and cucumbers, toss gently and chill well before serving.

Smoked Trout with Radishes
& Watercress

Recommended: Marynissen Estates Sauvignon Blanc
Serves 6

A lovely light supper or lunch dish, this preparation lends itself well to many variations. Smoked salmon or good-quality canned tuna (packed in olive oil) may be used in place of the trout, and you can also vary the greens by substituting frisée for the watercress. Serve with good crusty bread and boiled new potatoes cooked with lots of fresh mint, then tossed with butter.

⅓ cup (80 mL) fresh lemon juice
2 tsp. (10 mL) Dijon mustard
2 Tbsp. (30 mL) light mayonnaise
½ cup (120 mL) extra virgin olive oil
2 Tbsp. (25 mL) chopped fresh chives
salt and freshly ground black pepper
 to taste
1 lb. (455 g) smoked trout fillets

4 green onions, trimmed and chopped
¼ cup (60 mL) chopped fresh parsley
2 cups (475 mL) red radishes, trimmed
 and thinly sliced
1 cup (240 mL) white radishes (or red),
 trimmed and thinly sliced
2–3 bunches watercress, stems
 trimmed, washed and dried

Prepare the dressing by combining the lemon juice, mustard, mayonnaise, olive oil, chives, salt and pepper in a small mixing bowl. Whisk together until well blended. Set to one side.

Pull the trout fillets apart into rough chunks and place in a medium-sized bowl along with the green onions and half the parsley. Toss with half the dressing. In another mixing bowl, combine the radishes and watercress with the remaining parsley and dressing. Arrange the radishes and watercress on a large oval serving platter. Top with the trout mixture.

Cedar-Planked Salmon with Lavender Butter

Recommended: Pillitteri Estates Winery Chardonnay Family Reserve
Serves 6

This recipe is very close to my heart. In its original form, it appeared in another book that I co-wrote with grill chef extraordinaire, my buddy Ted Reader. The book in which it is featured won a Silver Award from Cuisine Canada. In that version, Ted crusted the fragrant fillets with a shallot and dill mixture. Here the planked fillets are each adorned with a circle of flowery lavender butter.

A word about purchasing cedar planks: due to the popularity of this method of cooking fish and seafood, you can often find cedar planks at fishmongers or at the seafood counters of large supermarkets. Failing that, head to your local lumberyard or building supply outlet and ask for construction-grade, untreated cedar planks, no more than 1-inch (2.5-cm) thick, 8–10 inches (20–25 cm) wide and 10–12 inches (25–30 cm) long. Serve the salmon with a rice salad or a salad of new potatoes tossed in an herb vinaigrette.

For the lavender butter:

2 shallots, minced

2 Tbsp. (25 mL) white wine vinegar

2 Tbsp. (25 mL) lavender blossom
honey (or other floral honey)

½ cup (120 mL) unsalted butter,
softened

24 fresh lavender flower heads,
minced

salt and freshly ground white pepper
to taste

Combine the shallots, vinegar, honey, butter and lavender in a bowl. Cream until well blended and season to taste with salt and pepper. Lay out a piece of plastic wrap on a clean, dry surface. Using a rubber spatula, arrange the butter along the length of the wrap to form a log. Partially cover with half of the wrap and roll back and forth with your hands until it begins to take the shape of a log (this will result in neat, coin-shaped pieces of butter once it has been chilled). Wrap tightly at both ends and refrigerate until well chilled. Butter will keep for about a week in the refrigerator.

For the salmon:

2 untreated cedar planks, soaked in water for a few hours (use a weight to fully submerge the planks)

6 6-oz. (170-g) skinless fillets Atlantic salmon, about 2 inches (5 cm) thick

½ cup (120 mL) Pillitteri Estates Winery Chardonnay Family Reserve

juice and finely chopped zest of 1 lemon

sea salt and freshly ground black pepper to taste

Lay the salmon on a baking sheet with raised sides. Combine the white wine, lemon juice and zest in a small bowl and whisk together. Pour this mixture over the fish, then give all the fillets a good seasoning with salt and freshly ground pepper. Loosely cover with plastic wrap and set to one side for 30 minutes.

Preheat the grill to high. Remove the planks from the water and season with a bit of salt. Place the planks on the grill, close the lid and heat for 3–5 minutes until they start to crackle and smoke. Carefully lift the lid (there will be smoke!) and place the salmon fillets on the hot planks. Close the lid and cook the salmon for 12–15 minutes, longer if you prefer your fish well done. Check periodically to ensure that the planks are not on fire. Use a spray bottle to extinguish any flames.

Carefully remove the planks from the grill and, using a metal spatula, transfer the fish to a serving platter. Garnish each piece with a slice of the lavender butter.

Who Will Buy My Lavender?

Lavender comprises a large family of aromatic, evergreen perennials and shrubs, some hardier than others. The two most well-known are *Lavandula angustifolia*, the botanical name for English lavender, and *Lavandula dentata*—French lavender. While any lavender can be used in the kitchen, for culinary purposes English or true lavender is recommended. Lavender flowers have a sweet, perfumed flavour with a slight lemony accent. Don't use too much, however, because it can be quite intense. Where lavender is concerned, less is definitely more.

Peller Estates Winery

Peller Estates Winery is located on 40 acres in the heart of Niagara-on-the-Lake wine country. A huge wine boutique features Peller's award-winning wines, and there are wide vineyard views from the winery's spacious restaurant complete with handsome French doors that open out onto an adjoining outdoor patio. Chef Jason Rosso, inspired by the surrounding countryside and all it has to offer, has developed a creative Niagara wine country menu matched with Peller's VQA wines.

Summer days in Niagara-on-the-Lake

Lime & Spice-Rubbed Flank Steak
with Oyster Mushrooms (page 145)

Grilled Rosemary Lamb Medallions with Goat Cheese Scalloped Potatoes & Fava Beans

Recommended: Cave Spring Cellars Cabernet Merlot
Serves 4–6

Chef Roberto Fracchioni of Cave Spring's Inn on the Twenty restaurant prepares this with the season's first fava beans, a lovely accompaniment to the tender lamb loins.

For the lamb:

¼ cup (60 mL) chopped fresh
    rosemary
¼ cup (60 mL) extra virgin olive oil
5 lamb loins, each cut into 5 or 6
    pieces

coarse salt and freshly ground black
    pepper to taste

Combine the rosemary, olive oil, lamb pieces, salt and pepper in a bowl. Using your hands, toss the ingredients together, making sure all the lamb is well-coated. Cover with plastic wrap and refrigerate for a couple of hours or as long as overnight. Let the meat sit, unrefrigerated, for about half an hour before grilling. When you're ready to cook the lamb, preheat the grill to high. Dab the excess oil from the lamb with paper towels. Season each piece with coarse salt and pepper and grill for 3–4 minutes per side. Keep warm while you prepare the potatoes and fava beans.

For the scalloped potatoes:

4 Yukon Gold potatoes, peeled
2 sweet potatoes, peeled
3 cups (720 mL) whipping cream

¾ cup (180 mL) goat's milk cheese
salt and freshly ground white pepper
    to taste

Lightly butter a 9 x 9-inch (23 x 23-cm) baking pan. Preheat the oven to 350°F (175°C). Use a mandoline, if you have one, to slice the potatoes and sweet potatoes in even, paper-thin slices. Warm the cream and goat cheese in a medium-sized saucepan, over medium heat, whisking until the cheese has dissolved and the mixture is creamy and smooth. Add a layer of potatoes to the base of the pan, making sure to overlap the slices. Season with salt and pepper and pour ¼ cup (60 mL) of the cream mixture evenly over the potatoes. Repeat this layering process with another layer of potatoes. Add a layer of sweet potato (there should just be one layer of the sweet potato in the centre), followed by the cream mixture and a final two layers of potatoes, cream and seasoning. Place in the preheated oven and bake for about 1 hour, loosely covering with foil if the top is browning too quickly.

To finish the dish:

2 cups (475 mL) fava beans, shelled	4–6 fresh rosemary sprigs for a
4 Tbsp. (60 mL) butter	garnish
salt and freshly ground pepper to taste	

Add the beans to a saucepan of boiling water and cook rapidly for 30–45 seconds, then transfer with a slotted spoon to a bowl of ice water. When cooled, slip the beans out of their skins and transfer to a little skillet to reheat along with the butter, salt and pepper.

To serve, place a portion of scalloped potato in the centre of each plate. Encircle the potatoes with the lamb medallions, leaving a space in between each slice. Place a portion of fava beans in between the lamb slices. Pierce the potatoes with a sprig of fresh rosemary and serve.

Lime & Spice-Rubbed Flank Steak with Oyster Mushrooms

Recommended: Inniskillin Pinot Noir Montague Estate Vineyard
Serves 4

Flank steak is a relatively inexpensive cut, considering how many steak lovers it will feed, and it's packed with flavour. A flank steak doesn't always need to be marinated; the most important thing to remember is to slice it thinly and against the grain. However, once in a while I like to treat it to a marinade of fresh lime juice and a few other ingredients, just to give it a boost. It is vital that you don't exceed the recommended marinating time, otherwise the lime juice will begin to "cook" the meat and turn it an unattractive colour to boot. Thinly slice the steak and pile it into warm flatbreads or plate it with a cooked grain (bulgur, rice, barley, quinoa) tossed with cherry tomatoes, chunks of cucumber and a little sesame oil.

For the spice rub:

2 Tbsp. (30 mL) salt

2 Tbsp. (30 mL) granulated sugar

2 Tbsp. (30 mL) light brown sugar

2 Tbsp. (30 mL) ground cumin

2 Tbsp. (30 mL) freshly ground black pepper

2 Tbsp. (30 mL) paprika

1 tsp. (5 mL) dry mustard

1 tsp. (5 mL) cayenne pepper

Combine all the ingredients in a small bowl and mix thoroughly. The spice rub makes about 1 cup (240 mL), far more than you will need for this recipe. But since it is a good all-round rub, you will find many uses for it. Store it in a jar with a tight-fitting lid.

For the steak and mushrooms:

2 cloves garlic, minced

2 Tbsp. (30 mL) chopped fresh cilantro

1 Tbsp. (15 mL) paprika

5 limes, juiced

4 Tbsp. (60 mL) olive oil

2½-lb. (1.1-kg) flank steak

½ lb. (225 g) oyster mushrooms,
  wiped clean

4 Tbsp. (60 mL) extra virgin olive oil

4 Tbsp. (60 mL) chopped fresh flat-
  leaf parsley

salt and freshly ground black pepper
  to taste

2 Tbsp. (30 mL) spice rub, or to taste

Combine the garlic, cilantro, paprika, lime juice and 4 Tbsp. (60 mL) olive oil in a small mixing bowl. Use a whisk to blend them thoroughly.

Place the steak in a large glass or ceramic dish. Pour the marinade ingredients over it. Cover with plastic wrap and marinate in the refrigerator for 4 hours, turning occasionally.

Preheat the grill to medium-high. A few minutes before the end of the meat's marinating time, trim the ends from the mushrooms and place them in a bowl with the remaining 4 Tbsp. (60 mL) oil, parsley and seasoning. Toss together, then grill the mushrooms for about 8–10 minutes until they are brown and the edges are crispy. Remove from the grill and keep warm.

Increase the grill heat to high. Remove the meat from the marinade and pat it dry. Rub the marinated steak on both sides with the spice rub and place on the preheated grill. Grill the steak for 5–7 minutes on each side (for medium rare). Remove from the grill and let sit for about 5 minutes before carving with a sharp knife on an angle across the grain into very thin slices. Serve with the mushrooms alongside.

Jenna's Sour Cream Sour Cherry Pie with Oat Crumble Top

Recommended: Sunnybrook Farm Estate Winery Cherry Wine
Serves 6–8

Wow, what a pie—that was the consensus when my daughter Jenna made this splendiferous dessert with our foraged sour cherries. Can she bake a cherry pie! Serve warm with unsweetened whipped cream or thick pouring cream.

For the topping:
½ cup (120 mL) all-purpose flour

½ cup (120 mL) light brown sugar

½ cup (120 mL) rolled oats

1 tsp. (5 mL) ground cinnamon

¼ cup (60 mL) melted butter

Combine the topping ingredients in a bowl and mix together until crumbly. Set aside.

For the pie:
pastry for a 10-inch (25-cm) single crust pie

4 cups (720 mL) sour cherries, stemmed and pitted

½ cup (120 mL) granulated sugar

½ cup (120 mL) light brown sugar

⅓ cup (80 mL) all-purpose flour

1 cup (240 mL) sour cream

Preheat the oven to 450°F (230°C). Arrange the cherries in the unbaked pie shell. Combine both sugars and the flour in a mixing bowl and blend together. Mix in the sour cream and pour evenly over the cherries. Sprinkle the topping over the top of the cherry mixture, pressing it gently into place. Bake for 15 minutes, then reduce the heat to 350°F (175°C) and continue to bake for about 30 minutes, or until the fruit is tender, the filling is set and the crumble top is golden brown. Let it sit for a few minutes before serving.

Lemon & Strawberry Cake
with Lemon Curd Cream

Recommended: Harbour Estates Winery Fragole or EastDell Estates Gamay
Serves 10–12

This is a lovely, impressive-looking cake, perfect for a special occasion in June since it makes the most of fresh, local strawberries. Use the recipe for Mum's Lemon Curd (page 44) for the lemon curd, an ingredient in the cake itself, the filling and the icing. The international sections of some supermarkets (and good food shops) sometimes offer a reputable commercial lemon curd. This cake will keep quite well, covered, in the refrigerator for a couple of days.

For the lemon cream filling:
½ cup (120 mL) whipping cream
½ cup (120 mL) lemon curd

Using an electric mixer, beat the whipping cream until firm peaks form, then fold in the lemon curd. Cover and refrigerate until ready to use.

For the icing:
½ lb. (225 g) soft cream cheese   ½ cup (120 mL) whipping cream
¼ cup (60 mL) icing sugar   ⅓ cup (80 mL) lemon curd

Using an electric mixer, beat the cream cheese until smooth. Add the icing sugar, whipping cream and lemon curd and beat on low speed until smooth and creamy. Cover and refrigerate until ready to use.

For the cake:

1¾ cups (420 mL) all-purpose flour

¼ cup (60 mL) cornstarch

1 tsp. (5 mL) baking powder

½ tsp. (2.5 mL) salt

½ lb. (225 g) unsalted butter,
    softened

1½ cups (360 mL) granulated sugar

4 eggs

¼ cup (60 mL) whole milk

1 tsp. (5 mL) pure vanilla extract

2 tsp. (10 mL) finely grated lemon zest

½ lb. (225 g) fresh strawberries,
    washed, hulled (halved, if large)

¼ cup (60 mL) finely chopped fresh
    mint

⅔ cup (160 mL) lemon curd

You will need two 8-inch (20-cm) cake pans for the cake; prepare them ahead of time by lightly buttering and lining them with parchment paper cut to fit the base. Preheat the oven to 350°F (175°C).

Sift the flour, cornstarch, baking powder and salt into a mixing bowl and set to one side. Using an electric mixer, beat the butter and sugar for about 3 minutes, or until light and fluffy. Add the eggs one at a time, beating well after each one. On low speed, beat in the milk, vanilla and lemon zest just until combined. Add the flour mixture in three separate batches, beating until just combined after each addition. Divide the batter between the prepared cake pans and bake for 30–35 minutes, or until a tester emerges clean. Let the cakes cool in their pans for a few minutes before turning out onto a wire rack to cool.

Place the strawberries in a bowl and gently toss with the chopped mint.

To assemble, halve each cake horizontally. Place the bottom layer of 1 cake on a serving plate. Spread with half the lemon curd, then add the top layer. Spread the lemon cream filling over this and top with the strawberries. Place the remaining cake bottom on top of the berries, spread with the remaining lemon curd and top with the final cake layer. Spread the cream cheese icing over the top and sides of the cake. If the kitchen is warm, refrigerate the cake until serving time.

Grasmere's Sour Cherry Cobbler

Recommended: EastDell Estates Summer Cherry Wine
Serves 4–6

One of summer's finest comfort desserts. Perfect for Canada Day weekend what with its patriotic red (cherries) and white (cream) tones. If you freeze sour cherries to use later in the year, you can also make this to provide a taste of summer during frigid February. Serve just warm with good-quality vanilla ice cream or whipped cream.

For the cherries:

2½ cups (600 mL) sour cherries, stemmed and pitted	¼ cup (60 mL) water
	1 cup (240 mL) sugar
2 Tbsp. (30 mL) unsalted butter	1 Tbsp. (15 mL) all-purpose flour

Preheat the oven to 425°F (220°C). In a stainless steel saucepan, combine the cherries, butter and water over medium-high heat. Bring to a boil, then remove from the heat. Blend together the sugar and flour. Add this to the cherries in the saucepan, stirring all the while to prevent lumps. Return the mixture to a boil, reduce the heat and cook for a minute or two until it has thickened slightly. Transfer the cherry mixture to a shallow, 4-cup (950-mL) baking dish.

For the topping:

1 cup (240 mL) all-purpose flour	3 Tbsp. (45 mL) chilled, unsalted butter
1 Tbsp. (15 mL) sugar	
1½ tsp. (7.5 mL) baking powder	¾ cup (180 mL) whole milk
½ tsp. (2.5 mL) salt	

In a mixing bowl, sift together the flour, sugar, baking powder and salt. Cut the butter into pieces and cut it into the flour mixture. When the mixture resembles coarse meal, add about ½ cup (120 mL) of the milk. Stir with a fork until the mixture resembles a thick batter, adding more milk gradually as needed (you may not use it all).

Use a large spoon to drop spoonfuls of the batter over the top of the fruit. Bake for about 25–30 minutes, until golden brown.

Pink Lavender Lemonade

Serves 4–6

Here is a lovely old-fashioned preparation that highlights the versatility and usefulness of lavender. The perfect beverage to enjoy in a hammock on a hot day.

1 cup (240 mL) chopped fresh
    lavender
2 cups (475 mL) boiling water
2 cups (475 mL) cold water

1 cup (240 mL) fresh lemon juice
¼ cup (60 mL) cranberry juice
1 cup (240 mL) sugar

Place the lavender in a large, heatproof measuring cup. Pour boiling water over it and let steep for 15 minutes. Pour through a coffee filter, then transfer to a glass jug. Add the cold water to the lavender water in the jug, along with the lemon juice, cranberry juice and sugar. Stir well to dissolve the sugar, then pour over ice into glasses garnished with a lavender stem.

View to a Vine

We are surrounded, totally, by masses of brilliant orange lilies that frame our entire property. There are hundreds, nodding in the breeze with all their profound greenery. They act as a house marker for anyone visiting for the first time. They are really to be enjoyed outside though; when I cut them for a vase they slap shut almost immediately and sadly die.

Ultra hot, hazy days, no rain for ages. There is no lack of sun or heat—everything is bone dry. Can't help but think about the farmers and growers around us and what they must do to ensure the success of their crops. We see farmers turning on their trickle irrigation and those spritz hoses showering over the vineyards and pick one up at our local country hardware store for our lawn.

An incredible variety of local produce is available now—just down the road. In the city, during the summer we always made the trek to the St. Lawrence Market of a Saturday to buy, probably from many of these same growers and farms.

We buy the first peaches, sweet cherries, golden plums, apricots, flat green beans, tomatoes, lovely first crop white potatoes with an incomparable flavour, corn, cucumbers, red and green peppers. And raspberries! We get some for eating straight up, but I cannot resist bringing home a flat of huge, dark raspberries that the friendly grower told me are the best for cooking. I make my Mum's old-fashioned raspberry vinegar. Using her recipe and the full flat of raspberries, I got three wine bottles full. This drink is also sometimes called raspberry shrub, and when it is blended with sparkling mineral water, ice and fresh mint, it makes the world's best summer thirst quencher. Hot and parched from serious gardening, Ted has his first glass and becomes an instant fan.

We discover wild garlic on our property! At least we think it's wild garlic, could be a big bed of garlic chives. Checking one of my herb books we learn it also looks a lot like sand leek (*Allium scorodoprasum*). Their small bulbs resemble tiny, unformed heads of garlic and have a distinct garlic scent. What the heck, I saute them along with onion, celery, carrot and tomato for a sauce to dress pasta—whether garlic, leek or chive, it has a lovely mild garlic flavour.

Our grapevine now holds marble-sized hard green grapes and the verdant canopy of leaves lends such beauty to the garden. I spy tiny plums, like little olives, on the wild plum tree at the back of our yard, which gets me to wondering why no one has grown olive trees in Niagara. I guess the winter would be just too harsh.

JULY 6. Planning Alysa's thirtieth birthday party next weekend here at Grasmere. Many guests are invited and she is organizing a Mexican barbecue with spit-roasted kid, grilled corn with two different butters, homemade corn tortillas, those cheese-filled peppers called *rajas*. We'll also do some shrimp and mussels on the barbecue and Jenna, our queen of tarts, is making a special dessert for her sister.

Mid-July and the three rose of Sharon trees bloom, one white, one mauve and one a deep majestic purple. In the driveway flower bed are pink and white flox and the tall, heavy yucca plant, looking like a giant asparagus.

The prolific trumpet vine, is simply growing everywhere. Ted tells me he saw a big old snapping turtle on the road near our house today and, forgive me, I think of *Babette's Feast*....

JULY 16. Looks as though we may soon have the last of the lettuce from the vegetable garden—must find out about "bolting." We will miss the wonderful convenience of picking a few greens to accompany supper. I will plant more fava beans next year, they were lovely but so few. Swiss chard is delicious, so clean and easy to cook quickly. One side of our garden—all of which receives full sun—does much better than the other, for some reason. I will also double or triple the number of the Sofia pepper plants bought from Niagara Nurseries . . . they have long, good-looking peppers, one or two per plant, but I will plant many more next year so Ted can smoke lots at a time for me to pack in olive oil. The potatoes are almost ready. Scarlet runner beans are in bloom, lovely with their showy red flowers. They were a staple of my Mum's garden every summer. The Sicilian eggplant finally looks as though it will really happen. It has taken a long time; this is definitely one to start earlier next year indoors.

The heat is extraordinary and no rain for weeks on end. From about mid-June there has been nothing save for the odd minute-long sprinkle. We call an arborist to come and tell us what is wrong with our horse chestnut trees, which have many brown-edged leaves. I think something is eating them but he tells us, "It's drought stress; you'll have to water the tree roots, they are giving off more water than they can take in through their root systems." So we opt to have them treated with a special solution to stimulate root system growth which, in turn, encourages them to take in more water. Again, I think about the fruit farmers and grape growers. No surprise that the first peaches are sweet but so much smaller than usual.

JULY 21. Ted comes home with a bag of spent grain from the brewery for me and my bread making. He tells me it is a combination of three different malts: Two Row Canadian, Carastan and Roasted Chocolate from the

U.K. Several chefs in the area like to use it in their bread recipes. It gives the bread a lovely nutty quality—even better when you substitute Niagara beer for the usual water in the recipe. So, on one of the hottest days of the year, I decide to make a batch of whole-wheat beer bread with Niagara Brewing's spent grain and Morningstar Mill's stoneground whole-wheat flour—unbelievably good.

Towards the end of the month, I toss a handful of arugula seeds in a large planter on my sunny side doorstep. It's no exaggeration to say green shoots come up within 24 hours. Before long, I am adding marvelous micro-sized arugula leaves to our salads. We snip a little basil here and there to top a slice of ripe tomato drizzled with good olive oil. Ted says the only thing better than the pungent green tomato scent on one's hands after picking them is that sun-warmed taste. I just want to sit in the midst of them with a salt shaker and eat. The crimson cherry tomatoes are over-whelming in quantity and perfect with absolutely every meal, especially when halved and tossed with chunks of ripe avocado and bits of green onion in a lemon-Dijon vinaigrette.

My nasturtiums! They grew so fast and every sweet little part is edible, even their pea-sized seeds, which you can pickle like capers. Peppery leaves and blooms are so pretty and rich in vitamin C.

Every other week or so, there seems to be another variety of peach that is ready. Alysa, the peach queen, shall have a peach croustade on her next visit.

In the Vineyard and On the Vine

"The big priority in the vineyard right now is shaping the vine—trellis-ing, we call it. This is when we have the most people out in the vine-yards, shaping, straightening, working towards giving us those neat, tidy rows. We cut off excess growth and pull off excess leaves to maximize sun exposure. And we do suckering, which is removing the unwanted shoot growth. We're doing everything we can now to keep weeds down—what we call vineyard floor management.

"Generally we're doing everything to ensure we capture every bit of sunlight we can, based on the ultimate wine that will be produced from that variety. This is adjusting the plants to the season, which might mean more sun exposure for some and not too much heat for others; it all depends on the variety.

"By the end of July towards August we're crop-thinning, especially for top end reds; 50–60 percent of the crop gets thrown on the ground.

"In the winery our goal is to finish bottling so we can start to plan for the coming vintage.

"In the store and hospitality area, this is the peak season. We have some events, like the Eight Unforgettable Weekends of Summer, that bring a lot of visitors. Along with Niagara Oyster, we've organized oyster-shucking events matched with summer releases, like our Chardonnay from the previous year, and other whites generally.

"This is also the time of year when we present our 'Shakespeare in the Vineyard' productions. These are very popular theatrical presentations that have been going on for four or five years now."

Matthew Speck, Henry of Pelham Family Estate Winery

Simple Seasonal Pleasure

New Potato Salad in Herb Vinaigrette

Steam up a potful of whole new potatoes and while they are cooking, chop up handfuls of fresh herbs—parsley, chives, tarragon, basil. Finely chop a few skinny green onions. When the potatoes are tender and while they are still warm, toss them together with the herbs. Whisk together a big spoon of coarse-grained mustard, salt and freshly ground black pepper, a generous splash of extra virgin olive oil, a little bit of brilliant green pumpkin seed oil (for colour and flavour) and just enough white wine vinegar to give it balance. Combine this with the warm potatoes and serve right away with grilled lamb, beef, chicken or any favourite summer grills.

In Season and On the Table

PEACHES, CHERRY TOMATOES, PLUMS, APRICOTS, RASPBERRIES, BLACKBERRIES, GREEN BEANS, FAVA BEANS, CORN, NEW POTATOES, GREEN ONIONS, MENNONITE SAUSAGE, NASTURTIUMS, PEPPERS, MUSSELS, CUCUMBER, WATERMELON

Chilled Sweet Pepper Gazpacho with Cucumber Granita *160*

Fire Roasted Corn with Chipotle & Nasturtium Butters *162*

Young Fava Bean & Pecorino Salad with Prosciutto *164*

Risotto of Grilled Summer Vegetables in Basil Lemon Olive Oil *165*

Campfire Cast Iron Potatoes Anna *168*

Barbecued Mussels in Niagara Millstone Lager & Garlic *170*

Grilled Shrimp with Tomato Plum Sauce *171*

Castle Rock Spiced Pepper Shrimp on Sweet Potato Cakes
with Fresh Mango Chutney *172*

Red Peppers Stuffed with Smoked Chicken *175*

Tuscan Bread Salad with Chardonnay Vine-Skewered Chicken *176*

Pork Ribs with Niagara Apple Ale & Mustard Glaze *178*

Grilled Mennonite Sausage with Pasta Ribbons,
Summer Vegetables & Parsley Pesto *180*

Peaches on Toast with Raspberry Butter *182*

Summer Pudding with Crème Fraîche *184*

A Cake for My Sister
(Victoria Sponge with Raspberries) *186*

Blackberry Fool with Poire William *188*

Niagara Peach Wine *189*

Watermelon Margaritas *190*

Chilled Sweet Pepper Gazpacho
with Cucumber Granita

Recommended: Cave Spring Cellars Sauvignon Blanc
Serves 6–8

A creative take on the traditional tomato-based summer soup, from chef Roberto Fracchioni at Cave Spring's Inn on the Twenty restaurant. Fresh-tasting and cooling on a sultry summer day. Make the garnish of cucumber granita first, as it needs time to freeze.

For the cucumber granita:

½ English (seedless) cucumber, peeled and diced (should equal 1 cup/240 mL)

1 green onion, trimmed and finely chopped

1 clove garlic, minced

2 Tbsp. (30 mL) lemon juice

1 Tbsp. (15 mL) finely chopped fresh basil

1 Tbsp. (15 mL) finely chopped fresh cilantro

dash hot pepper sauce

salt and freshly ground black pepper to taste

Purée all the ingredients in a food processor or use a hand blender. Transfer the mixture to the freezer. After an hour, gently stir the ice that is beginning to form. Return to the freezer for at least 4 hours.

For the gazpacho:

½ sweet onion (like Vidalia), chopped

1 English (seedless) cucumber, peeled and chopped

1 clove garlic, minced

2 yellow bell peppers, seeded and chopped

juice of 2 lemons

2 cups (475 mL) cold water

2 Tbsp. (30 mL) finely chopped fresh basil

1 Tbsp. (15 mL) finely chopped fresh chives

1 Tbsp. (15 mL) finely chopped fresh chervil

½ Tbsp. (7.5 mL) finely chopped fresh mint

½ tsp. (2.5 mL) finely chopped fresh thyme

dash hot pepper sauce

salt and freshly ground black pepper to taste

In a food processor or using a hand blender, purée the onion, cucumber, garlic, peppers, lemon juice and cold water until relatively smooth. Let the mixture sit for about 20 minutes until the vegetables release their liquid, then purée again. Stir in the fresh herbs, pepper sauce, salt and pepper. Chill until serving time.

To serve: scrape up the granita with a fork to loosen it. Ladle the gazpacho into individual bowls. Scoop out the granita and place it in the centre of each bowl of gazpacho.

Fire Roasted Corn
with Chipotle & Nasturtium Butters

Recommended: Konzelmann Estate Winery Gewürztraminer Late Harvest
Serves 8

You can follow this recipe that calls for grilling the ears of corn within their husks or you can grill the corn directly over the heat without the husks. If you opt for the latter, apply the butter at the table. Chipotles are large, dried smoked jalapeño peppers and are available in cans packed in a wonderful red sauce called adobo. Look for these in the specialty section of supermarkets, Latin American markets and food shops. The method for each of the butters is the same, so make the butters first and refrigerate until you need them.

For the chipotle butter:
½ cup (120 mL) softened butter
2 green onions, chopped
1 garlic clove, crushed
3–4 chipotles in adobo sauce (use
     more or less according to your
     heat tolerance)
1 tsp. (5 mL) fresh lime juice

For the nasturtium butter:
½ cup (120 mL) softened butter
1 cup (240 mL) nasturtium blossoms
1 tsp. (5 mL) fresh lemon juice

In each case, combine all the ingredients for the butter in a blender or food processor and process until well blended. Lay out a piece of plastic wrap on a clean, dry surface. Using a rubber spatula, arrange the butter along the length of the wrap to form a log. Partially cover with half of the wrap and roll back and forth with your hands until it takes the shape of a log. (Forming the butter into a nice log shape will result in neat, coin-shaped pieces of butter once it has been chilled.) Wrap tightly at both ends and refrigerate until well chilled. The butter will keep for about a week in the refrigerator.

For the corn:

8 ears fresh corn

Heat the grill to medium-high. Peel back the husks from the corn, but leave them attached at the base. Remove the corn silk. Spread one of the two butters over each ear of corn. Pull the husks back over the ear of corn and tie with a strip of corn husk or kitchen string. Soak the corn in cold water for about 15 minutes. Squeeze out the excess water and place the corn on the grill. Grill, turning frequently, for about 10–12 minutes (less time if the corn is without the husk). Serve with more of the chosen butter and a little salt.

Chef Mark Walpole

St. Catharines-born Mark Walpole heads up the kitchen at the Bench Bistro within EastDell Estates where his passion for local produce and products are teamed effectively with EastDell wines. "I love Canadian wines," he says, "and here in Niagara . . . we are also in the heartland for quality produce and meats. There aren't too many chefs in the world who have the opportunity to buy fresh-picked berries right at the source. It's a marriage of food and wine the way it should be." Besides his full-time involvement with EastDell, Mark and his wife, Angela, are the owners and operators of Keaton Manor, a B&B located just south of St. Catharines. Their restored 1830s house is set on eight acres of Carolinian woods next to a millpond that is home to turtles and white swans.

Young Fava Bean & Pecorino Salad
with Prosciutto

Recommended: Château des Charmes Estate Winery Cabernet Franc St. David's Bench
Serves 4

A summer salad with Italian overtones, this could also be made with any young fresh shelled bean or other cheeses, such as Emmental or a good-quality young Cheddar. Serve with lots of good crusty bread.

1 lb. (455 g) young fava beans, shelled
¼ cup (60 mL) extra virgin olive oil
2 Tbsp. (30 mL) fresh lemon juice
2 tsp. (10 mL) chopped fresh sage
2 tsp. (10 mL) chopped fresh chives
salt and freshly ground black pepper,
    to taste
1 small seedless cucumber, peeled
    and cut into neat ½-inch
    (1.2-cm) cubes

12 oz. (340 mL) young Pecorino
    Romano cheese, cut into neat
    ½-inch (1.2-cm) cubes
1 lb. (455 g) prosciutto,
    sliced paper-thin

Bring a large pot of lightly salted water to a boil over high heat. Cook the fava beans until tender and the skins slip off easily, about 5 minutes. Drain and rinse under cold running water, then remove and discard the outer skins. Place the beans in a large bowl and, while still warm, add the olive oil, lemon juice, sage, chives, salt and pepper and mix well to coat the beans. Add the cucumber and cheese and gently toss. Divide the prosciutto evenly among 4 plates and top with a serving of the bean and cheese mixture.

Risotto of Grilled Summer Vegetables in Basil Lemon Olive Oil

Recommended: Cave Spring Cellars Chardonnay Estate Bottled
Serves 4–6

You'd expect a chef with the surname Fracchioni to know a thing or two about risotto, so it's no surprise that this recipe is from the chef of Cave Spring's Inn on the Twenty restaurant. A perfect precursor to grilled summer fare, especially salmon or chicken. Read the entire recipe before proceeding, as the chef provides explicit instructions as to the best preparation for each vegetable. Be aware that the accompanying basil lemon olive oil requires 12 days to steep.

For the basil lemon olive oil:

6 large leaves fresh basil

zest of 2 lemons

$3\frac{1}{8}$ cups (750 mL) olive oil

Add the basil leaves and lemon zest to a large jar with a tight-fitting lid. Pour the olive oil over the basil and lemon. Attach the lid and allow to steep for 12 days in a cool, dry, dark place.

For the grilled vegetables:

olive oil as needed for brushing

1 green zucchini, sliced $\frac{1}{4}$ inch (.6 cm) thick lengthwise

1 yellow zucchini, sliced $\frac{1}{4}$ inch (.6 cm) thick lengthwise

1 red onion, cut into thick wedges, each attached to the stem

1 bulb fennel, sliced $\frac{1}{4}$ inch (.6 cm) thick lengthwise

1 leek, sliced in half lengthwise and thoroughly rinsed

1 red bell pepper, halved and stem, membrane and seeds removed

1 yellow bell pepper, halved and stem, membrane and seeds removed

2 portobello mushrooms, peeled and stems rubbed clean

salt and freshly ground black pepper to taste

balsamic vinegar to taste

Keeping the vegetables relatively large makes them easier to grill and work with. Try to keep the roots of the onion, fennel and leek intact when cutting. Preheat the grill to medium-high. Brush the vegetables liberally with the olive oil and place on the hot grill. Turn them once as they cook to produce an attractive cross pattern. The zucchini and mushrooms will cook quickly, about 6 minutes in total (3 minutes per side). Make sure to brush the mushrooms with more oil as they grill to keep them from drying out. The peppers will be about 2 minutes longer, followed by the leeks and onion at about 10 minutes. The fennel will take the longest, about 15 minutes (or par-boil it for 2 minutes and grill for about 6 minutes). As the vegetables are grilled, set to one side.

When the vegetables are cool enough to handle, cut them into small bite-sized pieces, or into small triangles or diamonds or cubes to make an attractive presentation. Place in a bowl and season with salt, pepper and a splash of balsamic vinegar. Set to one side while you prepare the risotto.

For the risotto:

5 cups (1.2 L) vegetable or chicken
  stock
¼ lb. (113 g) butter
2 tsp. (10 mL) olive oil
1 onion, finely chopped
1 clove garlic, minced
1½ cups (360 mL) Arborio rice (short-
  grained rice)

½ cup (120 mL) Cave Spring Cellars
  Chardonnay Estate Bottled
1 cup (240 mL) grated Parmesan
  cheese
1 tsp. (5 mL) chopped fresh rosemary
1 tsp. (5 mL) chopped fresh thyme
fresh basil for garnish

Pour the stock into a saucepan and bring to a boil. Reduce the heat and keep at a bubbling simmer while you work. In a large saucepan over low heat, heat half of the butter and the olive oil. Add the onion and cook until tender, about 5 minutes. Add the garlic and cook for another minute or two. Add the rice and stir, making sure every grain is coated with oil (add a little more oil if necessary). Add the white wine and stir until the liquid is absorbed. Start adding the hot stock, about 1 cup (240 mL) at a time, stirring continuously after each addition until it is completely absorbed. When just 2 cups (475 mL) of stock remain, add the reserved prepared vegetables. Continue adding the stock to finish cooking the risotto. When the rice is just tender, add the remaining butter, Parmesan cheese, rosemary and thyme. Stir vigorously for 2–3 minutes until the cheese and butter are melted and well incorporated. Drizzle with the basil lemon olive oil and garnish with a sprig of fresh basil.

Greaves

When I lived in the town of Niagara-on-the-Lake back in the early seventies, the Greaves storefront outlet on Queen Street was one of the best things about the town. If you didn't already know what fruit was in season, all you had to do was take a walk in the vicinity of Greaves and the wonderful aromas wafting out of the lovely old shop told you. Besides the sweet fragrance of strawberry, raspberry or peach jams and preserves, I remember most strongly the heady, pungent presence of tomato-based chili sauce wafting through the town. Nobody made it better. Today the storefront is still there but Greaves production is done off-site and anyone in the world can purchase their wonderful products online. The year 2002 will mark 75 years of Greaves pure jams, jellies, marmalades and more, and even though Mabel and William Greaves are no longer at the helm, their recipes are still used today—each batch is hand-stirred in open kettles using natural ingredients, the best of Niagara produce and no pectin, additives or preservatives.

Campfire Cast Iron Potatoes Anna

Recommended: Peninsula Ridge Estates Winery Chardonnay Reserve
Serves 4

Classic Potatoes Anna are usually finished in a hot oven, which is the last appliance you want to dally with during the steamy month of July. One hot day this past July, we had a hankering for the earthy goodness of this dish and, as Ted had a fire already in progress in our firepit, burning garden debris, I thought why not modify the recipe somewhat and finish cooking the sliced potatoes in a cast iron skillet over a rack on the outdoor fire? As they say in England, it worked a treat. If you are camping, do as I did and finish these over a campfire. Otherwise, preheat your barbecue grill to high, and place the cast iron skillet on the grill rack, close the lid, reduce the heat to medium and cook until the potatoes are golden and tender. You can lessen the amount of butter if you must but, as good as it will be, it won't be quite as unforgettable a dish. I used a 9½-inch (24-cm) cast iron skillet for this quantity of potato. If your skillet is larger, you could easily increase the quantities. Terrific accompaniment to steak.

3–4 large baking potatoes, peeled
¾ cup (175 mL) butter, melted
salt and freshly ground black pepper
to taste

Slice the potatoes crosswise very thinly (⅛ inch/3 mm or less) with a sharp chef's knife or on a mandoline. Put a medium-sized cast iron pan on medium-high heat and add a drizzle of melted butter, using a pastry brush to gloss the base of the pan. Start layering the potato slices in a spiral design, overlapping each slice. Drizzle a bit of butter over the layer, and add a sprinkle of salt and a grind of fresh pepper. Repeat this process (still working with the pan on the stove), layering the potatoes, drizzling with butter and sprinkling with salt and pepper, pressing the mass down with a metal spatula as you work. By the time you have finished, it will be time to remove the pan from the heat. (If you are working very slowly, take it off the heat before now.) End by drizzling the last bit of butter over the surface. Using a large metal spatula, press down on the cake.

Take the pan outside to the fire-in-progress. (The fire shouldn't be raging.) Place the pan on a rack about 9 inches (23 cm) above the fire, cover with an old pot lid (or foil) and cook until the edges of the potatoes are golden brown and the centre is tender when tested, about 25–40 minutes, depending on the heat of the fire. During this time, press down on the potatoes with a metal spatula every now and then to compress it into a cake.

Remove the pan and slide a thin spatula around the edge. Give the pan a bit of a knock. Place a plate on top of the skillet and quickly invert the cake onto the plate, then slip it back into the skillet to brown the other side for a few minutes over the fire. Serve in wedges right out of the pan.

Picard's

Billed as "home of the Canadian peanut," Picard's came as a big surprise to me when we first moved to Niagara. We live close to the Picard outlet in Fonthill (there are others in Niagara-on-the-Lake, Windham Centre, Elmira and Talbotville) where Picard's Ontario-grown peanuts— jumbo cocktail and extra fancy redskin—are sold. If you love peanuts— really fresh, quality peanuts—make sure to pay a visit to Picard's while in Niagara. Besides the unadulterated fresh nut itself, they offer wonderful peanut brittle, peanut and praline clusters, chip nuts, beer nuts, honey nuggets, peanut butter and other confections and more free samples than you can imagine. The Valencia peanut has been grown commercially in southwestern Ontario since 1980. Peanut seeds are planted in the middle of May and the peanuts harvested in late September before autumn frosts. I have to say these are the best, most addictive peanuts I have ever eaten.

Barbecued Mussels
in Niagara Millstone Lager & Garlic

Recommended: Niagara Brewing Millstone Premium Lager
Serves 6

You can vary this by adding shrimp or clams to the mussels. This is a very easy way to serve a lot of people a great first course outside. Add any fresh herbs you have on hand and, if you like heat, crush a few dried chili peppers and throw them in along with the garlic. Serve with lots of good bread and butter.

6 lb. (2.7 kg) mussels
4 cloves garlic, finely chopped
2 bottles, 12 oz. (341 mL) each,
    Niagara Brewing Millstone
    Premium Lager

¼ cup (60 mL) chopped fresh flat-leaf
    parsley
¼ cup (60 mL) chopped fresh chives
salt and freshly ground black pepper
    to taste

Preheat the grill to high. Scrub the mussels under running water, and debeard if necessary. Discard any mussels that are not tightly closed or have broken shells. Fold a length of foil in half to form a double thickness and use it to line a large roasting pan. Working in batches if necessary, spread the mussels evenly on the foil, scatter the garlic over the mussels and set the pan on the grill. Pour the lager over the mussels, close the lid and cook for 5–7 minutes. Discard any mussels that have not opened. Sprinkle the fresh herbs over the mussels, season to taste and carefully pour the mussels and their juices into a large, warmed deep platter or bowl. Serve at once.

Grilled Shrimp with Tomato Plum Sauce

Recommended: Inniskillin Gamay Noir
Serves 4

This recipe is from chef Izabela Kalabis of Inniskillin. Izabela says if you don't want to grill the shrimp, "you can also sauté it in a large skillet with a tablespoon of olive oil." Make the accompanying sauce ahead of time and allow to cool before proceeding.

For the sauce:

3 cloves garlic

1 tsp. (5 mL) minced fresh ginger

juice of 1 lemon

1 jalapeño pepper, seeded

3 plum tomatoes, skinned and seeded

3 Tbsp. (45 mL) plum jam

⅓ cup (80 mL) orange juice

1 Tbsp. (15 mL) honey

5 prunes, pitted

salt, to taste

Place all the sauce ingredients in a food processor or blender and process until smooth. Transfer the mixture to a saucepan and simmer gently over medium heat for 15–20 minutes, or until fragrant and thick. Remove from the heat and allow to cool while you prepare the shrimp.

for the shrimp:

1 Tbsp. (15 mL) olive oil

1 clove garlic, minced

1 lb. (455 g) large shrimp, shelled and
deveined

salt and freshly ground black pepper
to taste

Preheat the grill to medium-high. In a small bowl just large enough to hold the shrimp, stir the olive oil and garlic. Add the shrimp, coat well with the oil mixture and season with salt and pepper. (Do this with your hands as it distributes the oil evenly.) Grill the shrimp about 1–2 minutes on each side, until they are pink and begin to curl. Serve the shrimp on a large platter, with a bowl of the sauce in the centre.

Castle Rock Spiced Pepper Shrimp on Sweet Potato Cakes ·with Fresh Mango Chutney

Chef Neal Noble of Senses Restaurant in Toronto is often involved with preparing a special menu for opening night galas at Niagara-on-the-Lake's Shaw Festival. This first course was one he created for their production of Lord of the Flies. *Prepare the pepper sauce and the mango chutney a day ahead. Warm the chutney before serving.*

For the pepper sauce:

2 red bell peppers, roasted and skin and seeds discarded
1 Tbsp. (15 mL) olive oil
¼ cup (60 mL) sherry vinegar
1 Tbsp. (15 mL) coarsely ground black pepper

1 Tbsp. (15 mL) honey
½ cup (120 mL) finely chopped fresh chives

Place the roasted peppers in a blender, add the olive oil and purée until smooth. Scrape the pepper purée into a bowl and combine with the vinegar, pepper, honey and chives. Mix well, cover and refrigerate overnight to allow the flavours to develop.

For the mango chutney:

1 Tbsp. (15 mL) olive oil

2 shallots, diced

1½ cups (360 mL) diced fresh mango

¼ cup (60 mL) orange juice

2 Tbsp. (30 mL) lemon juice

1 Tbsp. (15 mL) honey

¼ tsp. (1.2 mL) dried chili flakes

Heat a small saucepan over medium-high heat and add the olive oil, shallots and mango. Sauté until the mango softens, about 8 minutes. Add the remaining ingredients and mix well. Bring to a boil, reduce the heat to a simmer and cook gently until the chutney has a jam-like consistency. Keep warm.

For the sweet potato cakes:

2 large sweet potatoes, baked until very soft, skin removed and discarded

4 eggs, lightly beaten

½ cup (120 mL) whipping cream

1 cup (240 mL) all-purpose flour

2 Tbsp. (30 mL) baking powder

2 pinches nutmeg

2 pinches ground cinnamon

½ tsp. (2.5 mL) pure vanilla extract

vegetable oil for frying

Place the sweet potato in a bowl and mash with a fork. Add all the remaining ingredients, except the oil for frying, and mix until smooth. Allow to rest for 10–15 minutes.

Heat a medium sauté pan over medium-high heat, and lightly coat the pan bottom with oil. Spoon the batter into the pan to form 3-inch (7.5-cm) cakes and pat down lightly. Cook until golden brown, turning only once when the surface begins to bubble. Remove from the pan and keep warm.

For the shrimp:
2 Tbsp. (30 mL) olive oil
24 large tiger shrimp, peeled and
    deveined, tail left on
salt to taste

Place a large sauté pan over high heat and add the olive oil. Sauté the shrimp quickly until they are firm and pink (don't overcook them). Add the prepared pepper sauce and sauté until just warmed through. Season with salt.

To serve, place a portion of warm mango chutney on top of each potato cake, arrange three shrimp on top of the chutney and spoon the pepper sauce over the shrimp. Serve immediately.

Shaw Festival

From April to November, Niagara-on-the-Lake's revered Shaw Festival presents polished theatrical productions with one of the largest repertory companies in North America—and the only theatre in the world that specializes in plays written by Bernard Shaw and his contemporaries. Three different theatre locations are utililized: the Festival Theatre, the largest and the first building visible when the town is approached from the Niagara Parkway, the Court House Theatre and the Royal George Theatre. The Shaw Festival adds the element of theatrical culture to a town steeped in history and a surrounding area filled with natural beauty.

View to a vine...dawn at Vineland Estates

Risotto of Grilled Summer Vegetables in Basil Lemon Olive Oil (page 165)

Red Peppers Stuffed with Smoked Chicken

Recommended: Magnotta Winery Pinot Gris
Serves 4

No fewer than four of the ingredients for this great-tasting dish have a smoke component, one of them being a smoked chili purée. If you can't readily obtain that particular condiment at a specialty food shop, any good Asian-style chili sauce may be used in its place. This recipe—perfect as part of an antipasto selection—is from chef Virginia Marr of Niagara-on-the-Lake's Pillar & Post.

For the stuffing:

½ lb. (225 g) smoked chicken, shredded

2 slices double-smoked bacon, diced and cooked

2 cloves garlic, minced

½ cup (120 mL) shredded smoked provolone

juice and finely grated zest of 1 lime

4 lengths of fresh cilantro, chopped

¼ tsp. (1.2 mL) smoked chili purée, or Asian-style chili sauce

salt to taste

pinch of nutmeg

Combine all the stuffing ingredients in a medium-sized mixing bowl and mix well.

For the peppers:

4 large red bell peppers, roasted, peeled, seeded and halved

flour for dredging

2 large eggs, beaten

olive oil for frying

Fill the pepper halves with the stuffing, then carefully roll the peppers in the flour, shaking off the excess. Preheat a non-stick frying pan over medium heat. Dip the floured peppers in the beaten egg and fry until golden brown on both sides. Remove from the pan and drain on paper towels before serving.

Tuscan Bread Salad
with Chardonnay Vine-Skewered Chicken

Recommended: Pillitteri Estates Winery Chardonnay Barrel Aged

Serves 6

I have seen boxes of imported vine cuttings in very upscale food shops in Toronto and New York City for absolutely ridiculous prices—ridiculous when you remember that grapevines have to be pruned whether there is a market for the cuttings or not. So, visit Niagara and gather ye cuttings at a local winery during pruning time. Buy a couple of bottles of wine and I'm willing to wager they'll throw the cuttings in with your purchase. They lend a subtle yet distinctive flavour to the chicken. If you can't obtain cuttings, soak wooden skewers for an hour in a little Chardonnay.

For the Tuscan bread salad:

12 thick slices day-old, coarse-grained, rustic bread	3 cloves garlic, minced
6 large ripe tomatoes	1 large seedless cucumber, cut into chunks
1/3 cup (80 mL) extra virgin olive oil	1 large white onion, quartered and thinly sliced
4 Tbsp. (60 mL) red wine vinegar	12 fresh basil leaves
salt and freshly ground black pepper to taste	

Cut the bread into rough chunks and place in a large bowl. Place a sieve over another bowl. Working over the bowl, skin, halve and seed the tomatoes, collecting the juice in the bowl beneath. Cut the tomatoes into rough chunks and set aside. Add the olive oil, vinegar, salt, pepper and garlic to the collected tomato juices, whisking the ingredients together. Pour this seasoned tomato juice over the chunks of bread and toss together until all of the liquid has been absorbed. (If the bread was exceptionally dry, add a little more olive oil.) Add the cucumber, onion and basil leaves to the bread mixture along with the reserved tomato. Toss together and taste for seasoning, adding a little more salt and pepper if needed. Let it sit in a cool place for about 2 hours before serving with the grilled chicken.

For the chicken:

6 boneless, skinless chicken breasts, cut lengthwise into 3 strips

6 Chardonnay vine skewers, 7–8 inches (18–20 cm) long, soaked in warm water for an hour

1 cup (240 mL) Pillitteri Estates Winery Chardonnay Barrel Aged

juice of 1 large lemon

4 Tbsp. (60 mL) olive oil

1 heaping Tbsp. (17 mL) paprika

3 cloves garlic, minced

salt and freshly ground black pepper to taste

Thread the chicken onto the presoaked vines and place in a shallow glass or ceramic dish. Whisk the Chardonnay with the lemon, olive oil, paprika, garlic, salt and pepper. When blended, pour over the chicken, cover loosely with plastic wrap and leave to marinate for an hour—no longer—at room temperature.

Preheat the grill to medium-high. Remove the chicken from the marinade and discard the marinade. Brush the chicken with a little more olive oil and grill on one side for 2 minutes, brushing with a little more oil or lemon juice if you like. Turn over and grill for another 2 minutes. Continue for 6–8 minutes, or until the chicken is cooked through. Serve alongside the Tuscan bread salad.

Pork Ribs with Niagara Apple Ale
& Mustard Glaze

Recommended: Niagara Brewing Apple Ale
Serves 4

Now these are pork ribs for beer lovers. I like to precook meaty pork ribs slowly in a quantity of Niagara Apple Ale because the beer helps to tenderize the meat and lends a distinctively fruity quality to it. Following this, the ribs are finished on the grill with a hearty beer and mustard glaze. Terrific with homemade coleslaw and lots of fresh corn.

4 lb. (1.8 kg) pork spare ribs, cut into sections
5 bottles (12 oz./341 mL each) Niagara Apple Ale
2 onions, roughly chopped
1 small head of garlic, separated

½ cup (120 mL) coarse-grain mustard
½ cup (120 mL) pure maple syrup
3 Tbsp. (45 mL) chopped fresh thyme
2 Tbsp. (30 mL) chopped fresh sage
salt and freshly ground black pepper to taste

Place the ribs in a large stockpot and cover with 3 bottles of the ale. Add the chopped onion to the pot, then smash each garlic clove, peel and add to the pot. Bring to a boil. Reduce the heat and simmer very gently for about 30 minutes. As the ribs are simmering, prepare the glaze.

In a large saucepan, bring the remaining 2 bottles of ale to a boil. Reduce the heat immediately and simmer for 15 minutes, until the liquid is reduced by half. Add the mustard, maple syrup, thyme, sage and salt and pepper. Stir together to blend all the ingredients and simmer for 5 minutes, then remove from the heat. Preheat the grill to high.

Drain the ribs and transfer to a baking sheet or roasting pan. Lightly oil the grill. Reduce the heat to medium-high and grill the ribs, brushing with the glaze and turning them to grill on all sides for a total of about 15 minutes, until they are brown and crusty. (If you run out of glaze, continue basting with more Niagara Apple Ale.) Serve hot from the grill.

 ### *Winemaker Jean Laurent Groux*

Born and raised in the French wine-producing region of the Loire Valley, J-L Groux joined Hillebrand in 1989 after studying winemaking in Burgundy and at the University of Bordeaux. His own particular style of winemaking has been encouraged by Hillebrand, whose state-of-the-art winemaking equipment and extensive barrel-aging facilities have helped J-L to consistently produce a wide spectrum of award-winning wines. In 1998 J-L received the Winemaker of the Year award from the Air Ontario competition and he was also honoured by the Vinitaly International Wine Competition, where Hillebrand Estates' Unfiltered Cabernet Sauvignon 1995 won the Grand Gold award.

Grilled Mennonite Sausage
with Pasta Ribbons, Summer Vegetables
& Parsley Pesto

Recommended: Hernder Estate Wines Cabernet Franc
Serves 4

I held a book signing at the opening of the Harvest Wine boutique not far from us, and prepared sausages in red wine with squares of polenta. The locally made sausages were obtained from the Harvest Barn with the only bit of information on the label referring to the hefty coils as "Mennonite sausage." With one taste, droves of people headed over to the deli section of the store and within no time every section of sausage was sold—they're that good. This recipe uses those sausages (or any good-quality lean sausage) sliced on an angle and tossed with pasta and the best summer vegetables. I like to use a flat ribbon pasta like tagliatelle or pappardelle for this, but any shape can be used. This is a very convenient summer preparation as it can be enjoyed at room temperature.

For the parsley pesto:

1 large bunch flat-leaf parsley, rinsed
    and stems trimmed
4 cloves garlic, smashed
1 cup (240 mL) Parmesan cheese

1 tsp. (5 mL) salt
½ tsp. (2.5 mL) freshly ground black
    pepper
½ cup (120 mL) extra virgin olive oil

Place the parsley and garlic in a food processor or blender and pulse until finely minced. Add the cheese, salt, pepper and olive oil and purée until the mixture is smooth. Transfer to a small bowl and set aside.

For the sausage, pasta and vegetables:

12 oz. (340 mL) tagliatelle or
   pappardelle

4 Tbsp. (60 mL) extra virgin olive oil

1 red onion, diced

2 cloves garlic, minced

2 young carrots, scraped and diced

1 green zucchini, trimmed and
   chopped

1 yellow zucchini, trimmed and
   chopped

½ lb. (225 g) slender green beans, cut
   into 1-inch (2.5-cm) pieces

1 yellow bell pepper, seeded and
   chopped

3 Tbsp. (45 mL) red wine vinegar

1 lb. (455 g) cherry, grape or pear-
   shaped tomatoes, halved

salt and freshly ground black pepper
   to taste

8 large lean sausages, grilled or pan-
   seared

Bring a large saucepan of water to a boil over high heat. When it is at a full boil, add a little salt and the pasta. Cook the pasta until tender but firm, about 8 minutes. Drain and rinse quickly under cold water, then set to one side.

Warm half the olive oil in a large skillet over medium-high heat. Sauté the onion and garlic for a few minutes until softened, then add the carrot and cook for about 3 minutes, followed by the zucchini, beans and yellow pepper. Stir-fry the vegetables together until they are crisp-tender, about 10 minutes, longer if you prefer.

Transfer the vegetable mixture to a bowl and let cool. Add the remaining 2 Tbsp. (30 mL) olive oil, vinegar, tomatoes and cooked pasta. Season with salt and pepper and toss gently until well combined. Slice the cooked sausages on an angle. Serve a portion of the pasta and vegetables, top with the sliced sausage and drizzle with a portion of parsley pesto.

Peaches on Toast with Raspberry Butter

Recommended: Peller Estates Winery Dry Riesling Private Reserve
Serves 4–6

For dessert, for breakfast, for any time at all, I love fresh peaches piled onto hot buttered toast. When there was "nothing for dessert" in my childhood home, my English-born Mum would make this comforting sweet with peaches or other fresh fruit, like raspberries or strawberries. I have gilded the lily a bit here with the addition of a simple-to-make raspberry butter. Go all the way and top with unsweetened whipped cream. Peaches are easy to peel if you just blanch them in hot water for a few moments, then plunge them into cold water before slipping the skins off.

For the raspberry butter:

½ cup (120 mL) chopped fresh
    raspberries
2 Tbsp. (30 mL) icing sugar, or to taste

1 Tbsp. (15 mL) raspberry vinegar
½ cup (120 mL) softened butter

Combine all the ingredients in a bowl. Cream together until well blended and smooth. Set aside.

For the peaches:

6 large ripe peaches, skinned and
    pitted
juice of 1 large lemon
2–3 Tbsp. (30–45 mL) sugar
    (depending on the sweetness of
    the peaches)
¼ cup (60 mL) Peller Estates Winery
    Dry Riesling Private Reserve

6 thick slices challah (egg bread) or
    English muffin bread
unsweetened whipped cream, for
    garnish
sprigs of mint, for garnish
1 Tbsp. (15 mL) raspberry vinegar
½ cup (120 mL) softened butter

Slice the peaches into a bowl. Add the lemon juice, sugar and Riesling and mix well. Let stand for 20 minutes or so to allow the flavours to develop. (The lemon juice will keep the peaches from discolouring.) When ready to serve, toast the bread and spread it with the raspberry butter. Pile the peaches on top, followed by a generous dollop of whipped cream and a sprig of fresh mint, if you like.

Malivoire Wine Company

"Interesting wines for interesting people" sums up the philosophy of Malivoire, the Beamsville Bench winery with the tiny red ladybug as a fixture on its label. My introduction to the wines of this small but important winery came via my daughter Alysa when she poured me a glass of their Ladybug Rosé as an aperitif at Avalon restaurant in Toronto one evening before we had moved to Niagara. "Try this," she said, "it changed my mind about rosé." It changed my attitude, as well. Malivoire's rosé was much more serious, more full-bodied and satisfying than any I had experienced and it triggered my interest in the winery that is now garnering awards thanks to the dedication of winemaker Anne Sperling and owner Martin Malivoire. The ladybug insignia refers to the fact that Malivoire uses sustainable agricultural methods in their vineyards—at one time employing more than a quarter million ladybugs to control an infestation of leafhoppers rather than using pesticides that would eradicate both good and bad insects. Coupled with softer and gentler vineyard and winemaking techniques—a gravity feed eliminates the need for the usual forceful pumping and handling of the grapes— these creative approaches are helping to raise the bar of quality winemaking in the region.

Summer Pudding with Crème Fraîche

Recommended: Hillebrand Estates Winery Trius Brut NV
Serves 4–6

I think of this classic English summer dessert as a variation on old-fashioned bread pudding. It calls for a mixture of soft, and mostly red, summer fruits, like strawberries ("ever-bearing" varieties ensure availability past June in our area), raspberries, blackberries, red and black currants and even cherries. If you use black currants, be careful how many you include, as their flavour and colour will dominate. You will need one of those lovely (1½ pint/3 cup/720-mL) pudding basins for this, or you could substitute a soufflé dish.

8 slices of homemade or bakery white bread, sliced ½ inch (1.2 cm) thick, crusts removed

1½ lb. (680 g) mixed soft fruits
½ cup (120 mL) sugar
crème fraîche (see page 124)

Line the bottom of the pudding basin with slices of bread to cover the base. Then line the sides with more bread cut to fit. Ensure that the pieces fit snugly together. After hulling and washing the fruit (if cherries are included, pit them), place in a large heavy saucepan and cover with the sugar. Over a low heat, bring to a gentle boil. Reduce the heat and simmer for 2–3 minutes until the sugar is dissolved and juice begins to appear. Remove from the heat and reserve 2 Tbsp. (30 mL) of the juice. Carefully spoon the fruit and the remaining juice into the bread-lined basin and cover the surface with the remaining bread. Set a small plate or saucer on top of the pudding and weight it with a heavy can. Refrigerate for approximately 8 hours or overnight.

When you're ready to serve, cover the dish with a serving plate and turn it upside down to unmould the pudding. Pour the reserved juice over any bits of bread that have not been soaked with juice. Serve with crème fraîche or loosely whipped cream.

Thirteenth Street

This small, premium wine co-operative is located in Jordan Station and is the result of a group of like-minded, talented amateur winemakers who decided to join forces in producing handcrafted wines. There are five partners in all, each one responsible for growing and producing their own particular vintage while keeping complete control over it from the ground to the bottle. Their intention is to stay small, partly because they all have retained their "day jobs" and partly because in this way quality is ensured. Particularly recommended: their G.H. Funk Riesling and Sandstone Gamay.

A Cake for My Sister
(Victoria Sponge with Raspberries)

Recommended: Peller Estates Winery Founders' Series Cristalle NV
Serves 6–8

Youngest daughter Jenna made this for eldest daughter Alysa on the occasion of her July birthday, when raspberries, blackberries, apricots and peaches abound. Vary the fruit as you like.

1 cup (240 mL) softened butter
1 cup (240 mL) fine sugar
5 eggs, at room temperature
1½ tsp. (7.5 mL) pure vanilla extract
1 cup (240 mL) all-purpose flour
1 tsp. (5 mL) baking powder

pinch of salt
4 cups (950 mL) fresh raspberries, rinsed
5 Tbsp. (75 mL) icing sugar
4 Tbsp. (60 mL) fruit liqueur
1½ cups (360 mL) whipping cream

Preheat the oven to 375°F (190°C). Lightly butter and flour a round 10-inch (25-cm) cake pan. In a large bowl, beat the butter until soft and creamy. Gradually add the fine sugar and cream the mixture until it is light and fluffy. Beat in the eggs one at a time, stirring well after each addition. Stir in the vanilla.

In another smaller bowl, sift the flour, baking powder and salt twice. Gradually incorporate the dry mixture into the wet mixture. Pour into a cake pan and bake for approximately 20 minutes. Reduce the heat to 325°F (165°C) and continue baking until the cake tests done, about 35–40 minutes. Cool. When the cake has completely cooled, cut it horizontally into 3 layers.

Pat the raspberries dry and reserve 10 or so for the garnish. Place the remainder in a bowl and cover with 2 Tbsp. (30 mL) of the icing sugar and 1 Tbsp. (15 mL) of the fruit liqueur. Crush slightly and gently mix. Set to one side at room temperature.

When you're ready to assemble the cake (an hour before serving), drain the berries in a sieve over a bowl. Keep the berries and juice separate. Whip the cream with 2 Tbsp. (30 mL) of the icing sugar in a chilled bowl until fairly stiff.

Place one sponge layer on a round serving platter or cake stand and sprinkle with 1 Tbsp. (15 mL) of the fruit liqueur and 1 Tbsp. (15 mL) of reserved berry juice. With a metal spatula, spread ½ the whipped cream over the sponge and follow with ½ the crushed raspberries. Place the second sponge layer on top and repeat the procedure. Finish with the third layer. Dust with the remaining icing sugar and decorate with the reserved berries. Serve with additional whipped cream if desired.

Daniel Lenko

The first time I drove past Daniel Lenko's modest winery I was struck by the portable sign positioned out front that read "good wines, friendly people, nice dog." Daniel Lenko, the 35-year-old proprietor is making serious strides in wine country with his hands-on approach to grape-growing, something that is clearly in his blood as the Lenko family has been in the business of supplying high-quality vinifera grapes to many top Niagara wineries for many years. The Beamsville vineyard boasts some of the oldest Chardonnay and Merlot vines in Ontario, and it is these vines that are contributing to the overall quality of the wines being produced by Lenko and his winemaker and mentor, Jim Warren, former owner and winemaker at Stoney Ridge Cellars. Due to limited production, Lenko's wines are available only at the winery. Reason enough to visit Niagara.

Blackberry Fool with Poire William

Recommended: Sunnybrook Farm Estate Winery Blackberry Fruit Wine
Serves 6

Well, I'm a fool for fools because they are made in a snap, taste wonderful and always capture the best of so many different seasonal fruits. Lovely after a feast from the summer grill.

6 cups (1.5 L) fresh blackberries, rinsed and drained	⅔ cup (160 mL) thick, plain yogurt, drained if necessary
⅔ cup (160 mL) sugar	1 cup (240 mL) whipping cream
3 Tbsp. (45 mL) Poire William or other fruit liqueur	6–8 langue-de-chat (ladyfinger-shaped biscuits)
1 Tbsp. (15 mL) lemon juice	

Reserve 18 berries for decoration. In a blender or food processor, purée the rest of the blackberries, in batches if necessary. Rub the mixture through a fine sieve to remove the seeds.

Combine the purée with the sugar in a heavy saucepan and carefully bring to a boil. Lower the heat and simmer, uncovered, until well-thickened. Remove from the heat and pour the mixture into a heatproof bowl. Let cool, stirring frequently. Cover with plastic wrap and refrigerate until completely chilled.

Stir the liqueur and lemon juice into the cooled mixture. Whisk the yogurt until smooth. In a separate bowl, whip the cream until soft peaks form and fold into the yogurt. Carefully fold the cream mixture into the berry mixture to create a marble effect; do not overmix. Transfer to individual serving glasses or one large serving bowl. Refrigerate, covered, for at least 4 hours, or up to overnight. Decorate with the reserved berries and serve with the biscuits.

Niagara Peach Wine

Makes about 5 cups (1.2 L)

Well, okay, this isn't really wine made from peaches but a lovely, refreshing con-coction of peaches poached in dry white wine and left to stand overnight. A perfect—and logical—beverage from Niagara fruit and wine country. Use recycled wine bottles that you have washed and sterilized beforehand. New corks can be purchased wherever wine-making equipment is sold.

6 ripe peaches, peeled and halved	1 cup (240 mL) fine sugar
4 cups (950 mL) Harbour Estates Winery Riesling	³⁄₄ cup (180 mL) eau de vie

Place the peaches in a heavy saucepan, add the white wine and bring to a gentle simmer over medium-high heat. Simmer for 15 minutes, until the peaches are soft. Remove from the heat, cover and let stand overnight. Remove the peaches from the liquid (reserve the poached fruit for another use) and strain the liquid through a coffee filter. Add the sugar and eau de vie and stir to completely dissolve the sugar. Pour the mixture into steril-ized, dry bottles. Insert the cork and store in the refrigerator. This bever-age should be enjoyed within 2 weeks of bottling. Make sure to serve it very well chilled.

Watermelon Margaritas

Serves 6

We made these for Alysa's July birthday. Actually, we made authentic margaritas for us and fresh watermelon juice for the kids and at some point in the festivities had the brilliant idea to meld the two components—outstanding.

3 lb. (1.35 kg) watermelon, peeled and seeded

¼ cup (60 mL) sugar

1 cup (240 mL) Tequila

½ cup (120 mL) fresh lime juice

12 fresh mint leaves

Cut the watermelon into chunks and pulse in a blender or food processor until the watermelon is reduced to a liquid. With the motor running, add the sugar, Tequila, lime juice and mint leaves. When well blended, transfer the mixture to the freezer to chill thoroughly and thicken. Serve in margarita-style glasses.

Vinehaven Bakery Artisan Breads and Catering

Chef Lenny Karmiol and his wife, Heather, also a chef, had a dream of opening a bakery featuring authentic rustic breads. At the time of writing, Lenny and Heather's dream is becoming a reality even as Lenny maintains his position as resident chef at the Good Earth Cooking School and the two continue to provide catering services. "We feel very excited about being part of a group of like-minded people committed to excellence and vision in wine country, especially as it continues to grow," says Lenny.

August

Country Kitchens & Roadside Stands

August and the heat continues, as they say, unabated. We cook and eat simply: halibut, salmon and chicken prepared over the open fire pit outside. The garden still provides salad greens every day and now our tomatoes are ripening—especially the cherry tomatoes. If we had planted full-fledged tomato plants bought from the local nursery, we might be further ahead by now, but it was a kick to grow them from seed and see those slender grass-like plants take root and shape. This past weekend I obtained wonderful peaches from Whitty Farms, along with apricots, corn and strawberries. Local strawberries at this time of the year, I couldn't believe my eyes. And they were perfect. Karen Whitty tells me they are the ever-bearing variety. I tell her the few we planted must be the never-bearing variety, we only had a handful, but then it was the first year for them. The magnificent Late Red Havens peaches will be ready at the end of next week.

AUGUST 5. They have issued a Heat Emergency warning in Toronto, a first. When I walk out our front door, I feel as though I have stepped into Jamaica. I want only to sit on the verandah and sip Mum's raspberry vinegar beverage with lots of soda and fresh mint.

Last month and this, we are enjoying much rosé—these are truly the days of rosé wine and roses. We've tried a number of them, from Malivoire's lovely Lady Bug to Henry of Pelham's and now an especially memorable rosé from the area's newest winery, Peninsula Ridge. It is palest rose and quite sophisticated—perhaps the best yet.

AUGUST 7. The potted basil is lush and bushy, and I love to run my hands through it whenever I pass by. We will have our first crop of potatoes tonight—Yukon Golds, fresh dug! I think we could have enjoyed them a little earlier, but I wanted to leave them in the ground a little longer for size. Now they're pushing up through the surface of the soil like partially covered gold bums. Ted will boil water outside over the fire pit and, after a quick rinse from the hose, I'll take them directly to the pot, cook them up and we'll eat them with quantities of butter and salt and want nothing more for dinner. Finally, we have a bit of rain. Not nearly enough, though.

AUGUST 8. The tropical heat continues. I try to keep things watered in the garden, but everything dries so quickly; the breeze is actually hot. Blue, cloudless sky all day and the cicadas buzz and whir at dusk. Old Molly, Middle-Aged Cider and Whippersnapper Kit-Kat, our resident cat collection, lie around in various states of over-heated ennui, looking as though they all expect to be given their own little chaise lounge.

It almost hurts to see the brown-edged leaves of the horse chestnut tree outside my window. Up to now these trees have looked so attractive, in leaf or not. Now they are parchment-dry. All we can do is follow the advice of the arborist and water as much as we can. Dave Perkins at Wyndym Farm near Niagara-on-the-Lake, who produces wonderful specialty greens and herbs, says he is watering constantly during this "bad summer."

AUGUST 11–12. A return to more moderate temperatures, but still hot. Tiny smidges of rain are just enough to settle the dust. Making lots of Tuscan-style bread salads with our cherry tomatoes, the bread made with Niagara Brewing spent grain. Made a variation on the theme, too: sticky rice with tiny tomatoes, leftover corn scraped from the husk, avocado, red onion, basil, parsley in a lemony vinaigrette.

Beginning to hear now what we feel daily, that the unrelenting rainless heat is affecting the harvest of everything here. Huge cracks in our land, on the lawn, in flowerbeds.

AUGUST 16. Finally a bit of steady rain late in the afternoon, about an hour's worth. Just enough to bring out the bits of green in that which has not totally given over to drought. Kit-Kat, the newest feline in our clan, is excited yet stymied by the drops—just what is this stuff? She hasn't seen any rain yet in her tiny life.

Now, at 8:15 p.m., I'm waiting for Ted to come home from an overnight trip to Ottawa. I sit on our side verandah, with a glass of Vidal from Henry of Pelham, listening to Miles Davis, and in awe of that special light in the sky, a leftover rain sky. You can almost see the air, moist, dusty, collecting around the length and breadth of the trees. A sudden breeze lifts leaves, pale grey clouds leave one part of the sky for another. The evening is still, yet full of sound: the crinkling, thrumming of crickets and evensong from a myriad of living things. Beautiful live theatre right in my backyard, with Casey, the cats and I the only audience.

AUGUST 24. It is almost the end of the month and there has been some rain, but nothing that has altered or improved the situation much. Have we got tomatoes! Cherry tomatoes and the Italian Romas by the score. We eat them at every meal and never tire of them. Standing on the upper deck I look down at a sea of red among the green. The Yukon Golds continue to thrill (unearthed another "boiling," as Mum would say). Alysa had them for the first time this past weekend. I made Niagara Apple Ale spareribs, our Swiss chard, spuds with butter, fresh corn scraped from the husk and sautéed with fresh herbs and butter.

AUGUST 27. Visited the Italian Ice Cream people in Niagara Falls to order the torrone gelati for our planned September party; also stopped in to Criveller Pastries to look at what they have. Have decided on Eisbock truffle, the wonderful layered pastries called *sfogliatelle* that are filled with sweetened ricotta and another called *caramellate* filled with hazelnut cream. Mmmmm.

Just talked to James Krieger at Niagara Oyster: he's happy to supply oysters *and* the shucker for us on September 15, which is now just around the corner. He is about to open his storefront on Cushman Road, perhaps by this weekend. Besides the seafood and fresh fish, eventually he plans to bring in wild mushrooms, foie gras and other specialty food items as the business grows.

AUGUST 28. A lovely rainy morning with a soft, coolish breeze—so good to hear and feel the rain. The scarlet runner vines have finally sprouted some tiny slender beans; lots of brilliant, deep coral-coloured flowers competing with the tomatoes to be noticed.

Just devoured half of a local muskmelon—good, juicy and so inexpensive considering that later in the year when we buy imported cantaloupe and honeydew they will be close to $4.00 each.

Ted and I enjoyed a wonderful dinner at Hillebrand last night, a chef's tasting menu of many really delightful courses, all with a strong emphasis on what is available now, and paired with the winery's best. Chef Tony de Luca started us off with a fresh pea soup with a tiny Parmesan cheese wafer hat that held a teaspoon of caviar. Then, foie gras with local white peaches on mizuna. Duck breast was teamed with these incredible little Sovereign Coronation grapes and tiny onions. Bison with Malabar spinach and blue ermite cheese. And for dessert, house-made ices—strawberry basil and cinnamon red currant, accented by a rich syrup based on strawberries and cabernet, and crisp wafers . . . wow.

Made wonderful quick apricot jam yesterday. Just a few jars, but what a flavour. A deep orange colour, like free-range chicken's yolks. It will make a wonderful filling for tarts or turnovers or a spread for hot toast or muffins. It's peach time, big time, now. I plan to make quantities of peaches in Riesling this Labour Day weekend, and something savoury with all the incredible tomatoes we have.

In the Vineyard and On the Vine

"In the vineyard we have a bit of a nice, quiet period in the month of August. I think of it as the calm before the storm of September. We are bunch-thinning if necessary, the fruit is ripening, and we are still performing crop adjustment to thin down excess crop depending on the type of wine. Everyone is pretty tired of bottling at this point! But we are striving to complete everything in readiness for next month. All of the harvest equipment comes out now to get cleaned up and ready and the cleaning of the tanks is done.

"More wine production in August, early reds and barrel-aged whites, but most of this takes place further into the fall."

Matthew Speck at Henry of Pelham Winery

Simple Seasonal Pleasure

Homemade Creamed Corn

Use the youngest, freshest corn for this summer comfort food. You can gussy it up as you like with chopped fresh herbs or bits of roasted red pepper, but I like it just as it comes. Base the number of ears on the servings: use a sharp chef's knife to scrape the kernels from the uncooked ears of corn, making sure to collect any of the milk that is released as you scrape. When you have as much corn as you want, add it to a large skillet along with a large knob of butter—I'll leave the amount up to you, but don't be stingy. Sauté the corn in the butter for 3–4 minutes and season generously with salt and freshly ground white or black pepper. Gradually add some whipping cream to the corn, stirring it into the corn over gentle heat. Using the back of a wooden spoon or a spatula, gently press down here and there to crush some of the kernels—not all, just some. Continue to cook and add cream until you have the creamy consistency you're after. Serve hot with more salt and pepper. Great with chicken, steaks or burgs.

In Season and On the Table

Chilled Cream of Mustard Soup
with Chicken & Chives

Recommended: Strewn Wines Riesling Terroir Strewn Vineyard
Serves 6

This recipe came about after we attended the annual Hamilton Mustard Festival, held during the Labour Day weekend each year at Ferguson Station. Not many realize that this area is responsible for most of the mustard grown in Canada. The name of this recipe always raises a few eyebrows, but wait until you try this wonderful, full-flavoured soup. Make sure to allow enough time for chilling. Very refreshing on a typically hot August afternoon.

1 large, whole chicken breast, halved	2 egg yolks
6 whole peppercorns	1 cup (240 mL) whipping cream
4–5 sprigs flat-leaf parsley	salt and freshly ground white pepper
1 small onion, unpeeled	to taste
4–5 cups (950–1.2 L) chicken stock	2 Tbsp. (30 mL) Dijon mustard
2 Tbsp. (30 mL) butter	¼ cup (60 mL) finely chopped fresh
1 Tbsp. (15 mL) all-purpose flour	chives
1 Tbsp. (15 mL) dry mustard	

Place the chicken breasts in a good-sized saucepan, scatter the peppercorns over the chicken and add the sprigs of parsley. Quarter the onion and add it to the saucepan (include the skin) and cover with about 3 cups (720 mL) of the chicken stock. Gently bring to a boil over medium-high heat, then immediately reduce the heat to low and simmer, loosely covered, for 20 minutes. Remove from the heat and let the chicken cool in the liquid. When cool, transfer the chicken with tongs to a cutting board. Remove and discard the skin and bones. Cut the chicken into strips, wrap and refrigerate until needed.

Pour the cooking liquid through a sieve and discard the solids. Wipe the saucepan clean and return the strained cooking liquid to it along with the remaining chicken stock (you need about 4 cups/950 mL of liquid in total). Return this mixture to a boil, then reduce the heat and keep warm.

Melt the butter in a medium saucepan over low heat. Whisk in the flour and dry mustard and cook for a minute or so. Ladle some of the hot chicken stock into the mustard mixture. Whisk as it thickens, gradually adding most of the stock. Remove from the heat for a moment as you beat the egg yolks with the cream and season with salt and pepper. Gradually pour this mixture into the hot stock. Whisk and return the saucepan to the heat. Reduce the heat and cook gently for 5 minutes or so. If it thickens too much as it cooks, add a bit more stock. Add the Dijon mustard to the soup mixture, blending it in well with a whisk.

Remove from the heat and transfer to a bowl. Let cool for 15 minutes or so, then loosely cover with plastic wrap and refrigerate for 4–5 hours until well-chilled. To serve, ladle the soup into bowls and garnish with the strips of chicken and a sprinkle of chives.

Winemaker Rob Scapin

Chief winemaker at Jackson-Triggs Niagara Estate Winery, Australian-born Rob Scapin comes to the job with almost 20 years of experience. He started by helping his Italian-born parents make wine from home-grown grapes, went on to study at his native country's Roseworthy Agricultural College and then to work at a number of Australian vine-yards. In 1998 he started with Jackson-Triggs Vintners and has played a significant role not only in the production of some of their award-win-ning wines but in the design of the new winery in Niagara-on-the-Lake. Rob maintains that the future of winemaking in Niagara will be very exciting with high-profile wineries such as Jackson-Triggs prepared to invest in quality "both in the choice of grapes and in advanced wine-making technologies."

The Good Earth Heritage Tomatoes in a Fresh Corn Crust

Recommended: Crown Bench Estates Cabernet Franc Vintner's Reserve
Beamsville Bench Estate Bottled
Serves 4

I love the simplicity and creativity behind this really beautiful summer dish that comes from the Good Earth Cooking School in Beamsville, owned by Niagara native Nicolette Novak. Based on a rustic pastry made with fresh corn and basil, filled with heirloom tomatoes, this pretty presentation defines what Niagara's produce and food is all about. Plan to make the crème fraîche and the corn crust shells ahead of time.

For the crème fraîche:

1 cup (240 mL) whipping cream	¼ tsp. (1.2 mL) salt
juice of ½ lemon	¼ tsp. (1.2 mL) white pepper
½ cup (120 mL) finely chopped fresh chervil	

Mix the cream and lemon juice together in a small measuring cup. Cover with plastic wrap and leave at room temperature for 24 hours.

Stir in the chervil, salt and pepper and refrigerate until needed.

For the corn crust:

4 ears fresh corn	1 tsp. (5 mL) salt
1½ cups (360 mL) all-purpose flour	½ tsp. (2.5 mL) freshly ground black
1 large egg	pepper
1 Tbsp. (15 mL) butter, melted	1 cup (240 mL) fresh basil, chopped

Preheat the oven to 350°F (175°C). Butter 4 3-inch (10-cm) tart moulds with removable bottoms and set to one side.

Using a hand grater, rub an ear of corn against the large-holed side to remove the top portion of the corn into a large bowl. After grating, use the back of a butter knife to scrape the corn "milk" out of the cob. Be careful not to scrape too hard or you may remove the husks as well. Repeat with the remaining ears.

Combine the corn with the remaining ingredients, mixing well. Don't be put off by the moistness of the dough. Flour your hands liberally and use your fingers to press the dough into the bottom and up the sides of the tart moulds. Refrigerate or freeze any excess dough.

Bake in the oven for 35–40 minutes, until firm and golden. Let the shells cool in the pans for 5 minutes, then remove them and cool on a rack.

For the tomatoes:

2 cups (475 mL) any variety of mini heirloom tomatoes (mini green grape, red and yellow striped, pinks, yellow and red pear and black currant)

1 Tbsp. (15 mL) rice wine vinegar
1 Tbsp. (15 mL) grapeseed oil
salt and freshly ground pepper to taste

Cut the larger tomatoes into halves and place in a small bowl with the remaining tomatoes. Sprinkle with the vinegar, oil, salt and pepper. Mix well and let sit for 15 minutes.

(Reserve black currant tomatoes on the stem and use as a garnish.)

To serve, plate a tart shell on a salad plate. Spoon ¼ cup (60 mL) of the crème fraîche into the tart shell. Arrange ½ cup (120 mL) of tomatoes over top of the crème fraîche and garnish with the black currant tomatoes. May be served with mixed greens or fresh chervil as additional garnish.

Grilled Oyster & Portobello Mushrooms on Greens with Asiago Crisps & Walnut Dressing

Recommended: Inniskillin Pinot Noir Reserve
Serves 4

From Chef Izabela Kalabis of Inniskillin, this satisfying first course could easily serve as a main course with the addition of a few sheets of silky prosciutto. Toast the walnuts in the oven before you make the cheese crisps; they will only take a few minutes, so watch them carefully or they will burn.

For the dressing:

1 tsp. (5 mL) Dijon mustard
1 Tbsp. (15 mL) sherry vinegar
1 tsp. (5 mL) finely chopped fresh
   thyme

salt and freshly ground black pepper
   to taste
4 Tbsp. (60 mL) olive oil
1 Tbsp. (15 mL) walnut oil

Whisk together the mustard, vinegar, thyme, salt and pepper. Slowly add the oils, continuing to whisk until slightly emulsified. Adjust the seasoning and set aside until needed.

For the mushrooms:

½ lb. (225 g) portobello mushrooms,
   wiped clean
½ lb. (225 g) oyster mushrooms,
   wiped clean
¼ cup (60 mL) olive oil

2 tsp. (10 mL) finely chopped fresh
   herbs (thyme, rosemary, parsley,
   sage)
2 cloves garlic, minced
salt and freshly ground black pepper
   to taste

Preheat the grill to medium-high. Brush the mushrooms with a mixture of olive oil, herbs, garlic, salt and pepper; grill until they are softened and beginning to crisp round the edges, about 12–15 minutes.

To assemble the salad:

¼ lb. (113 g) Asiago cheese

7 oz. (200 g) mixed salad greens (radicchio, watercress, endive, arugula)

¼ cup (60 mL) walnuts, toasted and roughly chopped

Preheat the oven to 375°F (190°C). Using a cheese slicer, shave wafer-thin slices of Asiago cheese. Place on a baking sheet lined with parchment paper and bake until melted. It should just take a few minutes. Using a spatula, remove the cheese immediately from the baking sheet. It will harden when slightly cooled. Wash and dry the salad greens.

To serve, toss the greens with the dressing. Place the mushrooms and Asiago crisps on top of the greens. Sprinkle with toasted walnuts and serve.

Birchwood Estates

This small estate winery in Vineland may not have the high profile of some, but in its own quiet way it's busy producing a relatively wide variety of wines, many from previous vintages of four and five years ago. The major 2000 vintage was Riesling, an interesting and highly recommended Gewürztraminer-Riesling blend, Pinot Gris, Chardonnay, Gamay, Cabernet Franc and three icewines.

Scarlet Runners with Couscous

Recommended: Lakeview Cellars Estate Winery Gamay Noir Beamsville Bench
Serves 4–6

You can vary this fresh-tasting bean and grain dish with whatever beans are plentiful, or a mixture if you wish. Almost any fresh herbs can be used—basil, mint, parsley, chervil and oregano all work well. Toast the pine nuts beforehand to add extra flavour and texture. This is particularly good with roast or grilled lamb.

2½ cups (600 mL) vegetable or chicken stock

1½ cups (360 mL) quick-cooking couscous

2 Tbsp. (30 mL) extra virgin olive oil

2 small onions, thinly sliced

1 lb. (455 g) scarlet runner beans or other fresh beans, washed, trimmed (halved, if very long)

2 Tbsp. (30 mL) chopped flat-leaf parsley

2 Tbsp. (30 mL) chopped mint

⅓ cup (80 mL) pine nuts

2 Tbsp. (30 mL) lemon juice

salt and freshly ground black pepper to taste

Heat the stock to a boil. Place the couscous in a large mixing bowl. Pour the stock over the couscous, stir once or twice and let stand for 10 minutes, or until the couscous is tender and the stock is absorbed.

Meanwhile, heat the olive oil in a skillet over medium-high heat. Sauté the onions until softened and beginning to colour, about 5 minutes. Add the beans and stir-fry with the onions until the beans are tender, about 10 minutes (less if the beans are particularly skinny). Add the parsley, mint, pine nuts, lemon juice, salt and pepper. Stir to combine well, then add the bean mixture to the couscous. Toss together and serve immediately.

Spaghettini Tomato Toss

Recommended: Thomas & Vaughan Vintners Baco Noir
Serves 4–6

A plethora, an abundance, a never-ending crop of sweet little cherry tomatoes was the inspiration for this simple summer pasta. Use any small, fresh, ripe tomatoes, making sure to include some red and yellow for contrast. You can also use regular-sized heirloom tomatoes and cut them into smaller pieces.

2 lb. (900 g) red and yellow cherry, grape or pear tomatoes, halved lengthwise
2 cloves garlic, minced
1 large onion, finely chopped
½ cup (120 mL) extra virgin olive oil
salt and freshly ground black pepper to taste

1 lb. (455 g) spaghettini or other fine-stranded pasta
1 tsp. (5 mL) coarse salt
½ cup (120 mL) loosely packed fresh basil leaves
¼ cup (60 mL) loosely packed fresh mint leaves

Bring a large pot of water to a boil over high heat. While it is coming to a boil, combine the tomatoes, garlic, onion, olive oil, salt and pepper in a large skillet. Simmer over medium heat until the tomatoes just begin to release their juices, about 6 minutes. Remove from the heat.

Add the pasta to the boiling water along with the coarse salt. Cook until it is tender but firm—don't overcook it. As the pasta is cooking, stack the basil and mint leaves and slice them into fine strips. Add them to the tomato mixture, stirring gently so as not to break up the tomatoes. Drain the pasta thoroughly and return it to the pot. Give the pot a shake or two over low heat to ensure all the water has evaporated. Add the tomato mixture and toss well but gently. Serve immediately with more extra virgin olive oil at the table for drizzling.

Cool Crab Cakes with Lemon Chive Cream

Recommended: Henry of Pelham Family Estate Winery Dry Riesling
Serves 4

These crab cakes are the real deal, possessing just enough of everything besides crab to keep body and soul together. The Niagara region is blessed to have the likes of Niagara Oyster Company in our midst, offering all manner of oysters, shellfish, fresh and smoked fish and more. This recipe just makes four sumptuous little cakes, so choose your dining companions with care. Old Bay seasoning is a great mixture of herbs and spices especially designed for crab and shrimp. Look for it at specialty food shops and good fishmongers.

For the lemon chive cream:

1 large egg

1 Tbsp. (15 mL) roasted garlic (see page 103)

2 Tbsp. (30 mL) fresh lemon juice

$\frac{1}{2}$–$\frac{3}{4}$ cup (120–180 mL) extra virgin olive oil

1 Tbsp. (15 mL) capers, drained

$\frac{1}{4}$ cup (60 mL) finely chopped fresh chives

salt and freshly ground black pepper to taste

Combine the egg, garlic and lemon juice in a blender or food processor and process for a few seconds. With the motor running, slowly add the olive oil (you may not use it all) until the mixture is thick, creamy and pourable. Transfer to a bowl and stir in the capers and chives. Season with salt and pepper, cover and refrigerate until needed.

(continued on page 207)

Roadside stands house Niagara's bounty of beautiful fruit

The Good Earth Heritage Tomatoes in a Fresh Corn Crust (page 200)

For the crab cakes:

1 large egg

2 tsp. (10 mL) lemon juice

¼ tsp. (1.2 mL) Worcestershire sauce

⅔ cup (160 mL) good quality
    mayonnaise

½ tsp. (2.5 mL) dry mustard

¼ tsp. (1.2 mL) celery seed

2 tsp. (10 mL) Old Bay seasoning

salt and freshly ground black pepper
    to taste

1 lb. (455 g) fresh lump crabmeat

1 Tbsp. (15 mL) chopped fresh flat-
    leaf parsley

1¾ cups (420 mL) fine dry
    breadcrumbs

2 Tbsp. (30 mL) unsalted butter

2 Tbsp. (30 mL) olive oil

Whisk the egg in a bowl, and whisk in the lemon juice, Worcestershire sauce and mayonnaise. In a separate little bowl, combine the dry mustard, celery seed, Old Bay, salt and pepper. Stir to blend and add to the egg mixture, blending thoroughly.

Remove and discard any shell or cartilage from the crabmeat and pull it apart into large chunks; don't overdo this, as you want big chunks of crab. Combine the crab with the parsley and 2 Tbsp. (30 mL) of the breadcrumbs, and mix gently with your hands. Carefully combine the crab mixture with the egg and seasoning mixture until just blended. Make four cakes from the mixture (fat, rather than flat), dip into the remaining breadcrumbs and transfer to a plate. Cover the cakes loosely with plastic wrap and let chill for about an hour.

Warm the butter and oil in a large skillet over medium-high heat. Fry the crab cakes for about 4 minutes on each side, until golden brown on both sides, turning once with a spatula. Drain on paper towels and serve with the lemon chive cream.

Vineyard Lamb Burgers
with Wine-Roasted Tomatoes
& Arugula Salad

Recommended: Hillebrand Estates Winery Collector's Choice Merlot Cabernet
Serves 4–6

Hillebrand Estates Winery hold their annual Vineyard Blues Concert during August, set against the backdrop of their Stone Road Vineyards and the beautiful Niagara Escarpment. Blues fans enjoy some of the best wine country cuisine from chef Tony de Luca of Hillebrand's Vineyard Café, great wine and terrific music. More casual fare is also offered, like these hefty lamb burgers that I have paired with the season's ripest tomatoes and peppery greens. Offer some tzatziki with the burgers in place of the usual condiments.

For the roasted tomatoes:

18 small ripe tomatoes	1 Tbsp. (15 mL) walnut oil
¼ cup (60 mL) dry white wine	1 Tbsp. (15 mL) balsamic vinegar
juice of 1 lemon	salt and freshly ground black pepper to taste

You can roast the tomatoes in your oven or outdoors on your grill. Preheat the grill or oven to a relatively low heat, about 212°F (100°C). Pierce each tomato a few times and place in a shallow baking or grill pan. Whisk the white wine, lemon, oil and vinegar in a little bowl. Pour this mixture over the tomatoes and season generously with salt and pepper.

Place in the oven or on the grill with the lid closed and roast for 45 minutes to an hour, checking from time to time to make sure they are not charring or roasting too fast, and adding additional wine if necessary. When they are rather soft and somewhat sunken, turn off the heat and allow to cool in the grill or oven.

For the burgers:

2 lb. (900 g) ground lamb
1½ tsp. (7.5 mL) ground cumin
1 white onion, grated
2 Tbsp. (30 mL) chopped fresh flat-
    leaf parsley

2 Tbsp. (30 mL) chopped fresh mint
1 large egg, lightly beaten
1 tsp. (5 mL) salt
½ tsp. (2.5 mL) freshly ground black
    pepper

While the tomatoes are cooling, prepare the burgers. In a large bowl, combine the lamb with the cumin, onion, parsley, mint, egg, salt and pepper. Mix gently to incorporate all the ingredients; don't overmix. Shape the lamb mixture into 4–6 patties about ¾ inch (1.9 cm) thick. Preheat the grill to medium-high. Place the patties on the grill and cook for a total of 8–10 minutes, turning once, or until nicely browned and a bit pink at the centre.

To serve:

1 bunch arugula, rinsed and trimmed
lemon wedges
4–6 small, warmed pita breads (with
    pocket)

thinly sliced white onion, cucumber
    and tzatziki, for garnish

Arrange the greens on a serving platter, placing the lemon wedges on the side for guests to squirt onto the greens and tomatoes, if they wish. Place the cooled tomatoes (they can still be somewhat warm) next to the arugula. Place the burgers in the pocket of the warmed pita breads and add some sliced onion and cucumber. Pass the tzatziki at the table.

Sicilian-Style Sirloins

Recommended: Pillitteri Estates Winery Cabernet Franc Family Reserve
Serves 6

In deference to the Sicilian heritage of the Pilliterri Estates Winery family just outside the town of Niagara-on-the-Lake, this recipe is inspired by a traditional Sicilian method of marinating and breading the steak before grilling on a hot fire. Absolutely superb summer fare. Serve with a ripe tomato and white onion salad and small potatoes dressed in a garlicky vinaigrette. Plan to make this the day before to allow time for the steaks to marinate.

6 sirloin steaks (3–3½ lb/
   1.35–1.6 kg)
1 cup (240 mL) olive oil
½ cup (120 mL) red wine vinegar
3 cloves garlic, finely chopped
2 Tbsp. (30 mL) chopped fresh
   oregano

freshly ground black pepper to taste
salt to taste
1½ cups (360 mL) Italian-style
   breadcrumbs
½ cup (120 mL) freshly grated
   Parmesan cheese
2 Tbsp. (30 mL) olive oil

Choose a glass dish large enough to hold all the steaks in one layer. Combine the 1 cup (240 mL) of olive oil, vinegar, garlic, oregano and pepper in a bowl. Whisk together and pour over the steaks, rubbing the marinade well into the meat on all sides. Cover with plastic wrap and refrigerate overnight, turning once or twice during that time. Remove the steaks from the refrigerator about half an hour before grilling.

Preheat the grill to high. Transfer the steaks from the marinade to a cutting board and season on both sides with a little salt. Combine the breadcrumbs with the cheese, mix together well and start to apply it to both sides of the steaks, patting the coating onto the meat to help it adhere. Carefully transfer the steaks to the hot grill, drizzle with the remaining 2 Tbsp. (30 mL) olive oil and grill for about 5 minutes. Turn and grill for another 5 minutes on the other side (or to the desired doneness).

Whitty Farms

A fixture at the corner of 7th Street and 4th Avenue in St. Catharines since 1908, Whitty Farms grow fruits and vegetables with a strong focus on flavour, and they pride themselves on their friendly, informed service. Throughout the growing season you'll find strawberries, peaches, nectarines, sweet cherries, grapes, pears, plums, sweet corn, tomatoes, peppers, peas, watermelon, musk melon, raspberries (red, purple, black and yellow!), blackberries, red, white and black currants, gooseberries, northern kiwi, apricots, flowers and fresh herbs. You can purchase produce straight from their roadside stand or take advantage of their pick-your-own program that includes strawberries, peas, raspberries, blackberries, currants and gooseberries.

Venison Chops from Arden with Northern Rice Spaetzle & Shallot Juniper Jus

Recommended: Vineland Estates Winery Reserve Cabernet Merlot
Serves 4

Arden Vaughn of Lake Land Meats provides wonderful farm-raised game to Niagara-area chefs and home cooks. "The advantage of farm-raised deer is that it is available all year round," she says. This recipe is from chef Mark Picone of Vineland Estates Winery. He maintains it will work well during summer, fall or winter; at this time of the year, do as the chef recommends and team it with a variety of grilled peppers and the little irregular dumplings known as spaetzle. You will need a spaetzle press for this preparation, which you should be able to find at cookware shops, country or farm hardware stores.

4 venison chops ($\frac{1}{2}$ rack)
$\frac{1}{4}$ cup (60 mL) extra virgin olive oil
2 Tbsp. (30 mL) chopped fresh herbs
    (rosemary, thyme, sage, parsley)
salt and freshly ground black pepper
    to taste
$\frac{3}{4}$ cup (180 mL) all-purpose flour
$\frac{1}{2}$ cup (120 mL) wild rice flour (grind
    wild rice in a coffee grinder or
    look for this flour at specialty
    food shops)

$\frac{1}{2}$ tsp (2.5 mL) salt
4 eggs
1 Tbsp. (15 mL) water
1 Tbsp. (15 mL) extra virgin olive oil
salt and freshly ground black pepper
    to taste
$\frac{1}{2}$ cup (120 mL) extra virgin olive oil
5 shallots, peeled
$\frac{1}{2}$ cup (120 mL) rich beef stock
1 tsp. (5 mL) juniper berries

Trim the chops of excess fat and place in a glass dish. Mix the $\frac{1}{4}$ cup (60 mL) olive oil, chopped herbs, salt and pepper. Pour over the chops and let sit while you prepare the spaetzle.

Bring a large pot of water to a boil over high heat. Combine the two flours and salt in a bowl and mix well. In another bowl, whisk together the eggs, water and 1 Tbsp. (15 mL) olive oil until well combined. Add the dry ingredients to the wet. When the combination begins to get thick, beat with a wooden spoon. Continue beating the dough until it is elastic and gelatinous, about 2–3 minutes.

Place the spaetzle press over the boiling water, add the dough and press the spaetzle dough into the water. When the spaetzle float to the surface, they are cooked. Remove with a slotted spoon and place on an oiled tray; keep warm.

Heat the ½ cup (120 mL) olive oil in a saucepan to 350°F (175°C). Add the shallots, reduce the heat and cook until tender, about 5–6 minutes. Remove the shallots from the oil (keep the oil for sautéeing, dressings or other uses). In another saucepan, cook the beef stock and juniper berries until reduced by half. Add the shallots and season to taste; keep warm.

Preheat the grill to high. Grill the venison chops for about 4–5 minutes per side (the chef recommends they be cooked to medium rare). To serve, place a portion of spaetzle on a plate, drizzle with a little of the beef reduction, top with a venison chop and drizzle with more of the beef reduction.

Grilled Quail with Peach Salsa

Recommended: Jackson-Triggs Proprietor's Grand Reserve Merlot
Serves 4

"Peaches are such a sexy food," says Michael Olson, whose recipe this is. "They have a beautiful colour, lovely curves and an intoxicating aroma. Going into a walk-in cooler filled to the ceiling with fresh peaches gives you the sensation of drinking in that air, jam-packed with the floral scent of the tender fruit." Try this recipe, too, with 4 boneless chicken breasts.

For the quail:

8 boneless quail

1 Tbsp. (15 mL) chopped fresh thyme

2 Tbsp. (30 mL) olive oil

juice and zest of 1 lime

salt and freshly ground black pepper
  to taste

Place the quail in a bowl. Add the thyme, olive oil, lime juice and zest, salt and pepper, and rub into the quail. Transfer to the refrigerator for about an hour.

For the peach salsa:

4 ripe peaches, peeled and diced

½ red onion, finely chopped

2 Tbsp. (30 mL) olive oil

juice of 1 lime

2 Tbsp. (30 mL) chopped fresh cilantro

2 Tbsp. (30 mL) chopped fresh mint

2 Tbsp. (30 mL) chopped fresh basil

salt and freshly ground black pepper
  to taste

While the quail is marinating, prepare the salsa. Toss all the ingredients together in a bowl and season to taste. Set aside.

To finish the dish:

Remove the quail from the refrigerator. Preheat the grill to medium-high. Season the quail with salt and pepper. Grill, skin side down, for 5 minutes. Turn, season again and grill for another 2 minutes. Serve the quail warm, placed over a portion of the peach salsa.

Grasmere's Apricot Jam

Makes about 3 cups (720 mL)

There is a lovely little coffee shop in St. Catharines called Cream and Sugar, Please. One morning, I arrived there just as the owner had taken a tray of muffins out of his oven. They were moist and sweet and the centre held a piece of warm, melting cream cheese. No muffin has ever impressed me more. That weekend, I made this apricot jam and, inspired by those muffins, baked a batch of muffins of my own and filled them with a bit of cream cheese and a spoonful of this apricot jam. This is a no-fuss jam; it doesn't require processing and just makes a small amount that keeps in the refrigerator. Plan to use it within a month or so. It's also wonderful as a tart filling. If you prefer sweeter jam, add a little more sugar.

2 lb. (900 g) ripe apricots, rinsed,
    unpeeled
1 cup (240 mL) sugar
½ tsp. (2.5 mL) lemon juice

Halve the apricots, discard the pits and place in a fairly wide saucepan (not too deep). Add the sugar, stir together, and cook over medium-high heat. As the mixture begins to simmer, stir fairly continuously so the fruit doesn't stick to the bottom of the pan. Simmer about 10–14 minutes, until it is thickened and jam-like but still has some chunks of fruit. Stir in the lemon juice, then remove from the heat. Let cool before transferring to one large container with a good lid or separate, sterilized jars with tight-fitting lids. Keep refrigerated.

Sunnybrook Farm Blackberry Wine Jellies

Serves 6–8

Sunnybrook Farm Estate Winery is just outside the town of Niagara-on-the-Lake. When next you visit Niagara, make sure to include a foray to this little winery that specializes in capturing the essence of ripe fruit in their collection of carefully produced fruit wines. You won't find Sunnybrook's wines anywhere else; they include wines made from damson plums, black raspberries, cherries, pears, plums, apples, strawberries, peaches, nectarines, blueberries and black-berries. This is not a recipe for a jarred jelly preserve, but rather one for making your own jelled dessert. Jell-o for grown-ups! Serve with a few fresh blackberries and a spoonful of barely whipped, unsweetened cream or a scoop of good vanilla ice cream.

2 oranges
2½ cups (600 mL) water
½ cup (120 mL) sugar
3½ Tbsp. (46.5 mL) gelatin (about
   3½ packets)

1 bottle (750 mL) Sunnybrook Farm
   Estate Winery Blackberry Fruit
   Wine
fresh blackberries and whipped
   cream, for garnish

Use a vegetable peeler to carefully peel the zest from the oranges. Place the zest, water and sugar in a saucepan over medium heat. Bring to a boil slowly, stirring now and then to dissolve the sugar. After 15 minutes or so, remove the saucepan from the heat and whisk in the gelatin all at once. Set to one side for about 10 minutes, stirring now and then to completely dissolve the gelatin.

Squeeze the peeled oranges and add the juice to the gelatin mixture. Pour this mixture into a large bowl—discarding the orange zest—and leave for about 45 minutes, or a little longer, until it has thickened somewhat, but not completely set. (You don't need to refrigerate it during this period.)

Gently and slowly add the bottle of blackberry fruit wine, carefully mixing the wine into the gelatin. Using a ladle, divide the mixture into serving glasses or custard cups. Cover each with plastic wrap and chill in the refrigerator for at least 4 hours, or until set. You can serve the jellies directly from their jelling glass or cup or unmould them by running a thin knife around the edge of each jelly, then carefully inverting onto individual serving plates. Garnish with blackberries and a dollop of whipped cream.

Joseph's Estate Wines

Once upon a time, Joseph Pohorly had a winery named Newark Wines, which he sold in 1982. That winery was renamed Hillebrand Estates. Ten years later Joseph decided to get back in the wine business and in 1996 he opened his second winery, just down the road from his first venture. Using his own grapes and those of neighbouring grape growers, Joseph has built a number of notable wines—a 1999 estate-grown Pinot Noir, Pinot Gris, a non-oaked Chardonnay and Gewürztraminer among them. A number of fruit wines are also available.

Lemon Lime Icebox Cake with Cream

Recommended: Inniskillin Wines Sparkling Icewine
Serves 6

This really delicious sweet would be called a semifreddo *in Italy. It is a refreshing combination of citrus, gelatin and cream that sits in the freezer overnight to set. Perfect for hot summer days and especially nice with the addition of some fresh late summer berries. Make sure to use ultra-fresh, preferably organic eggs for this recipe. Serve with whipped cream, a sprig of fresh mint and a strip of lemon zest.*

4 digestive biscuits or graham wafers, crushed
⅔ cup (160 mL) Grape-Nuts cereal
2 Tbsp. (30 mL) light brown sugar
2 Tbsp. (30 mL) butter, melted
3 large eggs, separated
juice and finely grated zest of 1 large lemon

juice and finely grated zest of 1 lime
⅓ cup (80 mL) granulated sugar
1 Tbsp. (15 mL) powdered gelatin (about 1 envelope)
⅔ cup (160 mL) whipping cream

Choose a 9 x 5-inch (23 x 12.5-cm) loaf pan (preferably ceramic or glass) for this recipe and spray it with a little non-stick cooking spray or oil. Combine the crushed biscuits or wafers with the cereal and the brown sugar and mix well. Add the melted butter and mix again. Use ⅓ of this mixture to line the base of the loaf dish. Put a saucepan of water on to boil over medium-high heat.

In a heatproof mixing bowl, whisk the 3 egg yolks with the lemon and lime zest and juice. Add the granulated sugar and gelatin, continuing to whisk. Place the bowl over the saucepan of just simmering water and continue to whisk (use a hand-held blender if you have one) for about 10 minutes as the mixture thickens. Once it has thickened, remove it from the heat and continue to whisk for another 8 minutes or so, until it's cool.

Beat the egg whites until stiff and set to one side. In another bowl, whip the cream just until softly whipped. Fold the egg whites carefully into the lemon-lime mixture, followed by the whipped cream. Pour the mixture into the loaf dish over the crumb base. Top with the reserved crumb mixture. Cover with plastic wrap and place in the freezer to set overnight.

The next day, transfer the loaf dish to the refrigerator (about 3 hours before you plan to serve). At serving time, dip a thin-bladed knife in hot water and run it around the edges of the cake. Turn it out onto a platter. Cut into serving slices, dipping the knife in hot water and wiping clean in between slices. Keep leftovers refrigerated for up to 2 days.

Winemaker Sue-Anne Staff

In the heart of Niagara-on-the-Lake, Pillitteri Estates Winery is home to winemaker Sue-Anne Staff. Niagara-born, Sue-Anne comes from a juice grape-growing family and took her love of the fruit a step further by studying at South Australia's Roseworthy College. As young as she is, Sue-Anne is responsible for an outstanding 1998 Merlot and 1997 Cabernet Franc and for such reds as her 1998 Pillitteri Estates Family Reserve Cabernet Franc, which won gold at the Challenge International du Vin 2000, Blaye-Bourg, France.

Pickled Peppery Peaches

Makes about 2 pints (950 mL)

This is a great recipe that uses just a few peaches, although you could easily double it. Because the peaches aren't processed in the traditional canning sense, the finished product must be refrigerated. Choose peaches that are just slightly underripe for this recipe so they will retain a bit of firmness. Don't worry about peeling the fruit, just use a coarse towel to rub off most of the fuzz. Wonderful with ham, sausage or any rich meat.

1 cup (240 mL) white wine vinegar
2 Tbsp. (30 mL) sugar
2 Tbsp. (30 mL) coarsely cracked black
    peppercorns

4 small to medium-sized peaches, left
    whole

Have ready two clean and sterilized pint jars, lids and seals. In a mixing bowl, whisk together the vinegar, sugar and peppercorns. Stir until the sugar is completely dissolved. Pack the peaches into the two pint jars. Add the vinegar mixture until it comes ¾ of the way up the peaches. Cover with the lids and turn the jar upside down a few times to evenly distribute the liquid. Refrigerate the peaches, giving the jars the same upside-down treatment once or twice a day. After about a week, the peaches will be ready to serve. They will keep for about 2 weeks in the refrigerator.

Peach Blackberry Frangipane

Recommended: Cave Spring Cellars Late Harvest Riesling Indian Summer
Makes 1 10-inch (25-cm) tart

A beautiful combination of local ingredients results in a stellar sweet from Anna Olson. She says, "the simplicity of the ingredients works well with summertime cooking—spending more time outside than in. Peaches that have some firmness are ideal for this as riper fruit will disintegrate while baking. Serve with quality vanilla ice cream."

2 cups (475 mL) ground almonds
6 eggs, at room temperature
1/2 tsp. (2.5 mL) almond extract
1 3/4 cups (420 mL) granulated sugar

2 peaches, peeled and sliced
1 cup (240 mL) blackberries
icing sugar, for dusting

Preheat the oven to 350°F (175°C). Toast the ground almonds on a baking sheet until lightly toasted, about 12 minutes, stirring occasionally. Allow to cool. Whisk together the eggs, almond extract and granulated sugar in a bowl. Add the ground almonds and blend well.

Pour the mixture into a greased 10-inch (25-cm) tart pan or pie plate with a removable bottom. Arrange the peaches and blackberries on top. Bake for 30–40 minutes, until golden brown and set. Serve at room temperature dusted with icing sugar.

Peach Blush Rosemary Vinegar

Makes 2 cups (475 mL)

You won't find an easier recipe than this or one with more summer appeal. All this requires is a big, fresh, ripe peach, some fresh rosemary, a few pink peppercorns, good cider vinegar and the patience to wait a few days before using it. If you're feeling ambitious and you've picked up a basket of Niagara's wonderful peaches, make a few bottles, and hand out to your best friends at Christmas. Choose a bottle or jar with a wide enough opening to accommodate the chopped peaches. Wash and sterilize beforehand. Choose a clear wine bottle for the final decanting so you can enjoy the beautiful pink blush of the finished vinegar.

1 large (or 2 smaller) ripe peaches, unpeeled, pitted and coarsely chopped

3 sprigs of fresh rosemary
6 pink peppercorns
2 cups (475 mL) apple cider vinegar

Place the chopped peach in the bottle or jar. Add the rosemary and peppercorns, then pour the vinegar over all. Seal the bottle or jar, give it a good shake and store in a dry, dark, cool place for 10 days. Shake it once a day or when you think of it. After 10 days, pour the mixture through a sieve (discard the chopped peaches), Return the rosemary and peppercorns to a sterilized wine bottle (3 cups/750 mL) and seal. This will keep for up to 3 or 4 months in a dark, cool place. Use as the basis for summer vinaigrettes.

September & October

Harvest of Orchard, Field & Vine

Today is September 12. The month has brought the cataclysmic events of the 11th, and the plans for our mid-month outdoor wedding party seem so trivial now. After much thought and talk with each other, family and close friends, we have decided to keep fast to our plans. Jenna echoed the thoughts of many when she said, "Mum, people need a celebration of life and love now, more than ever," and so we do.

With 150 on the guest list, there is much to do. I start by sitting in the gazebo to discuss the menu with my daughters—the first of many gazebo-and-wine meetings on the subject. Must have oysters from Niagara Oyster and I was hot on the idea of a classic pig roast until I chatted with Michael Olson. He quietly pointed out, "Y'know, everybody thinks a big old pig roast is a great idea, but at some point in the festivities, when the guy who's supposed to be tending it has disappeared, all the best bits have been taken and the back yard is a river of melted fat, suddenly the bean salad looks awfully good." Point taken. We've opted for porchetta, the wonderful stuffed pork specialty that I remember having on a visit to Umbria. It is marinated in red wine, partially boned and filled with a fresh herb and meat stuffing made using the pork shoulder. Chef Mario Pingue is going to make it for us. It takes a few days to prepare and needs a huge industrial oven in which to cook it, but Mario will bring it ready to be presented on the morning of the party. Sounds good to me. Mario's father, Mario Sr., is renowned in the area for his prosciutto. It is the best I have tasted outside of Italy. I was planning on making those tiny Italian rice balls filled with fontina cheese—arancini—as an appetizer to go with Vineland Estates Winery Riesling Cuve Close. But having a daughter whose partner is chef Chris McDonald clearly has its perks, as he has generously offered to prepare them at Avalon, his Toronto restaurant. Am I lucky. As for the remainder of the menu, after much debate we're going with Tuscan bread salad; chick peas with finely chopped Swiss chard and carrots; creamy polenta with sage, fresh corn, cream and Parmigiano-Reggiano and poached salmon with smoked red pepper mayo based on Ted's intensely flavoured smoked peppers. Then a big green salad with mustardy vinaigrette, lovely treats from Criveller Candies and Pastries in Niagara Falls and peaches that I steeped in Henry of Pelham Dry Riesling. We'll fill them with torrone gelato from the Italian Ice Cream place in Niagara Falls. Zweigelt-Gamay from Henry of Pelham and their Vidal and, of course, lots of brew from Niagara Brewing Company. As for the *pièce de résistance*—the cake—well, I'm lucky again.

SEPTEMBER 14. Leading up to the main event and as I rush about, I take time now and then to watch Jenna fully engrossed in the production of our beautiful wedding cake—three tiered, round cakes, sandwiched with her own lemon curd and iced so beautifully with palest yellow butter icing. She has her Gran's way with cakes and pastry; so patient and methodical and careful as it comes together beautifully. Alysa and Jenna decorate it with slim branches holding clusters of tiny navy blue berries and lengths of delicate white lysianthus. It takes my breath away.

SEPTEMBER 15. The day is here, the sun is shining, the sky blue, the temperature pleasant. Best of all, the unmistakable scent from the farmer's fields up the road has happily dissipated—it was pungent, to say the least.

Once again, Alysa is the hard-working queen of organization and delegation—if it wasn't for her, I'd still be sitting in the gazebo in a daze, wondering what to tackle first. She decorates the tables with beautiful, rather old-fashioned roses. They have an antique quality about them, dusty red, edged with cream. She sets them around white candles within glass domes tied with translucent ribbons of green and burgundy. The brewery has generously loaned us the large wooden bar they use at beer festivals and events and Ted happily sets it up just at the entrance to the garage—his very own private Niagara Brewing bar. Malpeque oysters are being shucked, the piper plays, we open the bubbly from Vineland and the show begins. The food is remarkable, the wine wonderful, our family and friends generous and loving. We dance and sing the night away and begin to run out of steam late in the evening just as the cool night thickens around us. Let's do this at the close of every summer!

SEPTEMBER 25. Where has the month gone? The big Grape and Wine Festival parade is this weekend in downtown St. Catharines.

We have had earlier-than-usual shows of colour on trees, due, I think, to the extreme dryness of the summer. Our own grapes have grown fat and deep blue. The rain we have had for the last two days and nights continues this morning. It is cool—definitely pack-the-shorts-away weather. *The Old Farmer's Almanac* predicted it would be a little cooler than September is meant to be. This is an especially welcome change after the unusually intense heat experienced during the previous months. As if to underline the switch, the fuel oil truck made its first scheduled delivery today.

Every evening features a sky made beautiful with sunset, no matter the weather. All month we have been enjoying the last of our vegetable garden: tomatoes, parsley, chard, carrots, beans and collected herbs. And we are trying to process as much of the local fruit as possible.

Peaches! The likes of which I have never experienced, especially the Harrow Beauty variety. Karen Whitty of Whitty Farms says they are her

favourite of all the peaches. I think they just may surpass my beloved Red
Havens. I blanched and peeled at least a bushel, turned some into a wonderful peachy preserve with lemon and sugar and the rest into croustades,
pies and bags and bags for the freezer. After a quick blanching, the skins
slip off between my fingers, revealing the rosy, pale orange flesh. As I work,
their sweet, floral scent fills the kitchen. They are such a sensual pleasure
to work with. I slice them with Mum's little paring knife and remember
the last summer of her life and the peaches we prepared together. The slices
tumble quickly into my big stainless steel bowl, their perfume clinging to
my fingers. I shake a little sugar and ascorbic acid over the slices to preserve their lovely colour, add a splash of water, give them a toss and pack
them into freezer bags. Some cold wintry day, when we need a hit of summer on the table, I'll bake them with a cobbler top and their scent will
transport us back to these hot sultry days.

As for tomatoes, I can't resist them, irrationally buying a bushel of ripe
plum tomatoes from a nice Italian lady named Jemma outside of Niagara-
on-the-Lake. Our Pathfinder should have a bumper sticker that says "I
brake for fresh tomatoes." I blanch, peel and freeze them alongside the
bagged peaches.

Then I succumb to pepper lust, with a restrained purchase of just half
a bushel. We pick them up when visiting the newly reopened St.
Catharines Farmer's Market. They are shepherd peppers. Ted smokes them
in our smoker, along with some of the tomatoes, just to see what they will
be like. I peel and pack the peppers in olive oil with leaves from my bay
tree. And I cannot resist—and cannot remember ever seeing in Ontario
before—the Damson plums I also bring home. Just the same as those I
picked in England from a little ownerless tree. I will make more chutney,
I think, with these. So pretty, purple and petite.

SEPTEMBER 30. This has been the closing weekend for the Niagara Grape
& Wine Festival. The weather is sublime, everything the beginning of fall

in Ontario should be. The air shimmers with that special fall light, as though a filter has been removed from the sun. Again *The Old Farmer's Almanac* is right about the weather. Slight breeze, just enough to encourage the odd leaf to flutter and fly. We find a nest of baby mice and their parents in the little barn, nestled in a gardening bag. We buy fruit trees today (Bartlett pear and red plum) to go with the three (Italian plum, multi-pear and Red Haven peach) given to us by good friends Lori and Gail. Trying to decide where to place them.

Smoke-roasted tomatoes are whirred together with ripe plum tomatoes to reduce the intensity of the roasted ones, then combined with sautéed onion, garlic, celery, carrots, rough-chopped leftover ham. I use this smoky tomato sauce to dress tagliatelle, dust it with freshly grated Parmesan, drizzle with peppery olive oil. So good.

I also use some of the sauce in a beef stew made with chunks of beef and dry red wine. It gives it just the right balance of flavour, colour and body. Unmistakable smoke!

Thanksgiving weekend, with Jenna, Colsen and Adam. A perfect fall weekend, we visit a pumpkin patch and go for a trek through Short Hills. The park is resplendent this time of year. Fresh, free-range turkey from Klagers, the butcher in Fonthill, is very, very good. I make two stuffings, the usual one and a sausage stuffing with apricots.

Jenna makes her wondrous butter tarts as a special treat for Ted. Their taste and fragrance are of my childhood, tasting exactly as Mum's did. Jenna also makes Edna Staebler's whisky pumpkin pie recipe from *Food That Really Schmecks*. Still the best.

As the turkey roasts, we tackle the front yard, raking up pails full of chestnuts and leaves. The clear light of autumn continues. Between 6 or 7 p.m. it shafts through the branches and leaves of the two horse chestnut trees.

The grapevine outside my office window is now totally bereft of grapes (which bubble in a pot along with the damsons as I write, on their way to chutney). The remaining leaves have a lovely aged quality, the vines still so strong. It would be nice to make something with them, a wreath perhaps.

OCTOBER 13. We are overrun with crazy ladybugs in the house and outside. The weekend just past was unseasonably, strangely warm, and multitudes of them (some pale orange with no black dots) cling to the doors and windows. They fly bizarrely at us, oddly aggressive. On Saturday night, a cool, wild wind helped to disperse them. In the morning, just a few ex-ladybugs lay around.

Driving around the area, it is so beautiful to see fat bunches of grapes hanging on the vines, plump apples in trees. Ted planted our new fruit trees at the far end of our property. They look like slim sentinels, sparse leaves dutifully changing. He wants to plant more so that one day we will have a small orchard.

Monday morning brings bright sun and cool temperatures. Rain is apparently on the way for the next few days. We have brought some of the last green tomatoes into the house to hang, still on their vines, upside down. Apparently they will ripen this way. Plan to bring the parsley in and let it live in a pot in a kitchen window.

OCTOBER 25. A handsome, wild day, filled with a bright, cool, whistling wind, a holdover from last night's lightning, thunder, rain and wind that whined and whooshed all night. Serves to remind us that we live at the top of the escarpment. Temperature has dropped considerably and is expected to go lower this afternoon and tonight. Thousands of leaves have left the trees. I have found two bird's nests, thrown from their perches. How beautifully they are made, perfectly rotund interiors, ready for another batch of eggs next spring, I attempt to re-nestle them in the highest branches I can reach, hoping they will stay there. Casey and I walk the trail and I can't help but pick up as many of the fallen, somewhat sticky pine cones as my pockets can carry. Perhaps I'll make a wreath of pine cone, chestnut and grapevine. The tangle of grapevine outside my window is beautiful, almost matted. The leaves fly by my window like slim, coloured birds.

The black walnut trees have lost almost all their leaves, but we don't see any of the tennis ball-sized fruit; only a few since the end of the summer have fallen. Within the hard dome is the nut, almost impossible to get out, apparently, but the green fruit has a pleasant, fresh citrus-pine fragrance.

OCTOBER 31. There is a perfectly full moon for All Hallows Eve, which is breezy and wet. I hear the geese every night again. We burn never-ending leaves and eat the last of the tomatoes that have been hanging from our kitchen rafters to ripen on their vine. I find myself thinking already about vegetables I will grow next year. Fingerling potatoes for sure. The very mild weather is more like spring than fall. Yet I know winter is in the wind.

In the Vineyard and On the Vine

"Hopefully, this is our harvest period from mid to late September and October. This should be the core of the harvest. On the farm—the vineyard—picking grapes is the main occupation. This is when the farm, vineyard and winery really come together. Starting early in September we sample grapes. We don't grow all our own grapes, it's sort of a half-and-half operation. We have our own and about a dozen growers between here and Beamsville supply the rest. By the end of September and beginning of October, the harvest is in full swing. In the winery, this is absolutely the busiest time, unlike the vineyard's busiest time—that would be spring.

"The winery runs two shifts a day during harvest, 18 hours a day, seven days a week. Seventy-five percent of the wine making is in that precise harvest time. We're selecting vineyards, picking at just the right time and getting that fruit from vine into tank in as timely and efficient a manner as possible, and getting fermentation underway.

"We redo 'cap management,' that is, skin contact management. The wine is really started in the vineyard, but it is during this fermentation time that its structure is formed. The wines change daily, almost hourly, now—very quickly. From morning to evening it alters, and you have to be right on top of it.

"The crush, or harvest, is the make or break time; this is when you can do something really fabulous or really screw it up. Sort of like running a great restaurant or steakhouse—you can buy the best quality meat and have a great kitchen and other ingredients, but if the guy cooking it leaves it sitting on the grill too long—or not long enough—it will be ruined.

"In the hospitality area, the busiest time is September and October. All operations are in full swing. The Grape and Wine Festival makes for a very busy 10-day period, with lots of people coming out to see the harvest and experience our wines. Lots of tour groups, too, now.

"The top reds of two years ago will be coming out and reds from the previous year.

"In September we face an annual problem—most of the young people who have been working with us all summer head back to school, and that leaves us a little short-staffed.

"Christmas really starts for us right about now, as we begin to ship wine out and start thinking about our gift baskets and how they will be put together. We are heavily weighted towards restaurant sales, with 40 percent of our wine sold in restaurants, and they are getting ready for the busy end of year time, too."

Matthew Speck at Henry of Pelham Winery

Simple Seasonal Pleasure

My Fast Tomato Sauce

You can make this with fresh tomatoes or good-quality canned plum tomatoes. It is a snap to make and unfailingly good. Unlike meat-based tomato sauces, it doesn't need a long cooking time. Roughly chop a couple of good-sized onions and as much garlic as you like. Splash some good olive oil in a large, heavy skillet—one that is wider than deep. Heat the oil slightly and add the onions and garlic. Give it a good stir and leave it to simmer for a few minutes. Chop up about 8 or 10 ripe tomatoes (or open a couple of big cans and snip them with kitchen shears right in the can), and throw them into the pan (if using canned, use some of the juice and reserve the rest). Stir them together with the onion mixture and add a generous amount of sea salt and lots of grinds of black pepper. Add a smidge of sugar and stir again. Bring everything to a boil and then reduce the heat to allow it to cook slowly and gently, uncovered. Taste it after a few minutes and adjust the seasoning. (If you like your sauce spiced, now is a good time to throw in a few crumbled dry chilies.) Just before it completely thickens, add a couple of spoons of good balsamic vinegar and cook until thickened. Use with any pasta you like.

In Season and On the Table

Mini Arancini with Fontina *234*

Salad of Chickpeas, Swiss Chard & New Carrots *236*

Parmesan Cream with Grilled Red Wine Bread *238*

Roasted Garlic Charred Tomato Bisque *240*

Jerusalem Artichoke & Yukon Gold Chowder

with Sautéed Wild Mushrooms & Goat Cheese Croutes *242*

Grilled Caprese Salad *244*

Eisbock Mussels with Double-Smoked Bacon *245*

Creamy Polenta with Fresh Corn, Sage & Parmesan *246*

Duck Tamale with Red Pepper Coulis & Popcorn Seedlings *247*

Honey-Roasted Duck with Crisp Spring Roll & Soy Apricot Syrup *250*

Balsamic Vinegar & Herb-Marinated Pork Tenderloin *252*

Niagara Pear & Hazelnut Tart *253*

Whitty Farms Harrow Beauty Peaches

in Henry of Pelham Dry Riesling *254*

Wine-Poached Plums with Mascarpone Cream *255*

Green Zebra Tomato Pickle *256*

Grasmere's Grape & Peach Chutney *257*

Mini Arancini with Fontina

Recommended: Vineland Estates Winery Riesling Cuve Close
Makes about 24

Arancini is Italian for "little oranges," a name given to these savoury rice balls because of their shape and colour after they are fried. When formed smaller than is traditional, they make terrific appetizers. You can make them entirely ahead of time and then reheat them in the oven before serving.

2 cups (475 mL) Arborio rice (short grain)
½ tsp. (2.5 mL) saffron threads, crushed
4 cups (950 mL) chicken stock
4 eggs
½ cup (120 mL) freshly grated Parmesan cheese
½–¾ lb. (225–340 g) fontina cheese, cut into ½-inch (1.2-cm) cubes
2 cups (475 mL) fine dry breadcrumbs
olive or vegetable oil for deep-frying

Combine the rice, saffron and stock in a large saucepan. Place over medium-high heat and bring to a boil. Give it a good stir, reduce the heat to as low as possible, cover and cook until the liquid is absorbed and the rice is tender but still a little firm, about 15–17 minutes. Transfer the cooked rice to a bowl and let cool to room temperature.

Whisk 2 of the eggs and add them to the cooled rice, along with the grated Parmesan cheese. Mix thoroughly. Wet your hands and shape the rice mixture into little balls, using about 2 Tbsp. (30 mL) of the mixture for each ball (or make them a little larger if you prefer). Press the centre of each ball to make a little well and insert one cube of cheese into the indentation. Cup your hand around the rice and roll it into a ball, encasing the cheese. Continue with the remaining rice mixture and cheese. Whisk the remaining 2 eggs in a bowl and place the breadcrumbs in a shallow bowl or plate. Roll each rice ball in the beaten egg, then in the breadcrumbs, rolling it around to completely coat it. Transfer to a tray lined with parchment paper as you work.

Place a baking rack within a baking sheet. Preheat the oven to 175°F (80°C). Heat the oil in a heavy saucepan (or deep fryer if you have one). Use a candy thermometer to determine when the oil has reached 360°F (185°C). Fry the rice balls (no more than 6 at a time) in the hot oil, turning them often, until they are golden brown all over, about 2–3 minutes. Use a slotted spoon to transfer them to the baking rack and keep them warm in the oven while you finish frying the remaining rice balls. Keep testing the oil temperature as you work and, if necessary, allow it to return to the recommended heat before continuing. Serve the arancini warm.

Salad of Chickpeas,
Swiss Chard & New Carrots

Recommended: Thirteenth Street Winery Sandstone Gamay Noir
Serves 6–8

When we made this for 150 wedding party guests, we bought a lot of dried chickpeas. You can substitute canned, if you must, but it is so much better made with chickpeas you cook yourself and it really doesn't take long. Serve this just warm or at room temperature. When chilled it's not as flavourful. Great with pork, chicken or as part of an antipasto spread.

1 cup (240 mL) dried chickpeas, soaked overnight in water to cover

2 cloves garlic, peeled

⅓ cup (80 mL) olive oil

2 lb. (900 g) Swiss chard, rinsed and thick stems trimmed

1 red onion, peeled and chopped

3–4 young carrots, scraped and chopped

salt and freshly ground black pepper to taste

1 cup (240 mL) dry white wine

3 ripe plum tomatoes, peeled, seeded and chopped (canned is fine)

1 cup (240 mL) roughly chopped fresh flat-leaf parsley (leaves only)

½ cup (120 mL) roughly chopped fresh basil

juice of 1 large lemon

Drain the chickpeas and transfer to a saucepan with just enough water to cover. Add the garlic and 1 Tbsp. (15 mL) of the olive oil (don't add salt as it encourages them to split while cooking). Bring to a boil over high heat, reduce the heat and simmer for about 40–45 minutes or until tender.

As they are cooking, place the Swiss chard in a large pot, cover with boiling water, then drain immediately. Let cool slightly, then transfer to a cutting board and roughly chop. Set to one side.

In a large saucepan or skillet, warm the rest of the olive oil over medium-high heat and sauté the onion and carrot until tender, about 10–12 minutes. Season with salt and pepper. Add the wine and cook until reduced a little. Add the chopped tomatoes and continue to cook until the mixture has thickened.

Add the Swiss chard and the chickpeas, mix to combine well and cook for another 10 minutes. Remove from the heat and add the parsley, basil and lemon juice. Taste once more for seasoning, then transfer the mixture to a large, shallow serving bowl. Serve warm or at room temperature.

Criveller Candies & Pastries

Located on Lundy's Lane, right next door to the Niagara Brewing Company, you'll find one of Niagara's best-kept secrets. Criveller Candies & Pastries is an Italian sweet lover's dream come true. This chocolate and pastry boutique, filled with handmade chocolates, delicate and intricately made pastries and other delightful sweets, is more like an authentic European sweet shop than any I have found in Toronto or elsewhere in Canada. Splendid wedding cakes, too. Wonderful quality, beautiful craftsmanship, sublime tastes.

Parmesan Cream
with Grilled Red Wine Bread

Recommended: Malivoire Wine Company Old Vines Foch
Serves 4

This is a rustic sort of appetizer that you should reward yourself with after a hard day's gardening. Enjoy it outdoors on a late summer day. Make sure to use a good country-style bread for this, otherwise it won't stand up to the wine or the grill treatment. Plan to make the Parmesan cream the evening before. Garnish this with fresh thyme sprigs, if desired. This is also very good with prosciutto and ripe cherry or grape tomatoes.

For the Parmesan cream:

1 cup (240 mL) freshly grated
    Parmesan cheese
1 cup (240 mL) whipping cream

1–2 sprigs fresh thyme
freshly ground black pepper to taste

Place all the ingredients in the top of a double boiler over simmering water. Whisk as the cheese melts. Once it has melted, pour the mixture through a sieve into a bowl. Let cool, then cover with plastic wrap and refrigerate overnight.

For the grilled red wine bread:

4–6 thick slices rustic bread
1–2 cloves garlic, halved
Malivoire Wine Company Old Vines
    Foch, for drizzling

salt and freshly ground black pepper
    to taste
extra virgin olive oil, for brushing

(continued on page 239)

Harvest of the vine—captured

Whitty Farms Harrow Beauty Peaches in Henry of Pelham Dry Riesling (page 254)

Preheat the grill to high. Rub the bread on both sides with the garlic. Place your thumb halfway over the mouth of the wine bottle and drizzle both sides of the bread with some of the red wine (don't soak the bread). Season the bread with salt and pepper and brush both sides of the bread with olive oil. Grill the bread on both sides for a few minutes until toasted and browned lightly.

To serve, use an ice cream scoop to place a portion of the Parmesan cream next to a slice of the grilled bread.

Italian Ice Cream Company

Gelato lovers will swoon over the selection of housemade Italian-style ice creams at this little shop in Niagara Falls. We ordered torrone gelati (nougat) for our wedding party to serve with my Riesling-soaked peaches and it proved to be a fabulous combination. Besides the wide variety available, they are happy to customize something especially for you. Great place to stop for an espresso or capuccino, too.

Roasted Garlic Charred Tomato Bisque

Recommended: Thomas & Vaughan Vintners Baco Noir
Serves 4

From Virginia Marr, chef at the Pillar & Post in Niagara-on-the-Lake, comes this great late summer soup that features the smokiness of charred tomatoes along with fresh (or canned) tomatoes. This is one soup that can be enjoyed hot or chilled.

1 large onion, peeled and quartered
1 clove elephant garlic
8 medium plum tomatoes, cored
1 Tbsp. (15 mL) olive oil
2 Tbsp. (30 mL) brown sugar
2 cups (475 mL) peeled, chopped tomatoes, fresh or canned (with their juice)

½ cup (120 mL) rich chicken stock, heated
salt and freshly ground black pepper to taste
6 leaves fresh basil, cut into fine strips

Preheat the grill to high. Slide a toothpick through the onion quarters to keep them intact. Thread the garlic clove on 2 toothpicks or a skewer. Grill the onion and garlic until softened and slightly blackened. Remove the toothpicks or skewers, crush the garlic and set all to one side.

Place the tomatoes on the grill to char and blister the skin. Use tongs to turn them and char the skins evenly. Transfer to a plate and let cool slightly. Peel the skins off and coarsely chop the tomatoes.

Place the oil in a medium saucepan over medium-high heat, and sauté the grilled onions and garlic for 2–3 minutes. Add the sugar, being careful not to scorch it. Stir and scrape the bottom and sides of the pot, then add the grilled tomatoes, the 2 cups (475 mL) fresh or canned tomatoes and the heated broth. Turn up the heat and bring to a boil, then reduce the heat to medium-low. Cook until the mixture is reduced by half, stirring occasionally, about 20 minutes. Using a hand-held blender, purée the soup. Adjust the seasoning with salt and pepper and pour into soup bowls. Garnish with the fresh basil.

Grimo's Nut Nursery

It might be quicker to list the things that don't grow in Niagara than to recite the growing numbers of things that do. Nuts, for instance. At Grimo's Nut Nursery, located just outside the town of Niagara-on-the-Lake, they not only sell fresh nuts, they will supply you with butternut, Persian walnut, black walnut, northern pecan, American and Chinese chestnut trees and lots more. Owner Ernie Grimo is a member of the Society of Ontario Nut Growers and is co-author, with Robert Smith, of *Nuts About Heartnut Cooking*, a cookbook devoted to heartnuts, a "seed sport" of the Japanese walnut tree.

Jerusalem Artichoke & Yukon Gold Chowder with Sautéed Wild Mushrooms & Goat Cheese Croutes

Recommended: Inniskillin's Klose Vineyard Chardonnay
Serves 8

From Izabela Kalabis at Inniskillin, this is perfect as a precursor to a Thanksgiving dinner. A very satisfying soup, featuring some of the season's best—potatoes, parsnips and wild mushrooms.

4 Tbsp. (60 mL) unsalted butter

1 medium onion, peeled and chopped

2 cloves garlic, minced

2 parsnips, peeled and chopped

½ lb. (225 g) Yukon Gold potatoes, peeled and chopped

2 lb. (900 g) Jerusalem artichokes, peeled and chopped

4 cups (950 mL) chicken or vegetable stock

2 cups (475 mL) mushroom stock (fresh or use a stock cube)

salt and freshly ground black pepper to taste

½ cup (120 mL) whipping cream

pinch nutmeg

1 Tbsp. (15 mL) unsalted butter

1 cup (240 mL) assorted wild mushrooms, wiped clean and chopped

1 clove garlic, minced

salt and freshly ground black pepper to taste

1 Tbsp. (15 mL) chopped fresh flat-leaf parsley

8 small rounds of sourdough or egg bread

2 oz. (57 g) goat cheese

Melt the 4 Tbsp. (60 mL) butter in a Dutch oven or similar pot over medium heat, and gently cook the onion until translucent, about 5 minutes. Add the garlic and cook for another minute. Add the chopped parsnip, potato and Jerusalem artichoke and cook for a minute or two, stirring to mix well and coat the vegetables with the butter mixture. Add the two stocks, season with salt and pepper and bring the mixture to a gentle boil. Reduce the heat and simmer gently for about 30 minutes. Use a hand-held blender (or conventional blender or food processor) to purée the mixture. Add the cream and nutmeg and taste for seasoning. Keep the mixture hot at a very low heat while you prepare the garnish.

Melt the 1 Tbsp. (15 mL) butter in a sauté pan over medium heat and add the mushrooms and garlic. Season with salt and pepper and cook for a few minutes until the mushrooms are softened and cooked. Remove from the heat and stir in the parsley.

Preheat the broiler. Toast the rounds of bread, turning them once, until golden. Spread each one with a bit of goat cheese, then slip beneath the broiler again to melt the cheese. Ladle the chowder into bowls. Place a portion of the sautéed mushrooms in the centre and a croute on the side.

 ### *Willow Heights Estate Winery*

Perhaps the boutique winery with the strongest Mediterranean feel, Willow Heights is owned and run by the Speranzini family and employs traditional viticultural methods to produce novel whites and big reds, including a respected Pinot Noir. They feature tours and tastings and the chance to enjoy their wines on a sun-flooded patio. Billing themselves as "Niagara's best kept secret," many critics feel that this is one winery to watch mostly due to the Old World winemaking methods and philosophies employed by winemaker Ron Speranzini.

Grilled Caprese Salad

Recommended: Magnotta Winery Marechal Foch
Serves 6

If you like the classic caprese salad of sliced ripe tomato and thickly sliced buffalo mozzarella, you'll warm to this grilled variation. You will need to use hefty, meaty tomatoes, like beefsteaks, which are substantial enough to stand up to the grill. Easy, delicious and very pretty. Serve it with lots of good, crusty bread.

2 Sicilian (globe) eggplants
2 zucchini
6 green onions, trimmed
3 Tbsp. (45 mL) extra virgin olive oil
2 beefsteak tomatoes
salt and freshly ground black pepper
    to taste

2 large, fresh buffalo mozzarella,
    about ¼ lb. (113 g) each, sliced
2 Tbsp. (30 mL) chopped fresh flat-
    leaf parsley
extra virgin olive oil for drizzling

Slice the eggplant and zucchini crosswise about ⅛ inch (.3 cm) thick. Transfer to a bowl and add the green onions (left whole). Toss together with 2 Tbsp. (30 mL) of the olive oil and season with a little salt and pepper. Slice the tomatoes ¼ inch (.6 cm) thick and brush with the remaining 1 Tbsp. (15 mL) olive oil.

Preheat a lightly greased grill to medium-high and place the vegetables on the grill. As they start to soften, turn them just once (they should cook for 2 minutes per side). To assemble, drizzle a little oil on each serving plate and alternately layer the tomato, eggplant, zucchini and mozzarella (you should use 2–3 slices of cheese per serving). End by draping a length of green onion over the top. Scatter the parsley over the salad and finish with another drizzle of olive oil if desired.

Eisbock Mussels with Double-Smoked Bacon

Recommended: Niagara Brewing Limited Edition Eisbock
Serves 4–6

Chef Roberto Fracchioni of Inn on the Twenty likes to use Niagara Brewing's fabulous winter brew, Eisbock, when he steams fresh mussels—nothing better on a cool fall day. If you're feeling energetic, make a batch of frites to go with and you'll have one of the world's great food and beer combinations. Eisbock comes housed in a 750-mL bottle, so pour what you need onto the mussels and then enjoy the remainder as they cook—chef's perks. Serve this with lots of good, crusty bread and ice-cold Eisbock.

2 Tbsp. (30 mL) olive oil

1¼ cups (300 mL) diced double-smoked bacon

2 cloves garlic, minced

6 lb. (2.7 kg) mussels, scrubbed and debearded, if necessary (discard any that do not close when tapped)

1⅔ cups (400 mL) pearl onions, peeled and left whole

2½ cups (600 mL) diced tomatoes

2 sprigs fresh thyme, leaves only, chopped

2 sprigs fresh marjoram, leaves only, chopped

2 cups (475 mL) Niagara Brewing Eisbock

Choose a large pot for this recipe. Set it over low heat, add the oil and bacon and cook slowly to allow the bacon to release its fat. After a few minutes, increase the heat. When hot, add the garlic, mussels, onions, tomatoes and herbs. Sauté, stirring once or twice, for 2–3 minutes.

Add the beer, cover the pot and cook for 6–7 minutes or until all the mussels are opened. Discard any that are closed.

Creamy Polenta
with Fresh Corn, Sage & Parmesan

Recommended: Henry of Pelham Family Estate Winery Vidal
Serves 6

Even people who think they aren't fond of polenta swoon for it when prepared this way, with fresh corn, cream, Parmesan and sage. Delish. If you like, you can spread this mixture out to cool on a solid surface, cut it into squares, grill it, and top it with chopped, fresh tomatoes tossed with herbs and good olive oil. If you have cooked corn leftovers from another meal, use it here. And if it was grilled or roasted, so much the better.

2 cups (475 mL) whole milk
2 cups (475 mL) water
1 Tbsp. (15 mL) unsalted butter
1 Tbsp. (15 mL) coarse salt
1½ cups (360 mL) yellow cornmeal
½ lb. (225 g) fontina cheese, shredded

2 cups (475 mL) freshly grated Parmesan cheese
1 cup (240 mL) whipping cream
4 ears cooked corn, kernels cut from the cob (to make 2 cups/475 mL)
¼ cup (60 mL) roughly chopped fresh sage

Combine the milk and water in a heavy saucepan and bring to a boil over medium-high heat. Stir in the butter and salt. Reduce the heat to low and start to add the cornmeal in a slow, thin stream, whisking constantly. Switch to a wooden spoon and stir the mixture every minute or so until it pulls away from the sides of the pan in one mass, about 20–25 minutes. Stir in the fontina and Parmesan cheeses. When melted, add the cream, corn and sage. Stir to incorporate all the ingredients and serve when heated through.

Duck Tamale with Red Pepper Coulis & Popcorn Seedlings

Recommended: Pillitteri Estates Winery Family Reserve Merlot
Serves 6

Virginia Marr, chef at the Pillar & Post, created this inventive dish that combines two late-summer favourites: red peppers and fresh corn, along with that other chef favourite—Muscovy duck breast. Chipotle is a smoked jalapeño pepper most often sold in cans in combination with a wonderful tasting sauce called adobo. Look for these (and the corn husks) in specialty food shops or any markets selling Mexican-style foodstuffs.

To marinate the duck breasts:

4 large boneless Muscovy duck
    breasts, trimmed
juice and zest of 1 lime

1 tsp. (5 mL) mashed chipotle (see
    note above)

Place the duck breasts in a shallow glass dish. Combine the lime juice, zest and chipotle. Pour over the duck breasts and rub it in well. Cover with plastic wrap and refrigerate for 2–6 hours.

For the tamale mixture:

2 Tbsp. (30 mL) butter
8 ears corn, kernels cut from the cob
    (to make 4 cups/950 mL)
1 roasted red bell pepper, finely
    chopped
1 bunch fresh chives, finely chopped
2 Tbsp. (30 mL) all-purpose flour

⅓ cup (80 mL) whipping cream
1 egg, beaten
½ bunch cilantro, washed and
    chopped
salt and freshly ground black pepper
    to taste

Melt the butter in a skillet over medium-high heat and sauté the corn until cooked, about 3–5 minutes. In a blender or food processor, purée half the corn until smooth, then combine it with the remaining cooked corn kernels. Transfer to a mixing bowl and add the roasted red pepper, chives, flour, cream, egg, cilantro, salt and pepper. Mix well, cover with plastic wrap and chill in the refrigerator for 10 minutes or so.

For the red pepper coulis:

2 roasted red bell peppers, roughly
  chopped
1½ cups (360 mL) extra virgin olive oil

salt and freshly ground black pepper
  to taste

Blend the red peppers to a purée, adding the olive oil in a slow stream until you have a thick, emulsified mixture. Transfer to a bowl, season with salt and pepper and set to one side.

To assemble the dish:

7 dried corn husks
1 pinch saffron

popcorn seedlings or other sprouts,
  for garnish

Place the corn husks in a bowl, crumble the saffron over them and cover the husks with hot water. Let them sit for a few minutes, then transfer the soaked husks from the water to a clean kitchen towel. Use one of the husks to make 12 strips for tying. Lay the remaining 6 husks on a flat surface.

When you're ready to assemble the dish, preheat the oven to 350°F (175°C). Place a generous spoonful of corn mixture on each husk. Roll up the husk and tie it at each end to secure (like a Christmas cracker). Place the tamales on a baking sheet and bake for 15–20 minutes.

Meanwhile, prepare the duck. Place a sauté pan over high heat until hot. Sear the duck breasts, skin side down, for 3–5 minutes, then reduce the heat to medium-high. (This will render the fat from the duck to produce a crispy skin.) When the skin is crispy, turn the breast over and continue cooking for another 3 minutes, or to the desired doneness. Remove from the pan and let rest for a few minutes before slicing on the bias.

To serve, drizzle the plate with red pepper coulis, lay the sliced duck breast over the coulis and place one tamale on each serving of duck. Garnish with popcorn seedlings, other sprouts or any delicate greens. Serve immediately.

Lailey Vineyards

Long before the opening of their winery, Donna and David Lailey had a strong connection with the land. David's father, William Lailey, planted some of Niagara's first French hybrid varieties back in the 1950s and when the couple purchased the land from David's parents, they began the job of transforming the 20-acre fruit farm into a vineyard. At first their grapes were used by other wineries (like Southbrook Winery) to make a number of award-winning varietal wines. In addition to this, the Laileys have also supplied premium juice to amateur winemakers for the past 16 years. In 1991 Donna Lailey was crowned the Niagara Grape & Wine Festival's first ever Grape Queen, an award that is bestowed on the best vineyard of the season. Today Lailey Vineyard Winery has a brand-new winery building complete with retail store and a talented winemaker in Derek Barnett, the British-born winemaker who is responsible for much of Southbrook's success and shares co-ownership of Lailey.

Honey-Roasted Duck with Crisp Spring Roll & Soy Apricot Syrup

Recommended: Daniel Lenko Estate Winery Old Vines Merlot
Serves 4

A recipe from chef Stephen Treadwell of the Queen's Landing inn, who pre-serves his own apricots each season. Failing this ingredient, poach a few fresh apricots in a sugar syrup until soft and tender. Canned apricots (reserve syrup) could also be substituted. Parsley root—available at good fruit and vegetable markets—is a carrot-like root vegetable with a flavour that is a cross between carrot and celery. You can also use its leaves as you would parsley. Start prepa-ration for this dish a day ahead, as the duck breast requires a 12-hour season-ing period.

For the duck:

1 large boneless Muscovy duck breast
2 Tbsp. (30 mL) coriander seed
2 Tbsp. (30 mL) white peppercorns

4 tsp. (20 mL) unpasteurized Ontario honey

Trim the excess fat and skin from the duck breast. Place a sauté pan on high heat. When it's hot, sear the duck breast skin side down for 3–4 min-utes in total, turning it once, until the skin is golden brown. Grind the coriander and white peppercorns together, using a mortar and pestle or coffee grinder. Rub this mixture well into both sides of the duck. Drizzle the honey over both sides of the duck. Place on a plate, cover with plastic wrap, and use a heavy can to weight it down. Place in the refrigerator for 12 hours.

For the spring roll:

2 large leaves Savoy cabbage, trimmed and blanched

1 parsley root, trimmed and very thinly sliced in 2-inch (5-cm) lengths

1 young carrot, trimmed and very thinly sliced in 2-inch (5-cm) lengths

1 daikon radish (or regular radish), trimmed and sliced into thin lengths

1 Tbsp. (15 mL) chopped fresh ginger

4 sheets rice paper, blanched

Lay out the blanched cabbage leaves on a work surface. Divide the parsley root, carrot, radish and ginger evenly between the leaves. Roll up tightly, cover in plastic wrap and refrigerate for an hour. Remove the plastic wrap, slice each roll in half on the bias, then tightly re-roll each half in one of the blanched rice papers. Set to one side.

To finish the dish:

4 Tbsp. (60 mL) preserving syrup (from apricots)

1 Tbsp. (15 mL) light soy sauce

4 whole preserved apricots (or canned apricots)

fresh chervil or cilantro, for garnish

Wipe the excess spice rub from the duck breast. Place a sauté pan on high heat and when hot sear the duck breast, skin side down for 2 minutes. Flip and sear on the other side for about the same length of time (this will result in a rare duck breast, which is recommended). Keep warm while you warm the preserving syrup with the soy sauce in a small saucepan.

To serve, place one of the spring roll pieces in the centre of a plate. Cut the duck breast into 4 pieces and place a slice on top of the spring roll. Garnish with a preserved apricot and some fresh chervil or cilantro and drizzle a little warm sauce around the edge.

Balsamic Vinegar & Herb-Marinated Pork Tenderloin

Recommended: Inniskillin Chardonnay Schuele Vineyard
Serves 4

Inniskillin's chef, Izabela Kalabis, not only prepares dishes for special wine-makers' dinners at the winery in Niagara, but is involved in a number of events associated with the winery in Toronto throughout the year. Here is her recipe for an Italian-styled pork entrée that she likes to pair with roasted Yukon Golds and a summer squash stir-fry. Try it, too, with the Creamy Polenta with Fresh Corn, Sage & Parmesan (page 246). Allow 6 hours for the pork to marinate.

¼ cup (60 mL) balsamic vinegar
1 Tbsp. (15 mL) chopped shallot
½ cup (120 mL) mixed fresh herbs
(oregano, basil, thyme, sage, chervil, tarragon)

1 clove garlic, minced
¼ cup (60 mL) olive oil
1½ lbs. (680 g) pork tenderloin

Combine the vinegar, shallot, herbs, garlic and olive oil in a blender or food processor and blend to a paste. Cut little shallow nicks in the pork and spread the paste over the entire tenderloin, rubbing it in well. Transfer to a glass dish, cover with plastic wrap and leave to marinate for 6 hours in the refrigerator. Remove from the refrigerator about half an hour before grilling.

Preheat the grill to medium-high. Grill the pork about 10 minutes per side, or until the juices run clear—be careful not to overcook it. Transfer to a cutting board and let rest for 10 minutes. To serve, slice on the bias.

Niagara Pear & Hazelnut Tart

Recommended: Royal DeMaria Winery Vidal Icewine
Serves 6–8

This is a very simple tart with few ingredients, a good choice when you would like something pretty and impressive for dessert, but don't have time to fuss—thanks to the use of frozen puff pastry. Just make sure to roll the pastry out as thin as possible, because it will puff up considerably when baked. If you like, you can make six or eight individual tarts instead of a large one. You can also substitute peaches, apricots, apples or plums for the pears. Serve warm with unsweetened whipped cream or good vanilla ice cream.

½ package (375 g) frozen puff pastry, thawed

½ cup (120 mL) ground hazelnuts

3 ripe (but firm) pears, peeled, cored and thinly sliced

3 Tbsp. (45 mL) unsalted butter, melted

3 Tbsp. (45 mL) sugar

Roll out the pastry until it's very thin (⅛ inch/3 mm), and about 10–11 inches (25–28 cm) in diameter. Drape the pastry over the rolling pin and transfer it to a fluted tart shell. Use a fork to prick the pastry in a few places. Refrigerate for about 20 minutes.

Preheat the oven to 425°F (220°C). Remove the pastry from the refrigerator and sprinkle with the ground hazelnuts. Arrange the pears in a concentric pattern in the pastry shell, ending with a few set in the centre. Brush or drizzle with the melted butter and scatter the sugar over the surface.

Bake in the preheated oven for 30 minutes until lightly golden brown.

Whitty Farms Harrow Beauty Peaches in Henry of Pelham Dry Riesling

Recommended: Henry of Pelham Family Estates Winery Riesling Icewine
Serves 8

What could be more representative of Niagara than this lovely peach sweet? These are the peaches I prepared (in bulk!) for our wedding party. We filled them with wonderful torrone (nougat) gelato from the Italian Ice Cream Company in Niagara Falls. The peaches need a few hours standing time. Fill the peach cavity with ice cream or unsweetened whipped cream if desired and serve with biscotti, shortbread or other crisp biscuit.

1 bottle (750 mL) Henry of Pelham Dry
Riesling
½ cup (120 mL) sugar
4 strips of lemon zest

6 ripe (but firm) Harrow Beauty
peaches

Combine 1 cup (240 mL) of the wine, the sugar and the lemon zest in a saucepan over low heat. Stir to dissolve the sugar, then increase the heat slightly and simmer for 15 minutes. Remove from the heat and add the remaining wine. Stir to mix well, then set aside.

Bring a pot of water to a boil over high heat. Add the peaches carefully and blanch for about 30 seconds. Use a slotted spoon to transfer the peaches to a bowl of ice water and let chill. Drain and pull the skins from the peaches with the help of a paring knife. Halve the peaches, remove the stones and place the peach halves in the wine mixture. Make sure the peaches are completely submerged, cover and refrigerate for at least 1 hour and up to 6 hours, stirring now and then. To serve, place a peach half on a glass plate along with a generous spoonful or two of the poaching liquid.

Wine-Poached Plums with Mascarpone Cream

Recommended: Sunnybrook Farm Estate Winery Damson Plum Fruit Wine
Serves 6

Use ripe, red-skinned plums to make this easy dessert. Choose from one of a number of full-flavoured fruit wines from Sunnybrook Farm Estate Winery, located just outside of Niagara-on-the-Lake. Instead of the damson plum wine mentioned here, you could substitute the black raspberry, blackberry or cherry. Plan to make this the day before serving.

10 firm ripe red plums	1 cup (240 mL) mascarpone
3 Tbsp. (45 mL) sugar	1 cup (240 mL) plain yogurt
2 cups (475 mL) Sunnybrook Farm	1 tsp. (5 mL) pure vanilla extract
Damson Plum Fruit Wine	1 Tbsp. (15 mL) sugar
1-inch (2.5-cm) piece cinnamon	

Halve the plums and remove their pits. Combine the 3 Tbsp. (45 mL) sugar with the fruit wine in a saucepan, stir to dissolve the sugar, then add the plums and the cinnamon stick. Place over medium heat and gently poach the plums in the wine for about half an hour. Remove from the heat and let cool in the poaching liquid. When cooled, cover and refrigerate overnight.

When ready to serve, prepare the mascarpone cream by blending the remaining ingredients in a small bowl. Serve the plums in a glass dish or bowl, along with some of the poaching liquid and a dollop or two of the mascarpone cream.

Green Zebra Tomato Pickle

Makes about 6 pints

Green zebra tomatoes are grown exclusively for Niagara-on-the-Lake's Vintage Inns by Dave Perkins at Wyndym Farm. Substitute other ripe tomatoes if you wish. This pickle is good with grilled meats, cold ham or salami, with sausages, in sandwiches and with cheese. The recipe is from Oban Inn chef Andy Dymond.

7 lb. (3.2 kg) green zebra tomatoes (look for these at specialty produce markets)
1¾ lb. (800 g) Spanish onions, sliced
½ cup (120 mL) kosher or pickling salt
1⅔ cups (400 mL) brown sugar
¼ cup (60 mL) mustard seeds, toasted

2 Tbsp. (30 mL) ground cloves
3 cinnamon sticks
2 Tbsp. (30 mL) ground allspice
3 cups (720 mL) apple cider vinegar

Slice the tomatoes ¼ inch (.6 cm) thick. Layer the slices in a shallow dish with the sliced onions. Sprinkle generously with the salt. Refrigerate for 24 hours.

Remove from the dish the following day and allow to drain in a colander for 2 hours. Discard the liquid, then transfer the tomato mixture to a heavy saucepan. Add the remaining ingredients and stir. Place over medium-high heat and when the mixture begins to bubble, reduce the heat. Simmer until it has a jam-like consistency, about 1 hour, stirring often. Remove the cinnamon sticks. Pour into sterilized jars and seal according to jar manufacturer's directions. After opening, keep refrigerated.

Grasmere's Grape & Peach Chutney

Makes about 3 pints

I made this great-tasting grape chutney with the little Concord grapes that grow on our arbour just because I couldn't bear not to use them for something. I have to admit I didn't process the chutney in the recommended way—I simply poured it into sterilized jars, fastened with clean lids and placed all the jars in my big freezer. This is very good with so many things—try it.

2½ lb. (1.1 kg) Niagara Concord grapes
2 peaches, unpeeled, pitted and chopped
1 lemon, unpeeled and chopped
2 onions, peeled and chopped

2¼ cups (535 mL) packed brown sugar
2 cups (475 mL) malt vinegar
2½ tsp. (12.5 mL) salt
2 tsp. (10 mL) curry powder
2 tsp. (10 mL) ground ginger

Place all the ingredients in a heavy saucepan. Bring to a boil over high heat, reduce the heat and simmer for about 75 minutes, or until the mixture thickens and the lemon is quite soft, stirring occasionally. Pass mixture through a food mill or sieve. Transfer into hot sterilized jars and seal according to jar manufacturer's directions, or cool and freeze. Keep refrigerated after opening.

November & December

Celebrating the Winter Solstice

The beginning of November has brought very mild and damp weather, albeit with big winds that sent a lovely freshness through the house last night as we sat watching the World Series. It is being held for the first time in November due to September 11 and the awful aftermath.

The horse chestnut trees, my seasonal markers, are almost completely bereft of leaves. They've been that way some time, due no doubt to the intense summer drought. How many chestnuts have we collected? Untold numbers. They are a burnished shiny brown and feel so good in my hand. Today, November 2, is overcast and almost warm. I do hope it gets colder, as it should be at this time of the year. No matter the temperature, when the calendar says November I find myself wanting to make crispy roast chicken, braises, earthy comfort things, rustic French preparations, strong flavours to go with strong wine.

NOVEMBER 7. Today is as bright as bright can be, with a seamless blue sky. A lovely light glints off what is left of the leaves. Went for a walk with Casey on the other side of Lake Gibson, through the trees, over fallen branches and the carpet of oak leaves. I love the ancient grapevines, thick and substantial, twisting up the lengths and along the branches of trees to hang over the water. Where the water meets the clay bank, a grouping of assorted leaves float on the surface of the water, looking like a worn patchwork quilt. It is fresher, cold, see-your-breath weather this morning and first frost is evident on the grass. I see a brilliant cardinal and his dowdy wife pecking in the remnants of our vegetable garden. Must get some birdseed—the supper for which they have paid in song.

Otherwise November remains unseasonably mild, with much rain. We rake and rake the leaves into huge piles, gather the endless horse chestnuts and enjoy the woodsmoke from our leaf fire. The very definition of pungent, it is never smelled any more in the city. I remember it from my childhood, but as Toronto grew and grew, fires to burn garden waste were disallowed. Necessary, I guess, but what a shame to lose this fragrant essence of fall.

NOVEMBER 15. Alysa comes for dinner and we pick up boneless rib steaks to go with the earthy dish she plans to make. It must be the world's most outrageous potato and wild mushroom gratin. Red-skinned potatoes are sliced very thin before being bathed—submerged really—in heavy cream, which absolutely disappears once made. Within the middle it features a layer of sautéed chanterelles. Oh my, it is good and perfect with the beef and some simply cooked rapini. We eat it all and also much good cheese for dessert. Ted serves Daniel Lenko Estate Winery Warren Private Reserve Cabernet Sauvignon to go with.

NOVEMBER 26. At the end of this month, this year's Niagara Brewery's Eisbock 2002 is launched—looking forward to tasting it and comparing it to last year's. So good by the fire with cheese and fresh-cracked nuts after a brisk, early-winter walk.

Well, it is the beginning of December and I am disappointed by the mildness. Last year at this time there was snow. None yet. You could almost go without a jacket or coat at the beginning of this month and that's just not right. And by the side door our forsythia bush is blooming. That is definitely not right.

DECEMBER 10. Geese go back and forth in such earnest flight from one lake to another. They don't seem to know whether they are coming or going. What do they make of this mild weather, I wonder? Does it confuse their schedule? The lake behind our house is high, the trail soft and mucky, as Casey and I take our walks. The day is so pretty, just barely cold, but with a lovely clear sky and lots of ground frost making the grass appear dusted with fine sugar this morning. I have made a beef hot pot with Niagara Brewing's Olde Jack and added carrots—they are not traditional but they make it almost a one-dish dinner for tonight, which is tree-trimming night.

DECEMBER 13. Our Christmas Open House this Saturday. With our busy schedules and shrinking time frame, I am trying to keep it simple and classic with great cheese and wine, but I am envisaging a beautiful chicken liver mousse preparation I would like to make and goat's cheese tarts (little rounds of chèvre partially wrapped in puff pastry and baked . . . mmmmm). Also thinking of those lovely big Mennonite sausages in red wine with onions and served with squares of polenta with Parmesan, also little cheese puffs—*choquettes au fromage*—prosciutto and Fontina pastries and the like. Hmmm, definitely seems to be a cheese theme, here.

I met with chef Mark Picone at Vineland Estates Winery today. Mark came to Vineland in the spring of 1996. He often has young chefs from around the world—Holland, Italy, Germany, Scotland—coming to work in his kitchen. He grew up in Dundas, Ontario, and is a graduate of University of Guelph but says his first teachers were his parents. "I come from a food family," he says. He tells me about all his food suppliers, including a Japanese gentleman who grows Asian pears, regular pears, apples, kobacha squash (you can eat the entire thing, skin and all) and a Japanese vegetable called myoga (mee-O-ga), a root tuber that belongs to the ginger family. Mark spent five years in Italy and longs to be there often. He worked at two olive oil farms as well as one of Tuscany's best restaurants. "When I came back from Italy I never felt I would find local ingredients in this part of Canada like chestnuts, figs, pecorino and prosciutto [from the Pingue family] and arbutus berries. They are a strawberry-like fruit with soft mango-like flesh—amazing." We talk about good olive oil, one of my passions, and he tells me he holds an olive oil dinner (tasting) each spring. I joke that we have one every evening at home. He strives to use local ingredients almost exclusively at Vineland, because "the demand is here," and only brings in the most rudimentary supplies from outside this area. He has flour delivered every three days from a nearby Mennonite family, the Neufelds. They bring in white, whole wheat and buckwheat flour, the best Yukon Golds Mark has ever tasted and fresh eggs. And he is thrilled to know he can get spent grain from the Niagara Brewery for use in his bread baking.

DECEMBER 17. Ted's birthday is coming up—I think I'll cook him a classic bistro-style dinner. Perhaps duck with a stuffing of herby potatoes and maybe a first course of fat scallops in a sauce of crème fraîche and a little single malt. Maybe sticky toffee pudding for dessert instead of a cake. But then there is his perennial favourite, panna cotta. Wouldn't panna cotta be lovely with some sort of crimson sauce?

Today is December 18 and, like the days leading up to it, rather grey, damp and overcast. The only bright bit of outdoor goings-on have to do with the bird feeders and suet ball that hang outside my office window. The chickadees cling to the ball as they peck and swing; looks like a carnival ride for birds. The squirrels hang upside down to nibble at the sunflower seeds in one of the feeders, very dexterous. We had a dusting of snow on December 10, as we trimmed our tree. It could not have been lovelier or better timed. But later that night, the temperature rose slightly and rain washed all snow traces away. Looks like it might be a green Christmas.

This morning I made Ted a birthday fry-up complete with my home-made potato bread, fried tomatoes, mushrooms, egg, sausages and pro-sciutto. I got up earlier than him and made a sour cream coffee cake embedded with McIntosh apples. I don't think he'll need lunch.

We are looking forward to Christmas very much, an early one with Andrew, Ian and Emma, then Alysa, Jenna, Colsen, Ted and I, Ben and Chris to be at dinner on *the* day. Am thinking about the usual seafood preparations for Christmas Eve: some clams from Niagara Oyster as well as our favourite sautéed shrimps spiked with chilies and lemon.

As for baking, perhaps a yeast braid for Christmas morning, a Dundee cake for Win and Mac, Ted's parents. Potato bread and the traditional cookies, of course. Alysa and I talked about goose for dinner.

DECEMBER 24. As if ordered, it snows again, big fat feathery flakes, right on schedule, late at night. We have huge succulent clams from Niagara Oyster paired with garlic and butter tossed with linguine followed by wedges of hot smoked salmon with a lovely Pinot Blanc from Vineland Estates Winery.

Christmas dinner is prepared mostly by Alysa and Chris. And I have more time to play with Cole—what could be nicer? I make a cauliflower and potato soup, with Chris adding his own little touch, the leftover hot smoked salmon chopped up and crisped in a hot pan then mixed with chopped chives. Lovely garnish with the creamy soup. Alysa took full charge of the goose, stuffed it with a fragrant fruity stuffing filled with apples, prunes, and chestnuts. My bay leaf tree is growing profusely indoors, so we used its leaves to scent and flavour the stuffing, and before our goose was cooked Chris scored it like a ham and brushed it with some of my *nettare d'uva*—Italian grape nectar. This is a dark elixir that I brought back from the Slow Food Festival in Turin where I had it drizzled on creamy panna cotta. Braised endives, mashed potatoes with black pepper, pickled red cabbage. A true Dickensian feast, complete with dark and light fruit cakes, our holiday cookies, warm mincemeat tarts and wonderful English Stilton.

DECEMBER 30. The birds love the suet ball and sunflower seeds. Chickadees, woodpeckers, cardinals, blue jays . . . still waiting for those orioles to come back. Have to get different seed, I think. Not everyone loves the winter birds—certainly not the wineries with icewine grapes still on the vine, waiting for the three-day freeze. For them the hungry birds are decidedly unwelcome. This year, it seems as though the freezing weather will never arrive.

In the Vineyard and On the Vine

"Harvest is in and now we are busy fighting the birds, netting the icewine grapes to keep them well protected. We had a lot of rain this year in November but it didn't hurt because we had such intense drought during the entire summer. What we never want is lots of rain in October.

"We always hope to be picking icewine grapes in December, usually right around the holiday—preferably before, but it doesn't always happen that way. Scaring those birds off is the big priority right now.

"As far as the shop goes, we are busy with Christmas gift orders; this is the period when we traditionally sell lots of wine. Hopefully we're selling what we've bottled from the previous year.

"In the winery from early to mid November, we are busy doing cellar work with wine in tanks. We are involved in lots of barrel work, getting the reds into barrel and other cellar work. Otherwise December is a rather quiet time, other than the picking of the icewine grapes, if that is happening."

Matthew Speck, Henry of Pelham Winery

Simple Seasonal Pleasure

Mulled Wine

Chef Mark Picone of Vineland Estates told me how to make the best mulled wine I have ever tasted. You'll make it more than once during the winter. Choose a big saucepan and fill it with one bottle of Vineland Estates Cabernet Sauvignon, 2 cups (475 mL) of quality apple cider, ½ cup (120 mL) liquid honey, a 2-inch (5-cm) stick of Ceylon cinnamon (look for this at East Indian or specialty food outlets, or substitute regular stick cinnamon), 1 small orange and 1 small lemon, both unpeeled and sliced, 3 or 4 cloves, the same number of allspice berries and a fresh (or dry) bay leaf. Bring this mixture to a simmer and let simmer for about 10 minutes before straining and serving warm.

In Season and On the Table

APPLES, MULLED WINE, OYSTERS, SCALLOPS, TROUT, BUTTERNUT SQUASH,
CHICKEN LIVER PÂTÉ, GOAT'S CHEESE, QUAIL, FOIE GRAS, OXTAIL, PORK TENDER-
LOIN, CAULIFLOWER, GOOSE, BEEF, CRANBERRY, PEAR, TRUFFLES

Mr. & Mrs. Kingsmill's Far Superior Chicken Liver Pâté *269*

Niagara Oyster & Lemon Shooters *272*

Niagara Oyster Co. Clams Casino *273*

Gravlax of Trout with Dill & Mustard Sauce Kaiser *274*

Seared Scallops on Buckwheat Blinis *276*

Butternut Squash Soup with Maple Sage Cream *278*

Goat's Cheese Packets with Fresh Thyme *280*

Tortelli of Game & Reggiano in Oxtail Cabernet Broth *281*

Quail Timbale with Foie Gras, Chardonnay Pears & Maple Syrup Splash *284*

Pork Tenderloin with Smoked Apple Dumplings *286*

Classic Cauliflower Cheese *289*

Alysa Cooks a Goose with Chestnut, Apple & Prune Stuffing *290*

Short Ribs of Beef in Niagara Gritstone Ale "Ketchup" *292*

Grasmere's Peach Bread Pudding with Whisk(e)y Sauce *294*

Napoleon of Fresh & Preserved Figs with Benedictine Crème Fraîche
& Vanilla Almond Shortbread *296*

Apple Ginger Crisp with Honey Mascarpone *299*

Cranberry Pear Croustade *300*

Panna Cotta with Strewn Wines Cabernet Sauvignon Raspberry Sauce *302*

Icewine Apple Butter *304*

Gewürztraminer Granita 305

Cabernet Truffles *306*

Helen Lenko's World-Famous Apple Pie

Daniel Lenko's Mum, Helen, makes a terrific apple pie and, if you're lucky, when you drop in to the Lenko Winery to sample a wine or two, you might just be offered a slice. Daniel says it should be served with Daniel Lenko Select Late Harvest Vidal—and who are we to argue? Here is the recipe as it was given to me; I thought it was just too honest and home-spun to gussy up.

$\frac{1}{2}$ cup of butter, $\frac{1}{2}$ cup of Tenderflake Lard, 2 cups Five Roses Flour, pinch of salt, $\frac{1}{2}$ cup water. Mix flour, butter, lard, salt quickly by hand. Add water a little at a time. Work ball of dough quickly. Do not overmix !!!! Dust with flour. Divide dough in half . . . roll out bottom crust and top crust. Place in 10 inch pie plate; lightly greased.

Fill pie shell with [peeled] sliced Matsu apples. Sprinkle a few teaspoons of sugar and a dab of butter. Sprinkle cinnamon and/or nutmeg if you like. Apply top crust. Press edges together with fork. Prick holes in top with fork. Sprinkle a little white sugar on the top. Bake 1 hour in 400°F oven. Enjoy hot with vanilla ice cream and Daniel Lenko Select Late Harvest Vidal.

Mr. & Mrs. Kingsmill's
Far Superior Chicken Liver Pâté

Recommended: Henry of Pelham Family Estate Winery Gamay Noir
Serves 20

I often choose to live life on the edge; that's why I like to test recipes on my friends and loved ones. It tempts fate, I know, but what the hey, they still love me. I decided to try out my planned preparation for satin-smooth chicken liver mousse on a group of friends we had invited to a little informal Christmas gathering. My proposed silky mousse was, well, not. Furthermore it lacked that flavour oomph that makes you want to eat more than you really should. I was despondent, but my good buddy and good food lover David Kingsmill, said, "It just needs butter and lots of it—why don't you try Bonesie's recipe—far superior to any." Now, on matters of food and drink, I always listen to David because he is just so smart. So, off I went back to the kitchen armed with his recipe (that originated with his equally smart and wonderful wife, Bonesie, aka Marian). He was right. So here, with their very kind permission, is the Kingsmill recipe that was first introduced in David's really terrific book Home Bistro *(Key Porter 1996); it will change your mind forever about the humble chicken liver. Serve to very good friends (like David and Bonesie) with thinly sliced baguette or good white bakery bread, toasted and crusts trimmed. Don't forget a little dish of gherkins, too.*

4 Tbsp. (60 mL) olive oil

1 medium onion, chopped

1 medium shallot, chopped

3 rashers bacon, chopped

5 cloves garlic, finely chopped

$\frac{1}{4}$ tsp. (1.2 mL) salt

5 grinds fresh black pepper

1 tsp. (5 mL) dry chervil

$\frac{1}{2}$ tsp. (2.5 mL) ground coriander

1 Tbsp. (15 mL) finely chopped fresh flat-leaf parsley

1 Tbsp. (15 mL) finely chopped fresh oregano

4 fresh sage leaves, finely chopped

1$\frac{1}{4}$ lb. (565 g) chicken livers, cleaned of membranes

$\frac{3}{4}$ cup (180 mL) all-purpose flour

2 eggs

$\frac{1}{4}$ cup (60 mL) whipping cream

$\frac{1}{2}$ cup (120 mL) softened unsalted butter

2 Tbsp. (30 mL) crushed black peppercorns

3 rashers bacon

Heat 1 Tbsp. (15 mL) of the olive oil in a frying pan; add the onion, shallot and the chopped bacon and sauté for 10 minutes over medium-low heat, until the onions are limp and translucent but not browned. Add the garlic, salt, pepper, chervil, coriander, parsley, oregano and sage; sauté for 5–7 minutes or until the herbs have been absorbed into the mixture. Remove from the pan and set aside.

Add the remaining 3 Tbsp. (45 mL) olive oil to the frying pan and increase the heat to medium-high. Coat the chicken livers in the flour and place them in the frying pan. Brown the livers without burning them, about 3–4 minutes on each side, or until the edges appear beige and the livers start to bleed. Remove the livers from the pan and let cool.

Combine the eggs, cream and butter and beat with a whisk or electric mixer until well blended. Preheat the oven to 350°F (175°C). Place the onion mixture, the livers and the egg mixture in a food processor and pulse until it has a smooth and even texture.

(continued on page 271)

The barrel at work

Panna Cotta with Strewn Wines Cabernet Sauvignon Raspberry Sauce (page 302)

Sprinkle 1 Tbsp. (15 mL) of the peppercorns into an oiled pâté baking dish. (The more finely crushed they are the more peppery the taste.) Pour the liver mixture into the dish. Sprinkle with the remaining peppercorns, then cover with the remaining 3 bacon rashers.

Cover the baking dish and place it in a pan filled with hot water that comes halfway up the sides of the pâté dish. Bake for 1½ hours. Remove from the oven and allow to cool. To serve, run a hot knife around the edges of the pâté and unmould onto a serving platter.

Featherstone Estate Winery & Vineyard

Featherstone Estate Winery & Vineyard is set on 23 acres of prime grape-growing land of the Beamsville Bench and is winning accolades for a number of its wines, all of which are made using only the grapes the owners grow themselves. David Johnson, winemaker, and his wife, Louise Engel, are well-known in the Guelph area for their culinary expertise at the Guelph Poultry Gourmet Market, a company they established in 1986. They come to the wine industry from careers dedicated to excellence in food and a passion for wine. David was originally an accomplished amateur winemaker who now tends to the vines and the vinification of the harvest at Featherstone. His goal is to craft balanced, elegant wines true to their varietal characteristics and indicative of the vineyard's terroir. In 2001 Featherstone won a gold medal for their 2000 Off-Dry Riesling, a silver for their 2000 Vidal Blanc and their 2000 Barrel Fermented Chardonnay as well as a number of bronze medals, all from the Great Lakes Wine Competition.

Niagara Oyster & Lemon Shooters

Makes 6 cocktails

Like the best caviar, briny oysters are a good match for icy vodka. These are fun and festive—just the thing to kick-start holiday festivities or serve as a delightful precursor to a special dinner. This is easy to increase for extra guests.

6 fresh-shucked oysters (choose a
    smaller variety, like Kumamoto)
6 oz. (¾ cup/180 mL) ice-cold lemon
    vodka
hot sauce, to taste

Set out 6 elegant, chilled, shooter-style glasses. Add an oyster to each followed by 1 oz. (30 mL) vodka and a splurt of hot sauce. Serve and slurp.

Niagara Oyster Co.

In 1995, St. Catharines-born James Krieger started work at Rodney's Oyster House in Toronto and soon became synonymous with the place and the mollusk. For two years he shucked and served oysters, advising patrons and gathering knowledge along the way. Then he was promoted to manager of purchasing and got involved with caterers and the city's top chefs. He participated in shucking festivals, fundraisers and competitions and travelled around North America representing Rodney's, all the while learning all there was to know about the subject of oysters and seafood in general. Today, ever-smiling James and his wife, Tracy Vencel-Krieger, own and operate their own company, Niagara Oyster, bringing a wealth of experience—not to mention great fresh seafood—to the Niagara region.

Niagara Oyster Co. Clams Casino

Recommended: Peninsula Ridge Estates Chardonnay Barrel Aged
Makes 24

Tracy Vencel-Krieger of the Niagara Oyster Company knows a thing or two about clams, oysters, mussels and the like. She and her husband, James Krieger, are the owners of this great little company that is beloved by professional chefs, home cooks and oyster lovers alike. This is Tracy's recipe for a classic clam appetizer.

24 pieces East Coast clams (littleneck or topneck), scrubbed and rinsed
2–3 cloves garlic, minced
2 small shallots, minced
2 Tbsp. (30 mL) chopped fresh flat-leaf parsley
2 Tbsp. (30 mL) chopped dill
3–4 cups (720–950 mL) fresh breadcrumbs

$\frac{1}{2}$ cup (120 mL) melted butter
4 Tbsp. (60 mL) olive oil
$\frac{1}{4}$ cup (60 mL) grated Romano cheese
salt and freshly ground black pepper to taste
3–4 shots hot sauce

Place the clams in a pot with just enough salted water to cover the bottom. Place over high heat and steam the clams until they have all opened, about 10 minutes. Let cool; discard any clams that haven't opened. Scoop the clam meat from the shells and chop with a sharp chef's knife (don't use a food processor for this). Set the empty clam shells aside.

In a large mixing bowl, combine the chopped clams with all the remaining ingredients, adding more olive oil or butter if needed for moistness. Preheat the oven to 375°F (190°C). Stuff the mixture into the half shells and bake for approximately 15 minutes, until golden brown. Serve hot.

Gravlax of Trout
with Dill & Mustard Sauce Kaiser

Recommended: Inniskillin 2000 Late Autumn Riesling
Serves 15–20

Co-founder with Donald Ziraldo of Inniskillin Wines, Karl Kaiser kindly gave me his recipe for the classic Swedish specialty, gravlax. This curing method is usually applied to salmon, but Karl says it also works well with trout—and he's right. Start preparations for this 3 or 4 days in advance. You will need a large glass or enamel dish (about 10 x 18 x 2 inches/25 x 46 x 5 cm) and a couple of bricks wrapped in foil, to be used as weights. This is a great party piece.

For the trout:

¼ cup (60 mL) pickling salt
½ cup (120 mL) sugar
4–6 lbs. (1.8–2.7 kg) trout fillets
1 large bunch fresh dill, stalks
  removed, chopped

2 Tbsp. (30 mL) coarsely ground white
  pepper

Combine the salt and sugar in a bowl. Place half the trout fillets skin side down in the dish. Sprinkle half the salt and sugar mixture over the fillets. Scatter the chopped dill over top. Sprinkle with the white pepper. Place the remaining half of the trout fillets on top of this, cover with plastic wrap and weigh down with the foil-wrapped bricks. Twice a day, turn the fish and baste in the accumulating juices. Add a little of the extra salt and sugar mixture as needed. After 3 or 4 days, scrape the mixture off the fish, rinse and pat dry. Cover and refrigerate until serving time.

For the dill & mustard sauce:

3 Tbsp. (45 mL) Dijon mustard

1 Tbsp. (15 mL) Keen's dry mustard

3 Tbsp. (45 mL) sugar

1 Tbsp. (15 mL) white wine vinegar

3 Tbsp. (45 mL) extra virgin olive oil

salt and freshly ground black pepper
to taste

1 cup (240 mL) chopped fresh dill

Whisk the Dijon mustard, dry mustard, sugar and vinegar together in a bowl. Whisk in the olive oil gradually. Taste and season with salt and pepper, then add the chopped dill and mix well.

To serve, slice the fish on the diagonal, beginning at the tail end. Serve the gravlax on thinly sliced dark pumpernickel. Drizzle with the mustard and dill sauce.

Chef Michael Olson

Michael Olson was one of the first "food" people I contacted when we moved from Toronto to Niagara and what a smart move that proved to be. I knew Michael in his capacity as chef of Inn on the Twenty, the winery restaurant for Cave Spring Cellars in Jordan, through a number of food features I had written over the years for newspapers and magazines. Affable, outgoing, down-to-earth and unpretentious, Michael is a pleasure to know. I filled pages with information he supplied about food producers, chefs, bakers, growers, hiking trails, not-to-be-missed spots for pizza, schnitzel, homemade pie, Italian foodstuffs and just about anything else you can think of to do with food. Michael's list of achievements include the beautiful book he created with his wife, Anna Olson, the *Inn on the Twenty Cookbook* and his new career as a teacher at Niagara College's Niagara Culinary Institute. He loves the work he does now, teaching and inspiring young hopefuls to become chefs, and who better to teach them than someone who has the love and passion for food, the good humour and the knowledge that Michael possesses.

Seared Scallops on Buckwheat Blinis

Recommended: Cave Spring Cellars Chardonnay Reserve
Serves 6

If you're feeling financially flush, add the luxe touch of a little caviar to each of the sautéed scallops in this recipe from chef Roberto Fracchioni of Inn on the Twenty. This makes a lovely first course for a special evening and the blinis can easily be made ahead of time if you wish. The chef drizzles a little of his house-made roasted leek oil on the scallops before serving. If you have a flavoured olive oil that you prefer, use it here or choose an extra virgin olive oil with a peppery quality.

For the blinis:

1 cup (240 mL) all-purpose flour	1½ cups (360 mL) whole milk
1 tsp. (5 mL) baking powder	⅓ cup (80 mL) buckwheat flour
½ tsp. (2.5 mL) baking soda	pinch salt
1 egg, separated	3 Tbsp. (45 mL) plain yogurt
pinch sugar	2 Tbsp. (30 mL) melted butter

In a mixing bowl, combine the all-purpose flour, baking powder, baking soda, egg yolk and sugar with the milk; stir together and let sit in a warm place for 20 minutes to rise.

Add the buckwheat flour, salt, yogurt and butter to the mixture, mix well and let sit for an hour.

Whisk the egg white until stiff. Just before cooking, fold the egg white into the batter. Place a lightly buttered non-stick pan over medium-high heat. Pour enough batter to form 2-inch (5-cm) round blinis into the pan and cook for about 2 minutes, or until golden brown, before flipping and cooking the other side. Keep the blinis warm as you prepare them.

For the scallops:

2 Tbsp. (30 mL) vegetable oil

18 large sea scallops

½ cup (120 mL) Cave Spring Cellars
    Chardonnay Reserve

3 Tbsp. (45 mL) butter

olive oil, for drizzling

Place a heavy frying pan over high heat. When it begins to smoke, carefully add the oil and then the scallops. After one minute, loosen the scallops from the bottom of the pan (don't flip them) and continue to cook for just another minute.

Flip the scallops over and cook for 2 minutes on the other side. Remove from the pan and keep warm. Pour off any remaining oil from the pan and add the wine, scraping up any bits clinging to the bottom. Cook until the wine has reduced by half. Remove from the heat and whisk in the butter, heating it through.

Serve 2–3 blinis and 3 scallops per person. Drizzle with oil and serve immediately.

Butternut Squash Soup
with Maple Sage Cream

Recommended: Cave Spring Cellars Riesling Off Dry
Serves 4–6

At some point over the fall and winter months, you will dream of such a soup as this—satiny smooth with a beautiful colour, filled with the nuttiness of roasted squash. From chef Roberto Fracchioni at Inn on the Twenty in Jordan.

For the soup:

1½ lb. (680-g) butternut squash

3 Tbsp. (45 mL) vegetable oil

1 onion, finely chopped

1 stalk celery, finely chopped

1 carrot, peeled and finely chopped

1 clove garlic, minced

4 cups (950 mL) water

1 Yukon Gold potato, peeled and
    finely chopped

1½ tsp. (7.5 mL) chopped fresh thyme

¼ cup (60 mL) whipping cream
    (optional)

salt and freshly ground black pepper
    to taste

Preheat the oven to 350°F (175°C). Quarter the squash. Scoop out and discard the seeds. Peel each quarter, coat the pieces with 1 Tbsp. (15 mL) of the oil and place flesh side down on a buttered baking sheet. Roast for 30–40 minutes, or until tender.

In a medium saucepan, heat the remaining 2 Tbsp. (30 mL) oil over medium-high heat and sauté the onion, celery and carrot until tender, about 5 minutes. Add the garlic and sauté for another minute. Add the water, roasted squash (break the squash up a little), potato and thyme and simmer for about 20–30 minutes, or until the potato is tender. Using a hand-held blender (or food processor), purée the mixture, then pour through a sieve placed over a bowl, rubbing the mixture to force it through and scraping the underside of the sieve to get all the purée. Wipe the saucepan clean, then return the strained soup to it; add the cream if using, season with salt and pepper and keep at a low heat while you prepare the garnish.

For the maple sage cream:

½ cup (120 mL) whipping cream

1 Tbsp. (15 mL) pure maple syrup

1 tsp. (5 mL) finely chopped fresh sage

Whip the cream until it holds soft peaks, then fold in the maple syrup and sage.

Serve the soup in shallow soup plates with a dollop of maple sage cream in the centre of each serving.

Chef J. Mark Hand

Corporate chef J. Mark Hand of the Niagara Culinary Institute believes in simplicity of presentation and maximizing the flavours and freshness of foods, all of which help to define excellence in the Niagara hospitality industry. Whether inside the classroom or beyond the confines of the college, chef Hand shares his passion for the region's bounty and its highly acclaimed wines through television and personal appearances, and as one of the area's ambassadors of regional foods.

Goat's Cheese Packets with Fresh Thyme

Recommended: Peninsula Ridge Estates Sauvignon Blanc
Serves 6

Many years ago, I enjoyed this very simple appetizer at the home of a neighbour in a village in southwest England. She served it as the start to an equally simple meal that included those lovely ham steaks they call gammon in England and shirred eggs, an old-fashioned but very good method of cooking eggs in a shallow dish in the oven. I thought these cheese-filled puff pastries were the bee's knees—still do.

1 lb. (455 g) frozen puff pastry,
    thawed (you may not use it all)
8–9 oz. (225–255 g) goat cheese log
    (or 2 smaller logs), evenly divided
    into 6 pieces

1 large egg, beaten
6–8 fresh thyme sprigs
extra virgin olive oil, for drizzling

Preheat the oven to 425°F (220°C). Have ready a non-stick 6-cup muffin tin. Roll out the pastry and cut 6 pieces about 5 inches (12.5 cm) square. Line each of the muffin cups with a square of pastry. Place a piece of the goat cheese in the centre of each square of pastry, brush a little egg over the pastry, then gather it up to encircle the cheese, pinching it a bit to form 3 corners, leaving the top of the cheese exposed. Press a little sprig of fresh thyme into the top of each cheese. Bake for about 15 minutes, until the pastry is golden brown and the cheese is just beginning to ooze. Drizzle with a little olive oil and serve warm.

Tortelli of Game & Reggiano in Oxtail Cabernet Broth

Recommended: Cave Spring Cellars Cabernet Merlot
Serves 6

While this recipe from chef Roberto Fracchioni of Inn on the Twenty will take a little time to put together, the results are well worth it. It is a big, satisfying, rustic Italian preparation, just the sort of thing you would expect from a Niagara-born chef with Italian roots. Very, very good. (As the name would suggest, tortelli are big tortellini.) Start preparation for this dish by making the oxtail broth, as it does require a bit of time.

For the oxtail broth:

1 lb. (455 g) oxtail, cut into 2-inch (5-cm) pieces, trimmed of excess fat

1 large onion, cut into rough chunks

1 large carrot, cut into rough chunks

2 stalks celery, cut into rough chunks

½ leek, rinsed and cut into rough chunks

1½ cups (360 mL) Cave Spring Cellars Cabernet Merlot

2 Tbsp. (30 mL) chopped fresh thyme leaves

salt and freshly ground black pepper to taste

Preheat the oven to 300°F (150°C). Pat the sections of oxtail with paper towels to absorb excess moisture, placing them in a roasting pan as you work. Set in the preheated oven and leave to roast until they are dark brown, about an hour.

Transfer the meat from the roasting pan to a Dutch oven or similar heavy pot. Add the vegetables to the roasting pan, tossing them around to coat them with the fat rendered from the oxtail. Increase the oven heat to 400°F (200°C) and roast the vegetables until lightly coloured, about 20 minutes. Remove the pan from the oven. Using tongs, transfer the vegetables to the Dutch oven.

Add the wine and enough cold water to just cover. Add another 4 cups (950 mL) of water and place over high heat. Bring the mixture to a boil, reduce the heat and simmer for 5–6 hours, skimming off any foam or oil that accumulates on the surface. At the end of this time, pour the contents of the pot through a colander into a bowl. (Discard the vegetables, but reserve the cooked oxtail for another use.) Wipe the pot clean and return the strained liquid to it. Return to the heat, add the thyme and bring to a boil for another 10 minutes. Season with salt and pepper and set aside.

For the tortelli filling:

2 lb. (900 g) boneless stewing venison (or wild boar)

1 Tbsp. (15 mL) olive oil

1 onion, finely chopped

$\frac{1}{2}$ stalk celery, finely chopped

$\frac{1}{4}$ carrot, finely chopped

2 ripe tomatoes, peeled, seeded and chopped

2 cloves garlic, finely chopped

1 cup (240 mL) Cave Spring Cellars Cabernet Merlot

2 branches fresh rosemary

2 sprigs fresh flat-leaf parsley

$\frac{3}{4}$ cup (180 mL) grated Parmigiano-Reggiano cheese

$\frac{1}{2}$ cup (120 mL) ricotta cheese, drained

1 cup (240 mL) dry breadcrumbs

1 egg

2 Tbsp. (30 mL) water

salt and freshly ground black pepper to taste

Trim the venison or boar, if necessary, and cut into 1-inch (2.5-cm) pieces. Pat dry with paper towels. Warm the oil in a Dutch oven or similar heavy pot over medium-high heat and cook the onion, celery and carrot for about 3 minutes. Add the meat, tomatoes, garlic and wine. Stir together well, cover and cook over low heat for about 1 $\frac{1}{2}$ hours or until the meat is very tender and falling apart. Add the rosemary and parsley and continue to cook for another 10 minutes. (During the cooking time, add a little water if the mixture becomes too dry.) By the time the meat is cooked, most of the liquid should be evaporated. If there is excess liquid in the pan, slowly simmer until thickened. Pass the solid parts through a meat grinder or chop very finely by hand. To this add the cheeses, breadcrumbs, egg and water and mix thoroughly. Season with salt and pepper and check for consistency; the filling should be moist but not runny. If necessary add more breadcrumbs.

For the pasta:

4¼ cups (1 L) baby spinach leaves, trimmed and blanched very briefly

8½ cups (2.1 L) all-purpose flour

6 eggs

4 egg yolks

1 Tbsp. (15 mL) olive oil

1 cup (240 mL) finely chopped fresh flat-leaf parsley

Drain the spinach and chop it finely. Mound all of the flour on a clean, dry surface, making a well in the centre. Add the 6 eggs, egg yolks, olive oil, chopped spinach and parsley. Drawing the flour into the centre, thoroughly combine all the ingredients until a dough is formed. Cover and allow to rest in the refrigerator for an hour.

Pass the dough through a pasta machine or roll it by hand to ¹⁄₁₆ inch. Cut the pasta dough into 3-inch (7.5-cm) squares.

Whisk the egg with the water in a small bowl. Place 1 heaping teaspoon of filling in the middle of a pasta square and brush the edges of the pasta with the egg wash. Place another square of pasta on top, ensuring that no air is trapped inside. Press to seal the edges together. (You may cut or fold these pastas into many different styles, but a rustic dish like this looks good a little bit unpolished.)

To assemble the dish:

1 egg

2 Tbsp. (30 mL) water

freshly grated Parmigiano-Reggiano, for garnish

Reheat the reserved oxtail broth. Bring a large pot of water to a boil over high heat. Lightly salt it, add the pasta squares and cook for 3–4 minutes, or until they have floated to the top. Remove with a slotted spoon to a warmed pasta bowl. Pour the hot oxtail broth over. Garnish with grated Parmigiano-Reggiano and serve immediately.

Quail Timbales
with Foie Gras, Chardonnay Pears
& Maple Syrup Splash

Recommended: Vineland Estates Chardonnay Reserve
Serves 6

If you think you can only enjoy foie gras when dining out, you must try this recipe from chef Mark Picone of Vineland Estates Winery. Because the foie gras is combined with quail, a little goes a long way towards making an elegant first course for six. You will need ½ cup (120 mL) vegetable brunoise for this recipe. This is a mixture of finely chopped (⅛-inch/.3-cm cubes) carrot, celery and onion, sautéed with butter, salt and pepper and herbs (parsley, thyme, rosemary) until softened. You will need a food processor and 6 ramekin moulds for this recipe.

For the pears:

3 Bosc pears

3 cups (720 mL) Vineland Estates
    Chardonnay Reserve

¼ cup (60 mL) sugar

2-inch (5-cm) piece cinnamon stick

pinch of saffron threads

6 whole cloves

Wash, peel, core and quarter the pears. Place in a saucepan along with all the remaining ingredients and bring to a boil over medium-high heat. Reduce the heat and simmer for 10 minutes. Cool in the poaching liquid until serving time.

For the quail and foie gras:

1 Tbsp. (15 mL) olive oil

6 jumbo boneless quail, legs detached

1 egg white

½ cup (120 mL) whipping cream

½ cup (120 mL) vegetable brunoise
    (see above)

salt and freshly ground black pepper
    to taste

6-oz. (170-g) foie gras, cleaned of
    connective tissue, sliced into
    6 slices

Place a sauté pan over medium-high heat and add the oil. Sear the quail legs until lightly browned on both sides, a couple of minutes in total. Transfer from the pan to a plate and set aside.

Place the boneless quail breasts in the bowl of a food processor, add the egg white and pulse together until the meat is ground. Add the cream, pulse once or twice more to mix it in, then transfer the mixture to a bowl. Stir in the vegetable brunoise and season with salt and pepper.

Preheat the oven to 400°F (200°C). Use a bit of plastic wrap to line each ramekin, letting a little hang over the edge. Carefully spoon in some of the quail mixture, lining the bottom and the sides of the ramekins with equal amounts. Place two quail legs vertically on either side of the quail mixture and end with more mousse and a piece of foie gras laid carefully over the top. Place the filled ramekins in a baking pan large enough to hold them all without touching. Pull out the oven rack and place the baking pan on the rack. Carefully pour very hot water into the baking pan so that it comes a little more than halfway up the sides of the ramekins. Slide the rack into the oven and bake for 15 minutes.

For the maple syrup splash:

¼ cup (60 mL) pure maple syrup

2 Tbsp. (30 mL) white vinegar

¼ cup (60 mL) canola oil

½ cup (120 mL) toasted walnuts

salt and freshly ground black pepper to taste

While the timbales bake, whisk together the maple syrup, vinegar, canola oil, walnuts, salt and pepper.

Remove the quail ramekins from the oven and let sit for a few minutes before carefully inverting them onto serving plates (this should be relatively easy because of the plastic wrap). Carefully remove the plastic wrap. Portion some of the poached pears and their liquid around each quail timbale and follow this with a few drizzles of the maple syrup splash. Serve warm.

Pork Tenderloin
with Smoked Apple Dumplings

Recommended: Cave Spring Cellars Vineyard Chardonnay CSV
Serves 4–6

Chef Rob Fracchioni of Inn on the Twenty says if you don't have a smoker (or can fashion one using wood chips and your barbecue), you can add a little liquid smoke flavouring. "A couple of drops added to the apples as they cook will be plenty; it doesn't have nearly as good a flavour, but it will work in a pinch." The chef likes to serve this main course with carrots and parsnips roasted with thyme, basil and honey. Look for turbinado sugar (raw sugar) in specialty food shops or health food stores. Note that preparations for the smoked apple dumplings should begin the night before by salting the apples. Make the dumplings up to the point where they are removed from the cooking water, then finish them right after the tenderloin is cooked.

For the smoked apple dumplings:

3 Granny Smith apples, peeled, halved
   and cored
1 Tbsp. (15 mL) coarse salt
1½ Tbsp. (22 mL) granulated sugar
½ cup (120 mL) Cave Spring Cellars
   Vineyard Chardonnay CSV

5 eggs
3 Tbsp. (45 mL) whole milk
dash of nutmeg
6 cups (1.5 L) all-purpose flour

Sprinkle the apples with the coarse salt, cover and let sit overnight. Smoke the apples in a smoker for 20–30 minutes, until they have a distinctive smoky aroma (following manufacturer's instructions) or on a barbecue using soaked wood chips for about 15 minutes. Transfer the smoked apples to a saucepan, add the sugar and wine and place over medium heat. Cook the apples for about 5 minutes or so, until they fall apart, then set aside to cool, mashing them if necessary to help break them down.

In a mixing bowl, whisk the eggs, milk and nutmeg until blended, then add the apples, continuing to mix. Gradually add the flour, mixing all the while until a loose dough is formed. You may not require all the flour.

Place a pot of lightly salted water on to boil over high heat. Using about 1 Tbsp. (15 mL) of batter per dumpling, cook the dumplings in the boiling water for about 1 minute, or until they are set all the way through. Remove from the water and cool on a platter lined with paper towels.

For the pork tenderloin:

2 lb. (900 g) pork tenderloins (about 3)	4 Tbsp. (60 mL) hot chili sauce
2 Tbsp. (30 mL) granulated sugar	(Vietnamese or Chinese style)
2 Tbsp. (30 mL) turbinado sugar (see above)	4 Tbsp. (60 mL) chopped fresh thyme leaves
1 Tbsp. (15 mL) salt	1 Tbsp. (15 mL) chopped fresh rosemary
2 Tbsp. (30 mL) coarse salt	

Trim the tenderloins of any silver skin (very thin membrane that may be covering it) with a sharp knife, removing as little meat as possible. Combine the remaining ingredients in a little bowl, mix thoroughly, then rub well into the tenderloins. Place the meat in a glass dish, cover with plastic wrap and refrigerate overnight.

When ready to cook, preheat the grill to medium-high. Cook the tenderloins for 20–25 minutes in total, or to the desired doneness. (You could also pan-fry or oven-roast the meat.) Keep warm while you finish the dumplings.

To finish the dish:
1 Tbsp. (15 mL) butter
salt and freshly ground black pepper
    to taste

Preheat the oven to 375°F (190°C). Melt the butter in a sauté pan over medium-high heat and sauté the dumplings for about a minute, turning to sauté on all sides. Place in the preheated oven for 3 minutes. Slice the pork tenderloin and arrange on a plate with the dumplings.

Thomas & Vaughan Vintners

Beamsville is home to Tom Kocsis and Barbara Vaughan, the grape-growing husband-and-wife duo who decided to become winemakers themselves after supplying grapes to other wineries for some time. This family-owned estate winery has a strong focus on Cabernet Sauvignon, Merlot, Riesling, Chardonnay and Pinot Gris. Their Baco Noir, derived from French hybrid grapes, is a full-bodied favourite.

Classic Cauliflower Cheese

Recommended: Niagara Brewing Pale Ale
Serves 6

When cauliflower is in plentiful supply, make this rich, old-fashioned dish that is really splendid served alongside any roasted meat. Vary the cheese as you wish, but make sure it is full-flavoured.

1 large cauliflower, trimmed	pinch of nutmeg
1 tsp. (5 mL) salt	4 eggs, beaten
2 Tbsp. (30 mL) butter	3 rounded Tbsp. (50 mL) fresh
1 onion, chopped	breadcrumbs
1 cup (240 mL) whole milk	¼ cup (60 mL) grated Parmesan
¼ lb. (113 g) grated Gruyère cheese	cheese
salt and freshly ground pepper to taste	

Preheat the oven to 325°F (165°C). Break the cauliflower into small florets. Place in a large saucepan and cover with boiling water and the salt. Return to a boil, then reduce the heat to low and simmer gently for 5–8 minutes, until the cauliflower is tender but not soft. Drain and set aside.

Melt 1 Tbsp. (15 mL) of the butter in a small frying pan over medium-high heat, and sauté the onion until softened, about 5 minutes. Set aside.

Lightly butter an 11 x 7-inch (28 x 18-cm) baking dish and set aside. Bring the milk to a boil in a heavy saucepan. Reduce the heat, add the Gruyère and the remaining 1 Tbsp. (15 mL) butter, salt, pepper and nutmeg, whisking the ingredients together. Remove from the heat and cool slightly. Beat some of this mixture into the beaten eggs, then add all the egg mixture to the milk and cheese mixture. Fold the cooked cauliflower and onion into the mixture and pour everything into the baking dish. Top with breadcrumbs and the grated Parmesan cheese and bake for 40–50 minutes, or until golden brown.

Alysa Cooks a Goose
with Chestnut, Apple & Prune Stuffing

Recommended: Daniel Lenko Estates Winery Riesling Reserve
Serves 6–8

My daughter Alysa prepared a sumptuous goose for our Christmas dinner, complete with a rich stuffing of chestnuts, apples and prunes. It was fabulous and we all felt very Dickensian as we tucked into it, especially since it was followed by my mince tarts, dark fruitcake and a wonderful English Stilton.

For the stuffing:

3 lb. (1.35 kg) chestnuts

2 Tbsp. (30 mL) olive oil

6 cups (1.5 L) chicken or beef stock

2 Tbsp. (30 mL) butter

1 onion, finely chopped

2 tart apples, peeled, cored and chopped

10 oz. (285 g) pitted prunes, chopped

2 Tbsp. (30 mL) chopped fresh flat-leaf parsley

2 Tbsp. (30 mL) chopped fresh thyme

salt and freshly ground black pepper to taste

1 cup (240 mL) soft breadcrumbs

¼ cup (60 mL) brandy or cognac

With a little paring knife, cut slits in the flat side of each chestnut. Warm the oil in a frying pan and add the chestnuts. Cook over high heat, shaking the pan constantly, for about 3 minutes. Drain the chestnuts and set them to one side until they are cool enough to handle. With the paring knife, peel the chestnuts and remove the inner skin, transferring the peeled chestnuts to a saucepan as you work. Cover the peeled chestnuts with the stock and cook for about 20 minutes, or until tender. Drain (save the broth to use in soup), chop the chestnuts coarsely and place in a mixing bowl.

Melt the butter in a sauté pan over medium-high heat and sauté the onion until soft, about 5 minutes. Add the onion and butter to the chestnuts, then add all the remaining ingredients. Mix together thoroughly.

For the goose:

10–12-lb. (4.5–5.4-kg) goose

1 lemon, halved

salt and freshly ground black pepper
    to taste

½ cup (120 mL) prune nectar

Remove any loose or excess fat from the goose. Rinse the inside of the bird and wipe it dry thoroughly inside and out. Preheat the oven to 400°F (200°C). Rub the outside of the goose with lemon juice and season inside and outside with salt and pepper. Prick the skin all over with a needle, then fill the body and neck cavities of the goose with the stuffing. If you have any leftover stuffing, place in a buttered baking dish and bake it alongside the goose.

Place the goose on a rack or trivet in a roasting pan and pour 2 cups (475 mL) of hot water over it into the pan. Roast for 20 minutes, uncovered. Reduce the heat to 350°F (175°C) and roast for about an hour, then pour or spoon off the excess fat, taking care not to pour off the juices or browned bits; a bulb baster is useful for this. (Save the fat for other uses.) Continue to roast the goose for another 3 hours, pouring off excess fat as it accumulates and basting the bird from time to time. About 40 minutes before the end of the cooking time, remove the goose from the oven, score it with a sharp knife in a diamond pattern and brush with the prune nectar, then slip it back into the oven to finish roasting. Fifteen minutes before the end of the cooking time, increase the oven temperature to 400°F (200°C) to crisp up the skin. When done, let the goose rest for 20 minutes or so before removing the stuffing and carving. Serve hot.

Short Ribs of Beef
in Niagara Gritstone Ale "Ketchup"

Recommended: Pillitteri Estates Winery Trivalente Cabernet/Merlot
Serves 6

This is a big, full-flavoured dish, deliciously messy to eat, happily rough around the edges and terrific for the first cold winter day of the season. There are a couple of stages to it—short ribs do need a bit of time to cook—so start preparation for it the day before. The sauce is based on great beer and quite a bit of good old ketchup that we spiked further with seasonings and spices. You could also use your favourite barbecue-style sauce and combine it with the beer. Make sure to serve these ribs with a mound of deluxe mashed potatoes and maybe some oven-roasted root vegetables. This is what my Ted would call a "man dinner."

For the beef:
6 lb. (2.7 kg) beef short ribs, trimmed
    of excess fat
4 Tbsp. (60 mL) coarsely ground black
    pepper

2 Tbsp. (30 mL) coarse salt
3 bottles (12-oz./341-mL) Niagara
    Brewing Gritstone Premium Ale

Preheat the oven to 275°F (135°C). Blend the black pepper and salt in a small bowl. Rub well into the short ribs, coating them all over with the seasoning. Place the ribs in a roasting pan, pour the beer around the beef and cover the pan with foil. Bake for 2 hours. Remove from the oven, drain off and discard any liquid and set the ribs to one side to cool.

For the ale "ketchup"

2 Tbsp. (30 mL) olive oil	1 Tbsp. (15 mL) freshly ground pepper
1 large onion, finely chopped	1 Tbsp. (15 mL) salt
6 cloves garlic, minced	1 Tbsp. (15 mL) chili powder
$\frac{2}{3}$ cup (160 mL) brown sugar	1 Tbsp. (15 mL) dry mustard
$\frac{2}{3}$ cup (160 mL) honey	1 Tbsp. (15 mL) ground cinnamon
$\frac{2}{3}$ cup (160 mL) malt vinegar	2 Tbsp. (30 mL) coarse-grain mustard
$\frac{1}{3}$ cup (80 mL) Worcestershire sauce	2 cups (475 mL) canned puréed
3 bottles (12-oz./341-mL) Niagara	tomatoes
Brewing Gritstone Premium Ale	1 large bottle (4$\frac{1}{4}$-cups/1-L) ketchup

Place a large saucepan over medium-high heat, add the olive oil and sauté the onion until softened, about 5 minutes. Add the garlic and cook for a further minute. Add all the remaining ingredients—except the ketchup—stirring to blend well. Bring to a boil, then reduce the heat immediately so that the mixture is simmering. Finally, stir in the ketchup, blending well. Simmer at a low heat for about 30 minutes, stirring occasionally.

Pour the sauce over the cooled beef ribs, making sure they are all covered with sauce. Cover with foil or plastic wrap and place in the refrigerator overnight.

To finish the dish:

Preheat the oven to 400°F (200°C). Remove the ribs from the refrigerator and let sit at room temperature while the oven heats. Place the ribs in the oven and roast for 2 hours, or until they are ultra tender, basting them frequently with the sauce.

Grasmere's Peach Bread Pudding with Whisk(e)y Sauce

Recommended: Château des Charmes Estate Winery Estate Bottled Late Harvest Riesling
Serves 4

My Ted has a Scottish background, while my Celtic roots are Irish, but we are both inordinately fond of very good Scottish single-malt whiskies. However, I happen to like a bit of Irish now and then. The debate over who invented (and who perfected) the spirit of life goes on in our house, but the recipe that follows—for the best bread pudding in the world—tastes just as wonderful whether you use Scotch, Irish or Canadian rye. Be true to your roots and enjoy. I used the wonderful local peaches that I packed in freezer bags for this.

For the bread pudding:
2 cups (475 mL) whole milk

2 eggs

1 Tbsp. (15 mL) granulated sugar

1 tsp. (5 mL) pure vanilla extract

½ tsp. (2.5 mL) ground cinnamon

½ tsp. (2.5 mL) grated lemon zest

¼ tsp. (1.2 mL) grated nutmeg

2 cups (475 mL) day-old French or Italian bread in ½-inch (1.2-cm) cubes

2 cups (475 mL) sliced peaches, canned or frozen, drained and chopped

2 Tbsp. (30 mL) golden raisins

Preheat the oven to 350°F (175°C). In a large bowl, whisk the milk with the eggs, sugar, vanilla, cinnamon, lemon zest and nutmeg. Stir in the bread; let soak for 1 minute, then stir in the peaches and raisins. Pour the mixture into a lightly greased 8-inch (20-cm) square baking dish. Bake for 45–50 minutes, or until the centre is lightly set.

For the sauce:

½ cup (120 mL) cream

1 Tbsp. (15 mL) brown sugar

2 tsp. (10 mL) cornstarch

¼ cup (60 mL) whisky

In a small saucepan, whisk together the cream, brown sugar and cornstarch. Cook over medium heat for 3–5 minutes, whisking constantly, until the sauce boils and thickens. Stir in the whisky and remove from the heat. Spoon over the warm bread pudding.

Napoleon of Fresh & Preserved Figs
with Benedictine Crème Fraîche
& Vanilla Almond Shortbread

Recommended: Vineland Estates Winery Gewürztraminer Reserve Frontier Vineyard
Serves 6

David Berggren is the pastry chef at Vineland Estates. In this creative dessert, he treats dried figs to a poaching liquid of spiced Gewürztraminer, then pairs them with fresh figs and a wonderful flavoured crème fraîche, all of which is partnered with crisp shortbreads. Perfect seasonal Niagara fare.

For the preserved figs:

20 oz. (565 g) dried figs	10 cloves
8 cups (2 L) hot water	5 cardamom seeds
1¼ cups (300 mL) honey	1 cinnamon stick
1¼ cups (300 mL) Vineland Estates Winery Gewürztraminer Reserve Frontier Vineyard	

Snip the tips off the dried figs. Transfer the figs to a tall container and cover with the hot water. Let soak for 1 hour. Drain the figs well. Meanwhile, combine the honey, wine and spices in a saucepan set over medium heat. (Watch the mixture carefully as it will foam.) Skim off the foam as it appears, add the figs and reduce the heat to low. Simmer for 3 hours. When the figs appear dark and translucent, remove from the heat, cool and transfer to a jar with a tight-fitting lid. Cool and refrigerate until ready to use.

For the crème fraîche:

3½ oz. (100 g) Benedictine cheese
  (cave-aged blue cheese)
1¼ cups (300 mL) 30% sour cream
  (look for a brand called SnoWhite
  Crème Fraîche High Fat Sour
  Cream)

1 cup (240 mL) whipping cream
¾ cup (180 mL) icing sugar

Place the cheese in a small bowl and use a fork to break it into a fine consistency. In another bowl, combine the sour cream with the whipping cream and whip together until soft peaks form. Add the icing sugar and the cheese and re-whip to soft peaks. Chill until ready to use.

For the shortbread:

½ lb. (225 g) butter
⅓ cup (80 mL) icing sugar
1 vanilla pod

¾ cup (180 mL) almond flour (derived
  from grinding ground almonds to
  a flour-like consistency)
2¼ cups (535 mL) all-purpose flour

Cream the butter with the icing sugar in a mixing bowl. Slit the vanilla pod and use a paring knife to scrape the pulp into another bowl (save the pod to flavour custards or other desserts). Sift the flours over the vanilla pulp and blend the ingredients evenly together, making sure to distribute the vanilla pulp well into the flours. Combine the flour mixture with the butter mixture and mix to form a dough. Refrigerate until well chilled, about 1 hour.

Preheat the oven to 325°F (165°C). Roll out the dough to a thickness of about ¼ inch (5 mm) and cut into 18 3-inch (7.5-cm) rounds. Transfer to a baking sheet and bake until pale golden, about 11–14 minutes. Remove from the oven and cool on a rack.

To assemble:
6 fresh Black Mission figs
aged balsamic vinegar (optional)

Cut 2 preserved figs into quarters. Place 4 fig quarters on one shortbread, then repeat with a second shortbread and 4 more fig quarters. Place a dollop of the crème fraîche mixture on top of each. Transfer the two to a serving plate and stack one on top of the other. Top with a third shortbread and place a half-dollop of cream on top. Halve 1 fresh fig and place on top. Repeat for the remaining plates. When they are all ready to be served, drizzle with the aged balsamic vinegar, if desired, and serve immediately.

Sunnybrook Farm Estate Winery

Billed as "Canada's first fruit winery," Sunnybrook Farm Estate Winery is located precisely at the heart of Niagara's fruit belt, just west of the town of Niagara-on-the-Lake. Specializing in premium wines from 100 percent Ontario fruit—most of which is grown on their own farm— Sunnybrook has a remarkable collection of fruit wines available at its retail outlet. The Goertz family winery offers wines made from damson plums, peaches, pears, blueberries, cherries, nectarines, black raspberry, blackberries and more. If you've never tried a real fruit wine, drop by their winery and sample a few of these quality-made wines.

Apple Ginger Crisp with Honey Mascarpone

Recommended: Cave Spring Cellars Riesling Icewine
Serves 6–8

From Anna Olson, pastry and dessert chef at Cave Spring's Inn on the Twenty restaurant. She says, "I like to upscale this familiar dessert by serving it with a lightly sweetened mascarpone cheese. The mascarpone melts slightly when it hits the warm crisp and turns into a creamy sauce. Or try it with a scoop of vanilla ice cream or a piece of Cheddar cheese—equally delicious!"

1¼ cups (300 mL) rolled oats
1 cup (240 mL) brown sugar
¾ cup (180 mL) all-purpose flour
2 Tbsp. (30 mL) grated fresh ginger
½ tsp. (2.5 mL) ground cinnamon
¼ tsp. (1.2 mL) nutmeg
¼ tsp. (1.2 mL) salt
¾ cup (180 mL) unsalted butter, cut into pieces

6 Crispin or Granny Smith apples, peeled, cored and diced
½ cup (120 mL) granulated sugar
1 Tbsp. (15 mL) all-purpose flour
½ tsp. (2.5 mL) ground cinnamon
1 cup (240 mL) mascarpone cheese
2 Tbsp. 30 mL) honey

Preheat the oven to 350ºF (175ºC). Blend the oats, brown sugar, ¾ cup (180 mL) flour, ginger, cinnamon, nutmeg and salt together in a bowl. Cut in the butter with a pastry cutter or your fingers until it resembles the texture of coarse meal. In a separate bowl, toss the apples with the granulated sugar, 1 Tbsp. (15 mL) flour and remaining cinnamon. Transfer to a baking dish. Crumble the topping over the apples and bake for 40 minutes.

Blend the mascarpone with the honey until smooth. Chill until serving time.

To serve, spoon hot apple crisp onto a plate and add a generous spoonful of honey mascarpone.

Cranberry Pear Croustade

Recommended: Joseph's Estate Wines Iced Bosc Pear
Serves 6–8

Frozen puff pastry can be a real boon to the holiday cook. Certainly you can make your own (or other favourite pie pastry) for this recipe, but it is almost an effortless preparation when based on ready-made puff pastry. Croustades are open-faced pies that can hold any number of fillings, sweet or savoury (try a mixture of mushrooms, sliced potatoes, goat cheese and fresh herbs, for instance). This is very good, too, with apples in place of the pears or a combination of both.

½ package frozen puff pastry, thawed
    (or pastry for a
      14-inch/35-cm crust)
½ cup (120 mL) sugar
1 tsp. (5 mL) ground cinnamon
½ tsp. (2.5 mL) nutmeg
5 firm, ripe pears, cored and sliced
¾ cup (180 mL) cranberries, fresh or
    frozen

3 Tbsp. (45 mL) all-purpose flour
2 Tbsp. (30 mL) butter
1 egg yolk, beaten
sugar for dusting
2 Tbsp. (30 mL) white wine jelly,
    melted
whipped cream, for garnish

Preheat the oven to 425°F (220°C). Roll out the pastry on a lightly floured surface to a rough 14-inch (35-cm) round. Wrap the pastry around a rolling pin and transfer to the centre of a baking sheet.

Combine the sugar, cinnamon, nutmeg, pears, cranberries and flour in a mixing bowl. Toss well and pour into the centre of the pastry. Dot with the butter. Turn the edges of the pastry up over the filling, overlapping the pastry as necessary and leaving the centre of the filling exposed. (Pastry edges should be a little uneven.) Brush off any excess flour, brush with the beaten egg yolk and sprinkle with a bit of sugar. Bake for 15 minutes, reduce the heat to 375°F (190°C) and bake for another 25–30 minutes, or until the fruit is tender and the pastry lightly browned. Serve warm with unsweetened whipped cream.

Hernder Estate Wines

The Hernder family has a 50-year tradition of grape growing in Niagara. Now that tradition extends to the wine produced from the 500-acre vineyard located just beneath the brow of the Niagara Escarpment. A very visible presence due to their handsome wooden covered bridge that leads to a beautifully restored 1867 Victorian barn, Hernder's is a busy place year-round and a favourite venue for weddings, banquets and other special events. Hernder winemaker Ray Cornell prides himself on producing wines that are true representations of the particular character of the grape variety. Particularly recommended are the aromatic whites like Gewürztraminer, Riesling Proprietors Reserve and his family of icewines.

Panna Cotta
with Strewn Wines Cabernet Sauvignon
Raspberry Sauce

Serves 6–8

Ted would have panna cotta for dessert every night if it was offered. Undeniably rich, it is the simplest of sweets, Italian in origin, with a pristine whiteness just crying out for a brilliantly coloured accompaniment, like this beautifully flavoured wine and berry reduction. Everyone loves this. Start preparation the day before, or very early in the morning, to allow time for the little puddings to set. You will need 6 or 8 ramekins or custard cups for this recipe.

cooking spray	1 bottle (750 mL) Strewn Wines
4 cups (950 mL) whipping cream	Cabernet Sauvignon
¾ cup (180 mL) sugar	12 oz. (375 g) frozen raspberries,
1 tsp. (5 mL) pure vanilla extract	thawed (juice included)
2 Tbsp. gelatin (about 2 envelopes)	1 cup (240 mL) sugar

Spray the ramekins or cups lightly with cooking spray and place them on a tray. Warm the cream, ¾ cup (180 mL) sugar and vanilla in a heavy saucepan placed over medium-low heat, stirring to dissolve the sugar, just until the cream is beginning to ripple with the heat. Reduce the heat and simmer for 10 minutes. Remove from the heat.

Pour the gelatin in a small bowl and add ½ (120 mL) cup of boiling water, whisking to blend well. Let this sit for a minute then whisk in another ½ (120 mL) cup of boiling water. Continue to whisk to help it dissolve completely. Pour this mixture into the hot cream, stirring thoroughly to combine the two liquids. When well blended, pour or ladle the mixture into ramekins or glass custard cups. Transfer the tray holding the cups to the refrigerator for at least 4 hours or up to 24 hours.

Meanwhile, prepare the sauce. Combine the wine, raspberries and their juice and the 1 cup (240 mL) sugar in a large saucepan. Stir to dissolve the sugar, place over high heat and bring to a rolling boil. Reduce the heat slightly, but continue to cook vigorously for about 30 minutes, until the mixture is reduced by about half.

As the mixture begins to thicken, stir often and make sure it is not sticking to the bottom of the pan. When thickened and sauce-like, pour through a sieve into a bowl. Cool, pour into a glass jug or pitcher, then refrigerate for 4 hours, or until well chilled.

To serve, run a warm, narrow-bladed knife around the edge of the ramekins and turn the panna cotta out into the centre of a white or glass dessert plate. Carefully pour a portion of the wine raspberry sauce around the panna cotta.

Maleta Vineyards & Estate Winery

Stan and Marilyn Maleta left the city and came to Niagara-on-the-Lake to pursue Stan's love of winemaking. An amateur turned pro, Stan specializes in small batch premium wines at this cottage winery and vineyard that was originally called Sunnieholme Winery (which dates back to 1918). Since 1998, the couple have been replanting, specializing in Bordeaux varieties.

Icewine Apple Butter

Makes about 1 cup (240 mL)

Catherine O'Donnell, pastry chef at Hillebrand, makes this fragrant apple butter to fill tiny tart shells and offers them as part of a dessert platter. Make your own miniature tart shells ahead of time, then spoon this filling into each one.

3 cooking apples, peeled and cored
½ cup (120 mL) Hillebrand Trius
    Icewine
⅛ tsp. (.5 mL) nutmeg

⅛ tsp. (.5 mL) ground cloves
⅛ tsp. (.5 mL) ground cinnamon
¼ cup (60 mL) sugar

Slice the apples about ¼ inch (.6 cm) thick and place in a heavy saucepan along with the icewine. Cook over medium heat until the apple begins to soften, about 15 minutes. Remove from the heat and add the spices and sugar. Stir well into the apple mixture, return to the heat and cook over medium heat, stirring the mixture for 5 minutes or so, until it comes to a boil. Remove from the heat and set aside to cool. When cooled, transfer to a lidded container and keep refrigerated until ready to use.

Gewürztraminer Granita

Serves 10–12

While it is traditional to use an ice such as this one to refresh palates between courses at special dinners, this is also a very nice offering following a holiday dinner. I love ices and granitas because they are a snap to make and they don't require any special equipment. This also works well with an off-dry Riesling.

1 cup (240 mL) water
1 cup (240 mL) sugar
1 bottle (750 mL) Konzelmann Estate
    Winery Gewürztraminer Late
    Harvest, well chilled

3 Tbsp. (45 mL) rose water
a few rose petals (optional)

Combine the water and sugar in a large saucepan and stir to dissolve the sugar. Bring to a boil over medium-high heat and boil for a minute or so, stirring frequently, until a thin syrup forms. Remove from the heat, cool, then refrigerate until very well chilled.

When the mixture is chilled, combine it with the wine and rose water, stirring to blend well. Pour this mixture into a 9 x 13-inch (23 x 33-cm) baking dish and place in the freezer. After 3 hours, remove from the freezer and run a spatula around the edges to break up the crystals that are forming. Repeat this procedure every hour or so, until the mixture is completely frozen into crystals. Use an ice cream scoop to scrape up the granita and serve on chilled glass plates, garnished with rose petals if you have them.

Cabernet Truffles

Makes 30 truffles

While many of the local wineries offer icewine truffles in their winery shops, I have yet to see any influenced by red wine. A little bit of Cabernet adds another dimension to chocolate in these sumptuous little treats.

¼ cup (60 mL) whipping cream
7 oz. (200 g) bittersweet chocolate,
    finely chopped
2 Tbsp. (30 mL) Willow Heights
    Winery Tresette Reserve

4 Tbsp. (60 mL) softened unsalted
    butter
½ cup (120 mL) cocoa

Pour the cream into a very small saucepan placed over high heat and bring to a simmer. Reduce the heat to low and simmer the cream for about 2 minutes, until it is reduced by half, to about 2 Tbsp. (30 mL). Remove from the heat.

Melt the chocolate along with the reduced cream and the wine in the top of a double boiler set over simmering hot water. Stir frequently until the mixture is smooth. Remove from the heat and add the butter to the chocolate mixture, blending until smooth. Cover with plastic wrap and refrigerate until firm, about 5 hours. When ready to form the truffles, have the cocoa ready in a little bowl or plate. Use a melon baller or teaspoon to scoop out some of the chocolate mixture. Dip the tips of your fingers lightly into the cocoa, shaking off the excess. Roll it into a little ball, then roll in the cocoa to coat it on all sides. Place on a tray lined with waxed paper or parchment while you work. Store the truffles in an airtight container away from heat.

Sources & Directory

Andrés Wines
PO Box 10550
697 South Service Rd.
Winona, ON L8E 5S4
905-643-4131 or 1-800-263-2170
www.andreswines.com

Angels Gate Winery
4260 Mountainview Rd.
Beamsville, ON L0R 1B2
905-563-3942
www.angelsgatewinery.com

Beamsville Strawberry Festival
905-563-7403

Birchwood Estate Wines
4679 Cherry Ave.
Beamsville, ON
905-562-8463
www.birchwoodwines.com

Bruce Trail
P.O. Box 857
Hamilton, ON L8N 3N9
1-800665-HIKE (4453) or 905-529-6821
www.brucetrail.org

Cave Spring Cellars
3838 Main St., PO Box 53
Jordan, ON L0R 1S0
905-562-3581
www.cavespringcellars.com

Château des Charmes Estate Winery
PO Box 280, 1025 York Rd.
Niagara-on-the-Lake, ON L0S 1J0
905-262-4219
www.chateaudescharmes.com

The Cheese House
Jim & Rosemary Thompson
905-562-5774

Cilento Wines
672 Chrislea Rd.
Woodbridge, ON
1-888-245-9463
www.cilento.com

Cool Climate Oenology & Viticulture
Institute (CCOVI)
Brock University
Inniskillin Hall
500 Glenridge Ave.
St. Catharines, ON
905-688-5550
www.brocku.ca/ccovi

Creekside Estate Winery
2170 Fourth Ave.
Jordan Station, ON L0R 1S0
905-562-0035
www.creeksideestatewinery.com

Criveller Candies Canada—
Chocolate & Pastry Boutique
6853 Lundy's Lane
Niagara Falls, ON
905-356-9441

Criveller Company of Canada
6935 Oakwood Dr.
Niagara Falls, ON
905-357-2930
www.criveller.com

Crown Bench Estates Winery
3850 Aberdeen Rd.
Beamsville, ON L0R 2B6
905-563-3959
www.crownbenchestates.com

Cuvée
905-685-4577

Daniel Lenko Estate Winery
5246 Regional Rd. 81
Beamsville, ON L0R 1B3
905-563-7756
www.daniellenko.com

De Sousa Wine Cellars
3753 Quarry Rd., R.R. 2
Beamsville, ON
905-563-7269

Dougherty's Meats
2248 Centre St.
Allanburg, ON L0S 1A0
905-227-4737

EastDell Estates Winery
4041 Locust Lane
Beamsville, ON L0R 1B0
905-563-9463
www.eastdell.com

Featherstone Estate Winery & Vineyard
3678 Victoria Ave.
Vineland, ON L0R 2C0
905-562-1949

The Good Earth Cooking School
4556 Lincoln Ave.
Beamsville, ON L0R 1B3
905-563-7856 or 1-800-308-5124
www.goodearthcooking.com

Greaves Jams and Marmalades
55 Queen St.
Niagara-on-the-Lake, ON L0S 1J0
905-468-7831
www.greavesjams.com

Grimo's Nut Nursery
Harbour Estates Winery
4362 Jordan Rd.
Jordan Station, ON L0R 1S0
905-562-4639 or 1-877-HEW-WINE
www.hewwine.com

Harvest Barn Country Market
1179 Fourth Ave.
St. Catharines, ON
905-641-1666

Henry of Pelham Family Estate Winery
1469 Pelham Rd.
St. Catharines, ON L2R 6P7
905-684-8423
www.henryofpelham.com

Hernder Estate Wines
1607 Eighth Ave.
St. Catharines, ON L2R 6P7
905-684-3300
www.hernder.com

Hillebrand Estates Winery
R.R. 2, Highway 55
Niagara-on-the-Lake, ON L0S 1J0
905-468-3201 or 1-800-582-8412
www.hillebrand.com

Inn on the Twenty
Cave Spring Cellars
3836 Main St.
Jordan, ON L0R 1S0
905-562-7313
www.innonthetwenty.com

Inniskillin Wines
R.R. 1, Niagara Parkway & Line 3
Niagara-on-the-Lake, ON L0S 1J0
905-468-2187
www.inniskillin.com

Italian Ice Cream Co.
5458 Victoria
Niagara Falls, ON
905-356-3866

Jackson-Triggs Niagara Estate Winery
2145 Niagara Stone Rd.
Niagara-on-the-Lake, ON L0S 1J0
905-589-4637
www.jacksontriggswinery.com

Joseph's Estate Wines
1811 Niagara Stone Rd.
Niagara-on-the-Lake, ON L0S 1J0
905-468-1259
www.josephsestatewines.com

Kacaba Vineyards
3550 King St.
Vineland, ON L0R 2C0
905-562-5625
www.kacaba.com

Keaton Manor
1590 Regional Rd. 81
St. Catharines, ON L2R 6P7
905-688-6746

Kiely Inn
209 Queen St.
Niagara-on-the-Lake, ON L0S 1J0
905-468-4588

Kittling Ridge Winery & Spirits
297 South Servide Rd.
Grimsby, ON L3M 1Y6
905-945-9225
www.kittlingridge.com

Konzelmann Estate Winery
R.R. 3, 1096 Lakeshore Rd.
Niagara-on-the-Lake, ON L0S 1J0
www.konzelmannwines.com

Lailey Vineyard
15940 Niagara Parkway
Niagara-on-the-Lake, ON L0S 1J0
905-468-0503
www.laileyvineyard.com

Lake Land Game Meats
1226 Regional Rd. 81
St. Catharines, ON
905-688-4570 or 1-800-665-3547

Lakeview Cellars Estate Winery
R.R. 1, 4037 Cherry Ave.
Vineland, ON L0R 2C0
905-562-5685
www.lakeviewcellars.on.ca

Magnotta
4701 Ontario St.
Beamsville, ON L0R 1B4
905-563-5313
www.magnotta.com

Maleta Vineyards & Estate Winery
450 Queenston Rd., R.R. 4
Niagara-on-the-Lake, ON L0S 1J0
905-685-8486

Malivoire Wine Co.
P.O. Box 475
4260 King St.
Beamsville, ON L0R 1B0
905-563-9253
www.malivoirewineco.com

Marynissen Estates
R.R. 6, Concession 1
Niagara-on-the-Lake, ON L0S 1J0
905-468-7270
www.marynissenestates.com

Morningstar Mills & Decew Falls
www.infoniagara.com

New Vintage Niagara
www.grapeandwine.com

Niagara Blossom Festival
Niagara Parks Commission
7400 Portage Rd. S.
Niagara Falls, ON L2E 6X8
905-356-2241
www.niagaraparks.com

Niagara Brewing Company
6863 Lundy's Lane
Niagara Falls, ON L2G 1Y7
905-374-1166 or 1-800-267-3392

Niagara Culinary Institute
at Niagara College
5881 Dunn St.
Niagara Falls, ON L2G 2N9
905-735-2211
www.niagarac.on.ca
Note: as of September 2003, the
Niagara Culinary Institute will be
relocated to Niagara College's Glendale
Campus, 135 Taylor Rd. R.R. 4,
Niagara-on-the-Lake, ON L0S 1J0

Niagara Food Festival
Merritt Island, Welland, ON
905-735-4832
www.tourismniagara.com/welland

Niagara Grape & Wine Festival
905-688-0212
www.niagaragrapeandwine.com

Niagara Nurseries
1643 Regional Rd. 81
St. Catharines, ON
905-682-4783

Niagara Oyster Co.
12 Cushman Rd.
St. Catharines, ON L2M 6S8
905-682-0402

Niagara Parks Commission
7400 Portage Rd. S.
Niagara Falls, ON L2E 6X8
905-356-2241
www.niagaraparks.com

Niagara Presents
4000 Jordan Rd.
Jordan Station, ON L0R 1S0
905-562-1907 or 1-888-584-2387
www.niagarapresents.net

The Oban Inn
Box 1011, 160 Front St.
Niagara-on-the-Lake, ON L0S 1J0
905-468-2165
www.vintageinns.com

Olde Angel Inn
224 Regent St.
Niagara-on-the-Lake, ON L0S 1J0
905-468-3411
www.angel-inn.com

Peller Estates Winery
P.O. Box 1000, 290 John St. E.
Niagara-on-the-Lake, ON L0S 1J0
905-468-4678 or 1-888-673-5537
www.peller.com

Peninsula Ridge Estates Winery
5600 King St.
Beamsville, ON L0R 1B0
905-563-0900
www.peninsularidge.com

Picard's Peanuts
2467 Hwy. 20
Thorold, ON
905-892-9916

The Pillar & Post
P.O. Box 1011, King & John Sts.
Niagara-on-the-Lake, ON L0S 1J0
905-468-2123
www.vintageinns.com

Pillitteri Estates Winery
R.R. 2, 1696 Highway 55
Niagara-on-the-Lake, ON L0S 1J0
905-468-3147
www.pillitteri.com

The Prince of Wales Hotel
P.O. Box 46, 6 Picton St.
Niagara-on-the-Lake, ON L0S 1J0
905-468-3246
www.vintageinns.com

Quacker Box Farms, Grimsby
905-945-7963

Queen's Landing Inn
PO Box 1180, Byron St.
Niagara-on-the-Lake, ON L0S 1J0
905-468-2195
www.vintageinns.com

Reif Estate Winery
R.R. 2, 15608 Niagara Parkway
Niagara-on-the-Lake, ON L0S 1J0
905-468-7738
www.reifwinery.com

Royal Canadian Henley Regatta
Port Dalhousie
905-934-4636

Royal DeMaria Wines
4551 Cherry Ave.
Vineland, ON
905-562-6767
www.royaldemaria.com

Shaw Festival
10 Queen's Parade
Niagara-on-the-Lake, ON L0S 1J0
905-468-2172 or 1-800-511-7429
www.shawfest.sympatico.ca

Short Hills Provincial Park
www.infoniagara.com

Southbrook Farm & Winery
1061 Major Mackenzie Dr.
Maple, ON
905-832-2548
www.southbrook.com

Steve Bauer Bike Tours
PO Box 428
Vineland, ON L0R 2C0
905-562-0788
www.stevebauer.com

Stonechurch Vineyards
R.R. 5, 1270 Irvine Rd.
Niagara-on-the-Lake, ON L0S 1J0
905-935-3535
www.stonechurch.com

Stoney Ridge Cellars
3201 King St.
Vineland, ON L0R 2C0
905-562-1324
www.stoneyridge.com

Strewn Wines & Wine Country
Cooking School
1339 Lakeshore Rd.
Niagara-on-the-Lake, ON L0S 1J0
905-468-1229
www.strewnwinery.com

Sunnybrook Farm Estate Winery
R.R. 3, 1425 Lakeshore Rd.
Niagara-on-the-Lake, ON L0S 1J0
905-468-1122
www.sunnybrookfarmwinery.com

Tastes of Niagara
PO Box 22005
Town & Country Plaza
Niagara Falls, ON L2J 4J3
905-357-6104
www.tastesofniagara.com

Terroir La Cachette
1339 Lakeshore Rd.
(within Strewn Winery)
Niagara-on-the-Lake, ON L0S 1J0
905-468-1222
www.lacachette.com

Thirteenth Street Wine Co.
3938 13th St.
Jordan Station, ON L0R 1S0
905-562-9463

Thirty Bench Vineyard & Winery
4281 Mountainview Rd.
Beamsville, ON L0R 1B0
905-563-1698
www.thirtybench.com

Thomas & Vaughan Vintners
4245 King St.
Beamsville, ON L0R 1B1
905-563-7727
www.thomasandvaughan.com

Vinehaven Bakery Artisan Breads
& Catering
3543 King St. Box 197
Vineland, ON L0R 2C0
905-562-9333

Vineland Estates Wines
R.R. 1, 3620 Moyer Rd.
Vineland, ON L0R 2C0
905-562-7088
www.vineland.com

Vintage Inns
(Prince of Wales, Oban Inn, Queen's
Landing inn, Pillar & Post)
155 Byron St.
Niagara-on-the-Lake, ON L0S 1J0
905-468-2195
www.vintageinns.com

Warm & Wonderful Wool Farm
Wainfleet, ON L0R 2J0
905-386-6192 or 1-888-241-3923
www.warmandwonderful.com

Wellington Court Restaurant
11 Wellington St.
St. Catharines, ON
905-682-5518

White Meadows Farms
2519 Effingham St., R.R. 1
St. Catharines, ON L2R 6P7
905-682-0642
www.whitemeadowsfarms.com

Whitty Farms
1973 Seventh St.
St. Catharines, ON L2R 6P9
905-988-5380

Willow Heights Estate Winery
R.R. 1, 3751 Regional Rd. 81
Vineland, ON L0R 2C0
905-562-4945
www.willowheights.on.ca

Winona Peach Festival
P.O. Box 10505
Winona, ON L8E 5R1
905-643-2084
www.winonapeach.com

Wyndym Farm Specialty Produce
1133 Concession 2, R.R. 6
Niagara-on-the-Lake, ON L0S 1J0
905-468-0251
www.vaxxine.com/wyndym

Index of Recipes

E

Q

Index of People and Places